CONFUSION ARISES AS WISDOM

Confusion Arises as Wisdom

GAMPOPA'S HEART ADVICE ON THE PATH OF MAHAMUDRA

Commentary by Ringu Tulku

Edited by Ann Helm

TRANSLATED BY RINGU TULKU AND ANN HELM

Shambhala
Boulder
2012

Shambhala Publications, Inc.
2129 13th Street
Boulder, Colorado 80302
www.shambhala.com

Printed in the United States of America

Shambhala Publications makes every effort to print on acid-free, recycled paper.

Shambhala Publications is distributed worldwide by Penguin Random House, Inc., and its subsidiaries.
Designed by James D. Skatges

LIBRARY OF CONGRESS CATALOGING-IN-PUBLICATION DATA

Ringu Tulku.
Confusion arises as wisdom: Gampopa's heart advice on the path of Mahamudra / translated by Ringu Tulku and Ann Helm; commentary by Ringu Tulku; edited by Ann Helm.—First edition.
Pages cm
Includes translation from Tibetan.
Includes bibliographical references.
ISBN 978-1-59030-995-7 (pbk.: alk. paper)
1. Sgam-po-pa, 1079–1153. 2. Mahamudra (Tantric rite)
I. Helm, Ann, 1949– II. Sgam-po-pa, 1079–1153. Rje Dvags-po Rin-po-che'i tshogs chos chen mo. English. III. Title.
BQ7950.S437R56 2012
294.3'420423—dc23
2011051736

Contents

FOR HIS HOLINESS THE GYALWANG KARMAPA

Accomplisher of the buddha activity of the victorious ones,
who are victorious over the four maras.
Teaching as Karmapa, the essence of the teachings,
Pervading all directions, pervading and continuous,
May he always completely flourish,
and may this flourishing be auspicious.

May the dharma teachings of the Practice Lineage,
The blazing glory of auspiciousness, the ornament of the world,
Flourish west of the kingdom of Tibet, the Land of Snow.
May there be auspicious peace throughout the world.
I supplicate you to bring peace to the world.

Foreword

There is a special connection between the Kagyu lineage and the genre of dharma teachings known as *tsok chö,* which is translated in this book as "community talks." Such community talks, or public talks, have been part of the Dakpo Kagyu lineage founded by Lord Gampopa since its very beginning in the twelfth century.

After *dakinis* told him in a vision it would be better for him to spread the dharma than to do further retreat, Lord Gampopa attracted thousands of disciples, who sought the dharma from him at his main seat of Daklha Gampo. Like Marpa, Milarepa, and his other predecessors in the lineage, Lord Gampopa cared for the assembly around him by offering them the supreme form of care: dharma instruction. Lord Gampopa followed in his predecessors' footsteps in personally guiding many individual disciples in their meditative practice, and he also offered dharma teachings to the exceptionally large assemblies that came to hear the dharma from him. These public talks were known as tsok chö. The collected works of Gampopa include five separate collections of such tsok chö. In most cases, these were written down by students who themselves attended the teachings. Recognizing the exceptional value of the words they heard from their lama, Gampopa's disciples expressed their appreciation by preserving them for future generations of practitioners. The pattern continued in later generations as well: Lord Gampopa's disciple Dusum Khyenpa, the First Karmapa, in turn gave public teachings that were recorded as tsok chö, as did Phagmo Drupa and many subsequent masters in various Kagyu lineages as well.

As will be very clear to all who read this book, Lord Gampopa was an extraordinary teacher. He was able to reach the diverse hearts and minds of many, many practitioners with a single dharma discourse. Without leaving Daklha Gampo, Lord Gampopa was able to send the dharma forth into the world with such singular skill that the Dakpo Kagyu lineage he founded continues to thrive today, nearly a millennium later.

The world has changed a great deal since the day when people would leave behind their mundane concerns and flock in the thousands to train under great masters in Tibet's rocky hermitages. We of the Kagyu lineage left most of our mountain retreat places long ago. Nowadays we face the challenge of preserving our lineage's practice spirit while living in the bustling valleys and cities. Yet we also find an opportunity to offer the dharma wherever we are. In keeping with this modern adaptation of the Kagyu spirit, Ringu Tulku does not sit on a mountaintop guiding the disciples who have come to see him. Instead, he travels from country to country, seeking ways to offer the dharma wherever he can. I am pleased that Ringu Tulku has chosen to share in Gampopa's spirit of offering the dharma, by publishing this translation and commentary on *Gampopa's Great Teachings to the Assembly*. I am confident that the coming together of these two—root text and commentary, Gampopa and Ringu Tulku—will be a source of goodness in the world.

THE SEVENTEENTH KARMAPA
ORGYEN TRINLEY DORJE
June 16, 2011

Preface

This book contains eighteen short but profound teachings by Gampopa, one of the forefathers of the Kagyu lineage of Tibetan Buddhism. The original title of this text is *rje dvags po rin po che'i tshogs chos chen mo,* which could be translated more or less literally as *Great Community Talks of Je Dakpo Rinpoche* or *Gampopa's Great Teachings to the Assembly.*[1] Along with a translation of the root text, this book contains some commentary I gave on this text in Europe and America between 2004 and 2009.

Gampopa lived in Tibet from 1079 to 1153. He was the foremost student of Tibet's most famous yogi, Milarepa, who had been a student of Marpa the Translator. It was Marpa who brought the teachings of the Kagyu lineage from India to Tibet. From Milarepa, Gampopa received the main Vajrayana practices of the Kagyu lineage: Mahamudra and the Six Yogas of Naropa.

Before he met Milarepa, Gampopa trained as a monk in the Kadampa tradition, with its emphasis on the Mahayana qualities of bodhichitta, emptiness, and compassion. Gampopa brought together the Mahayana teachings of the Kadampas with the Vajrayana teachings of Mahamudra and the Six Yogas. The way he joined these teachings has shaped the study and practice of the Kagyu lineage to this day.[2]

This collection of Gampopa's teachings was compiled by a monk named Sherap Shönu. He was probably a direct student of Gampopa, although we can't be sure; we have no information about him. It's also possible that some of the teachings in this collection were added later by other students.

Although this book contains a few general instructions on Mahayana topics, most of the instructions are on Mahamudra meditation and the Vajrayana view and practice. Chapter 1 opens the book in a traditional way by giving the lineage history of these teachings and some background on Gampopa's life. Chapter 2 is a detailed discussion of the importance of devotion. The way devotion is described in seven categories is stylistically reminiscent of Gampopa's most influential book, the *Jewel Ornament of Liberation.* Chapter 3 tells a short story about a monk who was able to talk directly with Chenrezik, the bodhisattva of compassion, and ask him questions on behalf of Atisha Dipankara, the founder of the Kadampa lineage.

Chapter 4 is Gampopa's own explanation of what is popularly known as the Four Dharmas of Gampopa. This way of explaining the Four Dharmas is somewhat unusual, and the last section of this chapter forms a bridge with the upcoming Vajrayana teachings by introducing coemergent wisdom, a key term in Mahamudra.

The next three chapters discuss Mahamudra in more detail from different angles: chapter 5 is on applying coemergent wisdom to our experience, including some very practical advice on bringing negativity onto the path; chapter 6 is a pointing-out instruction on the nature of the mind; and chapter 7 discusses the meaning of Mahamudra in terms of experience and realization. Later in the book, chapters 9 and 12 also focus on Mahamudra: chapter 9 is on stabilizing recognition of the nature of the mind, and chapter 12 discusses the great significance of knowing *tamel gyi shepa,* the ordinary mind.

Chapter 8 is a detailed explanation of creation stage practice, or deity yoga, and emphasizes the way it transforms our perception of ourselves and our world. Chapter 10 discusses how to tell if a spiritual teacher is genuine or not, and chapters 11 and 13 examine the Vajrayana view, meditation, action, and result from two very different perspectives.

Chapter 14 is a pithy explanation of right and wrong motivation when listening to dharma teachings. Chapter 15, "Pitfalls in Experience and Deviations from the View," points out some typical mistakes people make in practicing meditation and understanding emptiness. Chapter 16 highlights the illusory, dreamlike nature of bodhichitta as the inseparability of compassion and wisdom.

Chapter 17 is Gampopa's heart advice to students doing long retreats. One can imagine Gampopa talking to a small group of dedicated practitioners, giving them very personal and pointed advice about what they must do to reach liberation. The final chapter, chapter 18, lists ten ways that students would ideally serve their teachers. The commentary is followed by an appendix, which contains the entire translation of the root text without commentary.

I translated this text with an American woman, Ann Helm, who also edited the commentary. I want to thank her for her work, and also to thank Lama Jinpa, my oral translator in Spanish, for the talks given in Barcelona, and Rosie Fuchs, my oral translator in German, for the talks given in Hamburg. Special thanks also go to Maria Huendorf-Kaiser, who coordinated the transcribing and the archiving of the sound files, and who transcribed many of the talks herself. These tasks are just a fraction of the work Maria has done over the years for Bodhicharya International, and I appreciate her efforts very much. I'd also like to add special thanks to Margaret Ford for all the publishing and organizational work she has done and continues to do. Many other students participated in transcribing the talks and producing the sound files for this book, and I thank them all: Gabrielle, Bernhard Kaiser, Ena Meyer, Rachel Moffitt, Jet Mort, Paul O'Connor, Rahima Sayer, Dave Tuffield, and Erik Vienneau.

Last but certainly not least, I would like to thank His Holiness the Gyalwang Karmapa—the Sixteenth Karmapa—for being the original inspiration for this book, and the Seventeenth Karmapa for very kindly writing the foreword. May this translation and commentary be a small contribution to the flourishing of the teachings of the Karmapa and the Kagyu lineage.

RINGU TULKU
Gangtok, Sikkim

ONE

The Lineage of These Teachings

A FEW YEARS AGO I met Sam Bercholz, the founder of Shambhala Publications, who told me about attending a meeting with Chögyam Trungpa Rinpoche and His Holiness the Sixteenth Karmapa. This must have been in the United States in the 1970s. They told Sam about a small book by Gampopa that contains some of his teachings to the public, which was not available in India at that time. If in the future Sam could find the book, then they wanted him to get it translated and publish it. When I met Sam, he asked me to look for the book and, if possible, to translate it.

Not long afterward, I came across the recent publication of the six volumes of the *Collected Works of Gampopa*. When I went through it, I found many fine, short teachings, and I couldn't tell which ones the Karmapa and Trungpa Rinpoche were talking about. However, this text I have translated is quite well known, and even if it is not the one they referred to, it is a very fine text.

Let's start with the words of the original title: *Gampopa's Great Teachings to the Assembly*. The Tibetan title begins with Gampopa's name in the form of "Je Dakpo Rinpoche." *Je* is the Tibetan word for "lord," *Dakpo* is the name of the area in which he lived, and *Rinpoche* means "precious one." His most familiar name—Gampopa—comes from "Gampo Dar," the place where his monastery was located. "Dakpo" and "Gampo" are both place-names, and they might have been the same place. Gampopa also had many personal names, like "Dao Shönu"

1

and "Sönam Rinchen," but in Tibet he is popularly known as Dakpo Rinpoche, which is how this text refers to him.

The next part of the title is *tsok chö chenmo*. *Tsok* means "gathering" or "community," *chö* means "teachings," and *chenmo* is "great," so this text contains "great community talks" or "great teachings to the assembly."

Next, there is a short homage: NAMO RATNA GURU. This short homage to the teacher literally means "Homage to the precious guru." The homage is written in Sanskrit rather than Tibetan to show that India is the source of the teachings. It is very common in Tibetan texts to use Sanskrit in the opening homage.

The lineage of these teachings stems from the sixth lord, great Vajradhara, the lineages of the four oral traditions, Jetsun Tilopa, Naropa, Maitripa, Tharlam, Lord Marpa, and Jetsun Milarepa.

The lineage of these particular teachings starts with great Vajradhara, the primordial buddha. Let's look at the term "primordial buddha," since it can be confusing. Many Vajrayana teachings say that the lineage goes back to Vajradhara, who is said to be the first buddha, the primordial buddha. Yet we also say that anyone who becomes enlightened does so as Vajradhara. How could this happen? It seems contradictory that you could become the primordial buddha. In order to become enlightened, you must study and practice the teachings of the enlightened ones who came before, so obviously you couldn't be the very first buddha.

The understanding here is that when people become enlightened, they don't feel, "Oh, great! Today I became enlightened." Instead they feel, "I have always been enlightened. Why didn't I realize it before?" They realize their ever-present buddha nature. This is how one becomes enlightened as Vajradhara, the primordial buddha.

All Buddhist teachings come from the actual experience of an enlightened being, so it is said that all the Vajrayana teachings trace their lineage back to Vajradhara. This is true even of teachings given by Buddha Shakyamuni, because the Buddha taught the Vajrayana in the form of Vajradhara. Even the tantras not taught directly by Buddha Shakyamuni say their source is the primordial buddha Vajradhara.

To sum up, the source of the Vajrayana teachings is called Vajradhara, sometimes Buddha Shakyamuni is called Vajradhara, sometimes your own root guru is called Vajradhara, and when you become enlightened by knowing your true nature, that is also called Vajradhara.

Tilopa is considered the founder of the Kagyu lineage, and sometimes we say that the lineage came straight from Vajradhara to Tilopa. In one sense, when Tilopa gained realization, it was as if no one had taught him what he knew, because his enlightenment was directly connected with the primordial buddha. But this does not mean that Tilopa did not receive teachings from human masters. He studied with many teachers, which is why the next line mentions the four oral traditions.

The four oral traditions refer to the four main lineages of the Six Yogas that Tilopa upheld: the lineages of Nagarjuna, Charyapa, Lavapa, and the great dakini Sukhasiddhi. From the lineage of Nagarjuna he received the teachings of the Illusory Body and Clear Light, and from Charyapa he received Tummo, or Inner Heat. Tummo practice uses the chakras and channels of the inner body to generate heat and bliss-emptiness. Milarepa and his followers used this technique to be able to wear only cotton cloth in the cold climate of Tibet. Tilopa received Dream Yoga from Lavapa, and from Sukhasiddhi (whom we sometimes call Kalpa Zangmo) he got the teachings on Phowa, the Transference of Consciousness, and the Bardo teachings, which are about the four or six intermediate states. We usually call these practices the Six Yogas of Naropa, but because they came from Tilopa to Naropa, they are actually the Six Yogas of Tilopa.

The next major lineage holder is Naropa. Earlier in his life he was one of the greatest scholars of Nalanda University, and later he became one of the greatest yogis of India. Naropa taught the Six Yogas to the Tibetan translator Marpa. While Marpa was in India, he also received teachings from Maitripa, particularly the teachings on Mahamudra, and from Tharlam.[1] As you may know, these two teachings—the Six Yogas and Mahamudra—are the ultimate teachings of the Kagyu lineage.

Marpa then passed these teachings to his student Milarepa, who is Tibet's most famous yogi. He is called the "singing yogi" because he used to give teachings in song, like those found in the *Hundred Thousand Songs of Milarepa*. So, these teachings were originally transmitted from Tilopa to Naropa, from Naropa, Maitripa, and Tharlam to Marpa, and from Marpa to Milarepa. Then they went to Gampopa, and from him they have come down to us.

This lineage was received by Dakpo Dao Shönu, or Gampopa, who was blessed by Milarepa. He attained supreme realization, and by giving these teachings, he sowed the seeds that covered the land of Tibet with realized beings.

From Milarepa the teachings on Mahamudra and the Six Yogas went to Gampopa. One of Gampopa's names was "Dao Shönu," which means "youthful moonlight." After attaining realization himself, Gampopa brought many others to enlightenment as well, so that the entire land of Tibet was filled with *siddhas,* or realized beings.

Gampopa gave these teachings to the First Karmapa, Lord Dusum Khyenpa, and from him they went to Drogön Repa Chenpo; from him to Loppön Rinpoche Pomdrakpa, and from him to the Second Karmapa, Karma Pakshi.

From Gampopa, these teachings were received by the First Karmapa, Dusum Khyenpa. This became an unbroken lineage, going from Dusum Khyenpa to Drogön Rechenpa; then to Pomdrakpa; and then to the Second Karmapa, Karma Pakshi. From then until now, this lineage has been unbroken. The text poetically says:

For these teachings, the river of empowerments has not diminished, the banner of maturing and liberating has not fallen down, the current of blessings has not been interrupted, and the plants of enlightenment have not dried up. These teachings have benefited beings impartially; they hold the royal seat of the Kagyu lineage.

What is being emphasized here is that the lineage is unbroken. A true lineage is not merely a teacher passing on teachings to a student. A true lineage refers to a realized being who teaches students, and some of the students attain realization from practicing the teachings. These students in turn transmit the teachings to others who also attain realization, and so on. There could be one lineage holder, or there could be many lineage holders. This is the meaning of the phrase "unbroken lineage."

In the past, the Buddha empowered the bodhisattva Dao

**Shönu for the benefit of beings, and he prophesied this bo-
dhisattva's rebirth in Tibet, the Land of Snow.**

In Tibet they tell a story about Gampopa, which comes from the
sutras. Gampopa was a special bodhisattva during the time of Buddha
Shakyamuni. One time when the Buddha was giving teachings about
the future, he prophesied that his teachings would fade away in the Land
of the Aryas, or India. It might be possible for his teachings to go north
and flourish there, except that the people in the north behind the mountains were as difficult to penetrate as hard shells. The Buddha described
them as barbarians, or the children of ogres. He must have been talking
about the Tibetans, since we are supposed to be the offspring of a monkey and an ogress.

Buddha went on to ask if any of the bodhisattvas would be willing
to go to such an unfavorable place with such difficult people. One particularly courageous bodhisattva stood up and said, "Yes, I will go there
and spread the dharma, no matter what." After he spoke, five hundred
other bodhisattvas felt so inspired by his bravery that they stood up and
said they would go to help him. It is said that Gampopa was the bravest
bodhisattva; he was the one who stood up first. Because of the strong
promise he made to the Buddha, he became a great teacher who could
benefit many beings. Not only that, but because many great bodhisattvas
were born in Tibet to help Gampopa, he created a very strong lineage.

**There, Gampopa became the spiritual friend known as Ratna
Guru Punya Ratna, or Precious Lama Sönam Rinchen. He
took to heart, with faultless certainty, the instructions coming
from glorious Atisha and the great guru Naropa, and he taught
them to others.**

Many people know the story of Gampopa's life, so I will mention
only a few incidents. Gampopa was born into a very good family, and he
became a physician with a wife and two children. Not only was he a
practicing doctor, he also developed various medical treatments. Some
of the medicines he created are still being used today. For instance, there
is one called *dakpo menmar,* the "red medicine of Dakpopa," which is
excellent for stomach problems.

What happened to change Gampopa's life was that his children died, and then his wife became terminally ill. Although her condition indicated she should be dead, she kept willing herself to stay alive. Gampopa said to her, "You must have a very strong attachment to something, which is holding you back. Please tell me what it is so I can fulfill your wishes."

She told him, "I am not attached to anything in this world except you. I cannot bear to let you go."

Then Gampopa told his wife that he had already decided to become a monk, whether or not she continued to live. He said he had seen enough of samsara, and he wanted to dedicate the rest of his life to practicing the dharma and becoming enlightened. His wife asked him to take a vow in her presence that he would definitely renounce the world and become a monk. He agreed, and after he made this promise, she died.

The next morning, Gampopa's uncle came to see him. His uncle thought Gampopa would be devastated from the loss of his wife, but he found Gampopa in a cheerful frame of mind. His uncle became very angry with him for being so callous, but Gampopa assured him that he was happy because now he could devote himself totally to the dharma. He was determined to become someone who could benefit a great number of beings.

Gampopa then divided his wealth into three parts: one part he distributed to the monasteries and the poor; one part he gave to the people practicing on behalf of his wife; and one part he kept for his own expenses. Then, Gampopa became a monk in the Kadampa tradition, which had been founded by the master Atisha. Gampopa became very accomplished in the Kadampa teachings because he was very intelligent and already a very learned man.

While Gampopa was living at a Kadampa monastery, he started dreaming of a blue-colored yogi coming to him, blessing him, and then going away. He dreamed this again and again, so he went to his teacher and asked his teacher what he thought this meant. His teacher told him, "I don't know, but maybe it indicates a need to do retreat practice on Miyowa." Miyowa, or Achala in Sanskrit, is a meditation deity with the ability to remove inner obstacles.

So, Gampopa did a retreat on Miyowa while staying on the outskirts of the monastery. This was during a time of famine, and there were many beggars in the area. In particular, there were three beggars sleeping below a large rock near Gampopa. One day, one of the beggars said, "I wish a sponsor would come to the monastery tomorrow and offer a very nice *tsampa* [roasted barley flour] soup, with big chunks of meat and bones, and invite everyone, including us. I really want some good soup."

The second beggar said to the first, "Don't think so small! Wish for something bigger than that. There is no harm in making a very big wish. You could wish to become the king of Tibet, like the great rulers of the past, Trisong Deutsen and Songtsen Gampo, who ruled over most of the world. They were powerful enough to attack China, and they brought the dharma to Tibet. They did tremendous good for people. Wish for something like that. Aren't you ashamed of wishing for something as small as a cup of soup?"

Then the third man said, "If you are going to make a wish, then wish for something better than being a king. Wish to be like Milarepa, who is completely free from samsara. He is totally enlightened and no longer has any need of food or clothing. He can fly from one village to another, and he teaches his students to become enlightened as well. Wish for something more like that. There is a retreatant up on that rock, and he usually circumambulates the monastery at this time of day. It would be embarrassing for him to hear us making such petty, worldly wishes."

It turned out that indeed, at that very moment, Gampopa was walking by and heard this conversation. When he heard the name "Milarepa," he became totally inspired. It was as if he had been struck by a thunderbolt. He had no doubt from that moment on that he should find Milarepa and study with him.

The next morning, Gampopa made a tsampa soup like the first beggar had described, and he offered it to the three beggars. He said, "I'm sorry, I couldn't help overhearing your conversation yesterday. Please tell me, where can I find Milarepa?" The elder beggar knew and gave him directions.

Gampopa had to make a long journey in order to meet Milarepa. Gampopa lived in central Tibet, and Milarepa lived far to the west, near Mount Kailash. Sometimes Gampopa got very sick on his journey, and Milarepa knew about this. Milarepa would tell his students, "I can see my heart son coming. He is a great bodhisattva who has incarnated to help Tibet by spreading the dharma. He is on his way here, and now he is sick. Please pray for him." Milarepa also told his students, "Whoever brings this bodhisattva to see me will never again be reborn in a lower realm, and instead will be quickly liberated."

When Gampopa arrived at Milarepa's place, he met an old woman who asked him who he was and where he had come from. When he said he was a monk from central Tibet, she said, "Oh, come in, come in! You must be the great bodhisattva my teacher has been talking about. He said that whoever escorts you to him will have no more lower births, so please allow my daughter to take you to Milarepa."

When Gampopa heard this, he thought, "Oh, really! I must be someone special!" and he became a little proud. The next day, when the daughter took Gampopa to meet Milarepa, Milarepa wouldn't see him. Milarepa was aware of Gampopa's pride, and he kept Gampopa waiting for fifteen days.

When Milarepa finally granted him an audience, Gampopa prostrated in front of Milarepa, who was flanked by two other *repas,* or cotton-clad yogis, and then Gampopa sat down. Milarepa handed Gampopa a skull cup full of *chang,* or Tibetan liquor, and told Gampopa to drink it. Of course, monks are forbidden to drink alcohol, and Gampopa was a monk. But Gampopa did not hesitate; he took the skull cup and drank every drop. Milarepa was pleased by this and told Gampopa, "You did very well. This is a sign that you will be a good vessel for my teachings."

Milarepa gave him all the teachings and meditation instructions, and he worked closely with Gampopa on his meditative experiences. Actually, Gampopa wasn't with Milarepa for very long, but he did learn the Six Yogas of Naropa and Mahamudra, and gained experience in them. At a certain point, Milarepa said he had given Gampopa everything he had, like pouring liquid from one cup to another, and he said that Gampopa should go back to his homeland and practice there. He also said that when Gampopa finally considered his old teacher Milarepa to be no different from the Buddha himself, then Gampopa should start to teach.

Before Milarepa and Gampopa parted for the last time, Milarepa gave him one final teaching. This has become a famous story, because what Milarepa did for his final instruction was to turn around, lift his skirt, and display the calluses on his bottom from many, many years of sitting in meditation. Milarepa's final instruction was that the only route to realization is to practice with great diligence.

I won't say any more about Gampopa's life here. You can read his biography, which goes into detail about his practice of the Six Yogas and Mahamudra, and how he performed miracles and taught his students.[2] The story of Gampopa's meeting with Milarepa is also recounted in the *Life of Milarepa* and in the *Hundred Thousand Songs of Milarepa*.[3]

In terms of the way Gampopa taught, he combined the general Mahayana teachings he received from the Kadampa tradition of Atisha with the quintessential Vajrayana teachings, like the Six Yogas and Mahamudra, which he received from Milarepa. These became the basis of the Kagyu lineage teachings. The Kagyu lineage is sometimes known as the Dakpo Kagyu, because all its branches stem from Gampopa, or Je Dakpo Rinpoche. This particular text, which includes both Mahayana and Vajrayana teachings, is representative of the classic teachings of this tradition.

Some of his teachings have been written down here, in a systematic way, by the monk Sherap Shönu.

This set of teachings was compiled by a monk named Sherap Shönu, who was probably a direct disciple of Gampopa. This completes the preamble, and now we will go to the actual teachings.

TWO

Understanding the Need
for Devotion

**The guru, Lord Gampopa, said: In general, in order to practice
the dharma, we need devotion, diligence, and wisdom. Devotion is the basis, diligence is the path, and wisdom is the assistant.**

GAMPOPA STARTS by saying that our practice must be based on devotion, that following the path takes diligence, and that these two qualities must be helped along by *prajna*, or wisdom. Gampopa supports
this statement with a couple of quotations. First, Nagarjuna's *Precious
Garland* says:

> *Because of having devotion, one diligently practices the
>   dharma.*
> *Because of having wisdom, one knows reality.*
> *Wisdom is the foremost of these two,*
> *But devotion is the foundation.*

Second, a verse from the *Sutra of the Ten Dharmas* points out why
devotion is necessary:

> *Positive qualities do not arise*
> *In people without devotion,*
> *Just like green plants*
> *Do not grow from burned seeds.*

Exactly what is devotion? The Tibetan word that I am translating as "devotion" is *depa*.[1] *Depa* is sometimes translated as "faith" or "trust," but it involves more than that. Depa has three special qualities: inspiration, aspiration, and certainty. The words "certainty" and "confidence" seem closer to the right meaning than "trust," because someone can believe in something and later find out it was untrustworthy. Depa is based on understanding, on having good reasons for devotion.

The actual basis is explained in seven points: (1) the causes that give rise to devotion, (2) how to gauge that devotion has arisen, (3) the categories of devotion, (4) the nature of devotion, (5) an analogy for devotion, (6) the activity of devotion, and (7) the way to measure the stability of devotion.

Gampopa describes devotion from seven different angles. Let's go through them one by one. First, he talks about four causes or activities that give rise to devotion.

a. When you read the sutras, devotion arises. It is recommended to initially make an offering and say a prayer, and then read the teachings.

When you read something that describes the way things are, you become inspired and think, "Yes, this is really true." Reading the Buddhist teachings can bring this kind of inspiration and certainty. When you are certain that something is true, it sparks your devotion to act accordingly.

I can remember being inspired by a Bible story about the wisdom of Jesus Christ. One time Jesus came upon some people throwing stones at a woman in order to kill her. She had misbehaved by being a prostitute or committing adultery, or something like that. He said to them, "Stop! Wait a minute. You can throw stones at her and kill her because she did something wrong. But the first stone must be thrown by someone who has never sinned. Look inside and see if you ever did something you shouldn't have. If you've never done anything wrong, then you can pick up a stone and throw it at her." Of course, nobody could pick up a stone. I found these words inspiring because I could see they were true.

Devotion is not the same as belief; it arises when something rings true to you. When something touches the core of your heart, you get inspired, and this leads to aspiration and certainty. Devotion is based on understanding the dharma. If you didn't understand the dharma, how could you be inspired by it? And without being inspired, why would you practice? You don't practice because someone said you should. Simply being told it is good to sit on a cushion for hours with your legs folded up is not particularly convincing. But if you know that sitting practice can bring tranquillity and wisdom, then you might do it. This is why inspired devotion is the basis of dharma practice.

Gampopa says devotion can arise from reading the sutras. He means not only the words of the Buddha but any words that are true. Then he says the best way to proceed is to make an offering, say a prayer, and then read the teachings. In other words, you begin your study by showing respect. In the Buddhist tradition, books are treated with great respect because they embody truth and show the way to liberation. Of all the miracles the Buddha performed—like turning water into fire, and fire into water—his most beneficial miracle was giving the teachings. Even going to heaven and reappearing surrounded by gods and goddesses would not be nearly as miraculous as the teachings he gave.

> b. Devotion also comes from spending time with friends who
> have devotion. It resembles the way you get blue color on you
> when working with blue dye, and red color on you when work-
> ing with red dye. It is important to have devoted friends.

The second cause is having friends with devotion. Since we are so easily influenced, if we spend time with people who are inspired and have conviction, then we gradually develop these qualities as well. That's why the sangha is so important; the sangha is a positive influence. Gampopa gives an analogy, saying that when you work with blue dye, you get blue color on you, and when you work with red dye, you get red color on you. Similarly, if you associate with people who have certainty and inspiration, you will become like them.

c. If you rely on a genuine spiritual teacher, that also produces devotion. A real spiritual teacher is someone who knows how to practice without going against any of the teachings. Devotion arises when you associate with someone like that.

Relying on a spiritual friend is another way to increase devotion. Gampopa defines a genuine spiritual friend as someone who knows how to practice without going against any of the teachings. A genuine teacher understands that all the Buddhist teachings, all the ways and means of the dharma, are connected without any contradiction.

This reminds me of a well-known story about Atisha Dipankara. After he arrived in Tibet, Atisha asked his translator what he had studied. The translator gave a long list of the sutras, tantras, and commentaries he had received. Atisha was very impressed and wondered why the Tibetans had felt a need to invite him to their country. Then, Atisha asked the translator how he practiced all those teachings, and the translator replied that he practiced each one according to the instructions in that particular teaching. When he heard this, Atisha realized that Tibetans certainly did need him, because they didn't understand how all the teachings are practiced with the same view.

A good teacher knows that all the Buddhist teachings are valid ways of working with the mind. The teacher sees how they fit together, and that there is no contradiction between them. Someone with this understanding sets the right example. Studying with a spiritual master who understands the teachings and knows how to practice them is yet another way to generate devotion.

d. If you meditate on death and impermanence, you will become devoted to practicing the dharma. You understand that the time of death is uncertain, death comes quickly, change happens rapidly, and there is no time to waste. Devotion arises from being completely certain about this.

Fourth, meditating on impermanence and death also generates devotion. Impermanence means that everything is changing in each instant. Since the time of death is uncertain and death can come very quickly, there is no time to waste. If you become certain about this, you will be devoted to dharma practice. When you truly recognize the reality of life and death, you feel inspired to use the time you have to do something positive for yourself and positive for others.

> **The second main point is how to gauge that devotion has arisen. By understanding death and impermanence, you stop taking the world to be real. Through conviction in karmic cause and effect, you are careful regarding positive and negative actions, and diligent in practices of accumulation and purification. Clearly, there is nothing more important to do than practice the dharma, and nothing more important to think about than the teachings of the dharma.**

After reading Gampopa's introduction to the topic of devotion, you might wonder whether you have devotion or not. When your devotion has become strong, several changes happen in your life. By understanding the impermanence of life and the reality of death, you become less attached to the affairs of this life and ordinary worldly concerns. In addition, certainty about cause and effect becomes stronger, so you become more mindful about acting positively rather than negatively. You have a clearer sense of how to practice—how to accumulate the merit that brings a more positive way of living, and how to purify your negative tendencies. Another sign that devotion has arisen is that you are utterly convinced that there is nothing more important to do than engage in dharma study and practice. With this kind of certainty, devotion is fully present.

> **Third, there are three categories of devotion: inspiration, certainty, and aspiration.**

The third point discusses the main aspects of devotion. First, inspiration comes from many different sources. One source of inspiration is seeing reality, seeing what is true. You can also be inspired from seeing or feeling certain qualities in other people, like their great compassion. This kind of inspiration is very clear. The second aspect of devotion is having confidence in the dharma. Your mind is certain; you feel the teachings are trustworthy and you can rely on them. The third kind of devotion is connected with longing for the dharma, with having the aspiration to embody the dharma.

Inspiration within devotion comes from seeing true teachers and genuine lamas, and from hearing the teachings. Inspiration also arises from visiting sacred sites that affect you so much that tears fill your eyes and your hair stands on end.

Gampopa says that inspired devotion arises when you see a genuine teacher or a real bodhisattva, like the Dalai Lama or the Karmapa. Many people start crying when they see great teachers, often without knowing why. I remember how the Sixteenth Karmapa affected people who went to see him. It didn't matter if they were Buddhists or not. He lived at Rumtek Monastery in the country of Sikkim, and Sikkimese government officials, army generals, and all sorts of people would come to see him. They simply liked him. They were not thinking about devotion or anything like that; they simply felt good in his presence. Often they wouldn't want to leave. What the Karmapa actually said was nothing much. Most of the time, he wasn't giving any teachings; he would just make little jokes or chit-chat. But people would get very inspired— sometimes they would be crying as they came out of the room. That often happened.

Inspired devotion also comes from listening to teachings and being affected by them. When you recognize that the words are genuine and the instructions truly useful, your heart is touched and you become inspired. Inspired devotion also arises from going to an inspiring place, like a pilgrimage spot. As Gampopa says, you can be so affected that your body hair stands up, and tears well up in your eyes.

Generally, we could say that inspired devotion opens your heart and moves you deeply. This comes from recognizing truth, and feeling its genuineness.

Certainty within devotion arises when you have no doubt about any of the Buddha's teachings, whether detailed or condensed, and so you practice the dharma.

The second type of devotion involves confidence. Devotion should not be regarded as simply emotional; it must be based on certainty. This kind of certainty often comes from study—first from reading and hearing, and then by reflecting on what you've read and heard. It's important to analyze and investigate the teachings. You need to test them for yourself. By thinking things over and looking at them from different angles, you can come to a conclusion about what is valid and what is not. When you reach the point where you have no doubts, then you have devotion based on certainty.

One of my favorite stories about certainty involves the First Karmapa, Dusum Khyenpa, who was a student of Gampopa. Dusum Khyenpa was already an advanced practitioner when he met Gampopa. Even as a child, he was known for his clairvoyance. When he was young, he looked after the family yaks. The other children tending their yaks would accompany him, and they would all play together while the animals grazed. When it was time to round up the yaks to go home, the children would ask Dusum Khyenpa where their animals had gone, and through his clairvoyance he would tell them where to find their yaks.

Later, Dusum Khyenpa studied and practiced in depth, and together with two men from Kham he went to central Tibet to become a student of Gampopa. Dusum Khyenpa practiced in retreat for many years. After he felt he had a good understanding of the nature of the mind, he went to discuss his experience with Gampopa. However, Gampopa was not impressed. He told Dusum Khyenpa that his understanding was wrong, and to go back to his cave, try again, and meditate for another year.

Dusum Khyenpa went back into retreat and practiced diligently. The next year he came back to see Gampopa, and he was in bad shape. He was unhappy and exhausted, and he told Gampopa that he was very sorry, but his experience of the nature of the mind was the same as before. This time Gampopa became angry and shouted at him. He told Dusum Khyenpa that his experience was completely backward and not to come back until he had a definite experience of the mind's true nature.

Another year passed, and Dusum Khyenpa returned to see Gampopa again. He was crying and despondent, and he fell at Gampopa's feet, begging for further instructions because there was nothing he could do to change his experience. Even if Gampopa were to beat him or kill him, his experience wouldn't change; it was strong and clear. Then, Gampopa smiled at him and congratulated him on his achievement. He said Dusum Khyenpa had been right all along, but it was extremely important for him to have conviction in the truth of his own experience. This is an example of the kind of certainty involved in devotion.

> Because of the aspiration within devotion, you long to purify
> your obscurations quickly to gain the results of your practice.
> This applies to whatever practice you do, whether it is a little
> or a lot. You aspire to have the positive qualities and happiness
> of the higher realms and liberation.

Due to our inspiration and trust, the third type of devotion arises—
the aspiration to practice the dharma. At this stage we want to work
toward enlightenment in order to attain the result. It becomes a high
priority. As Gampopa says, whether we do a small amount of practice or
a great amount of practice, we aspire to quickly purify the obscurations
preventing our accomplishment. Longing for the happiness of liberation and the higher realms is followed by the aspiration to attain these
qualities.

> Fourth, the essence of devotion is not mixed with a lack of de-
> votion. It should not be like cold water that is liquid on the
> surface but frozen underneath, or a container that has flour on
> top but ashes below. Those with devotion act in wholly posi-
> tive ways.

Next, Gampopa explains the essence of devotion as being very clear
and deep. It is not present only half the time or in a halfhearted way. He
gives two examples that were probably more familiar in his world than
ours. When water on a pond is melted on the surface but frozen underneath, then it is not really liquid. It may look like water, but there isn't
much water there. The other analogy refers to being sold a bag of tsampa,
or barley flour, which has flour on the surface but ashes underneath. In
the same way, halfhearted devotion is not certain enough or deep
enough.

The main point here is that devotion is not superficial. It's not infatu-
ation or a temporary inspiration that you have for a few days and then it
is gone. Sometimes devotion can be very emotional, and it can be hard
to tell the difference between a fleeting emotion and real devotion. It
can happen that a student feels strong devotion, but then some little
incident or provocation happens, and the devotion is gone. This isn't
real devotion; real devotion is based on deep understanding. On the

other hand, devotion is not merely rational or intellectual. There is room for devotion to be emotional and highly inspired, but it must also be clear and certain.

> The fifth point is an analogy: devotion is like a water-purifying jewel. When this type of jewel is placed in dirty water, the water becomes clear. Similarly, devotion removes defilements so the mind becomes clear.

The fifth point gives the example of a water-purifying jewel, which is something that supposedly existed in ancient times. This might seem strange; I don't know if there is such a thing or not. But when this type of jewel is put in water, the water becomes totally pure. Similarly, devotion removes defilements. When genuine devotion is present, our mind becomes clear and unconfused. We also find that when we are less confused, we have more devotion. Because of our inspiration and clarity, we know we're going in the right direction.

> Sixth, the activity of devotion causes negative deeds to diminish, like the waning moon, and causes positive deeds to increase, like the waxing moon.

The sixth point describes what devotion does for us. Gampopa says that it makes negative deeds diminish and positive deeds increase. Understanding how cause and effect operate is the key point of Buddhist ethics. We need to know how negative actions harm ourselves and others, and how positive deeds benefit ourselves and others, in both short- and long-term ways. Devotion helps us see this, and it makes us want to do more that is positive and less that is negative.

Of course, because of habitual tendencies, even when we know our actions aren't beneficial, sometimes we still do them. But the more mindful we are and the more certain we become of how karma works, the more our old habits fall away.

It's extremely important to understand how our actions are connected with their results. It's like knowing that if you put your hand in a fire, your hand will get burned. It is not a moral issue of right versus wrong but a matter of understanding cause and effect. From the Buddhist point of view, positive and negative deeds are not a moral issue; they are based on recognizing that positive actions bring benefit, and negative actions bring harm.

Seventh, for the way to measure the stability of devotion, it is said:

> *One who does not abandon the genuine dharma*
> *Due to desire, hatred, fear, or ignorance,*
> *Is said to have devotion.*

As it says, people with devotion do not abandon the dharma due to desire, do not abandon the dharma due to hatred, do not abandon the dharma due to fear, and do not abandon the dharma due to ignorance.

The final point is how to tell if your devotion is stable or not. For example, if someone says to you, "If you give up practicing the dharma, I will give you a million dollars," and you agree, then that would be abandoning the dharma due to desire. If someone in the sangha does something very negative, and you feel angry about it and stop practicing, that's an example of abandoning the dharma due to hatred. If you stop practicing because someone threatens to kill you, that would be abandoning the dharma due to fear. If people tell you there's something wrong with Buddhism, and you go along with them, that would be giving up the dharma due to confusion. On the other hand, if nothing can dissuade you from following the dharma, then your devotion is strong and well established.

Devotion is closely connected with diligence. Without devotion, you wouldn't keep going; devotion fuels your progress on the path. This is why devotion is emphasized in classical Buddhist texts, like the scripture Gampopa quoted at the beginning of this chapter:

> *Because of having devotion, one diligently practices the*
>   *dharma.*
> *Because of having wisdom, one knows reality.*
> *Wisdom is the foremost of these two,*
> *But devotion is the foundation.*

At the same time that we are cultivating devotion, we must use our critical intelligence. The Buddha said we should not believe anything until we have examined it, tested it, and know for ourselves that it is true. Some people find it difficult to connect these two approaches—that practitioners should have trust and devotion, and yet they should examine the teachings and not take them on faith. However, these approaches coincide when devotion is based on understanding, and consists of inspiration, certainty, and aspiration. We want to cultivate devotion rather than blind faith.

Even if something is trustworthy, you have to understand it for yourself. The teachings of the Buddha should not be accepted at face value. This is why we need to study as well as practice. We reflect on the teachings, and we practice meditation in order to apply the teachings to our own experience.

Without genuinely applying the dharma to our mind, it cannot transform us. Someone might think, "There are a hundred volumes spoken by the Buddha, and everything he said is true. This is unquestionably my view." Can inner transformation happen with an attitude like that? It's nice to appreciate the teachings, to make prostrations and offer incense in front of your books, but that won't transform you. You will continue to react in the same confused ways as before. But the more you understand the teachings, the more you change the way you see things and the way you react to them.

This is the main purpose of the dharma: to learn how to experience your life in such a way that you free yourself from suffering and problems. Unless you understand the teachings thoroughly and experientially, they will not transform you. Devotion is a key factor in this process.

The more we talk about the various aspects of devotion, the clearer it becomes how necessary it is. Devotion brings purpose and direction—we know what we want to do, what it will entail, and what we can accomplish for ourselves and others. We find ourselves moving in a definite direction, which makes the path straightforward. This is why devotion is so important.

THREE

The Monk Who Questioned Chenrezik

NEXT, GAMPOPA TELLS a very nice story. Once there was a novice monk in India who went to the great siddha Dombipa, one of the eighty-four *mahasiddhas*.[1] Dombipa is renowned for riding a tiger in the sky. When the monk went to see Dombipa, he made prostrations, offered a mandala, and supplicated Dombipa, who asked him, "What do you want?"

The novice monk said, "Please give me some instructions."

Dombipa replied, "No, I'm sorry. You have no karmic connection with me. Go to my student Atisha and ask him for instructions. You do have a karmic link with him."

So, the novice monk went to Atisha Dipankara, the great teacher who is known in Tibet as Jowo Je. The monk said, "Your teacher Dombipa said I should come to you. Kindly give me some instructions." Atisha gave him a small *sadhana*, or liturgical practice, of Chenrezik, along with instructions on how to practice it.

The monk practiced this sadhana so well that he had all the signs of accomplishing Chenrezik. He had visions of Chenrezik, he heard sound as Chenrezik, and he could touch Chenrezik. He became so accomplished in his practice that he could ask questions to Chenrezik, which Chenrezik would answer.

After a while, the monk went back to Atisha Dipankara and said, "It's like this: I can talk to Chenrezik and question him about anything. But what should I ask?"

Atisha told the monk to ask these six questions:

1. What is the essence of all dharma practice?
2. What causes obstacles?
3. What should we emphasize in practice?
4. Among all the views, which view is the most important?
5. How many consciousnesses are there?
6. What causes the perfection of the accumulations?

The student thanked Atisha, went and meditated on Chenrezik, and asked the questions. In reply, Chenrezik answered them one by one.

1. The essence of all dharma practice is *bodhichitta.*

The great Tibetan teacher Patrul Rinpoche said the same thing. He said he had read a great many sutras and tantras, as well as commentaries by the great masters of India and Tibet. He had received many pith instructions on various teachings and practices. But in all of these, he found nothing but teachings on bodhichitta. From beginning to end, from the four noble truths to the highest teachings of Dzogchen and Mahamudra, everything is included in bodhichitta. Some teachings lead to the understanding of bodhichitta; some teach how to increase bodhichitta; some teach the results of bodhichitta. He concluded that there is nothing besides bodhichitta in the entire Buddhist teachings.

What is bodhichitta? *Bodhi* is "enlightened" or "awakened," and *chitta* is "heart" or "mind." So *bodhichitta* is translated as "awakened heart" or "enlightened mind." We define bodhichitta as having two aspects: compassion and wisdom. These correspond to the two main types of bodhichitta: relative bodhichitta and absolute bodhichitta. Relative bodhichitta is the compassion aspect, which focuses on benefiting others. Absolute bodhichitta is the wisdom aspect, which focuses on perfect enlightenment.

Relative bodhichitta also has two aspects: aspiring bodhichitta and engaged bodhichitta. In a way, these two also reflect the aspects of compassion and wisdom. With aspiring bodhichitta, we have thoughts like,

"I want to become enlightened in order to help all beings have lasting peace and happiness." Compassion is the driving force of aspiring bodhichitta. Just as you don't want to suffer, no one else wants to suffer. No one wants pain or problems. Therefore, you generate bodhichitta by thinking, "I want to be free of suffering and pain, and I want others to be free of suffering and pain as well."

Engaged bodhichitta goes even further than this. Beyond simply having a great aspiration, it becomes engaged in the process: "Since I want all beings to become free from suffering, I will work diligently to help them reach enlightenment." This is engaged bodhichitta.

It sometimes happens that our compassion becomes frustrated compassion. We can see the pain and suffering of others and we want to do something, but we don't know what can be done, or what we personally could do. This is where the wisdom aspect comes in. Unless we can sense the possibility of being completely free from suffering, we would never say, "I will make this happen." With wisdom, we understand why we can be free of suffering, why lasting peace and happiness are possible. Bodhichitta must have both compassion and wisdom. With compassion, bodhichitta has a goal, and with wisdom, there is at least some understanding of what the goal is and why it is possible to reach it. So, even relative bodhichitta has both aspects of compassion and wisdom.

Bodhichitta brings wisdom and compassion together. One way this happens is that as our compassion grows, our self-centeredness lessens. With less self-absorption, our attachment and aversion decrease as well. The less attachment and aversion we have, the more our wisdom grows. In this way, compassion leads to wisdom.

It can also go the other way—wisdom leads to compassion. Wisdom is the direct experience of the true nature of our mind and our world. As our understanding becomes stronger, we become more fearless. As we become more fearless, we become less self-centered. This leads to less aversion and attachment, and this makes us more compassionate.

Bodhichitta is the awakened heart; it is the heart of a buddha. The buddhas are beings who have developed their wisdom and compassion to the greatest possible extent. The practice of Buddhism is the process of training in wisdom and compassion; it is all about cultivating bodhichitta. With highly developed wisdom and compassion, you have true peace of mind and true fearlessness, and you genuinely accomplish the welfare of all beings. This is how you can end suffering for both yourself and others. This is why bodhichitta is the essence of all dharma practice.

2. Obstacles are caused by ripening karmic effects. Even the tiniest ordinary action becomes a hindrance when it ripens.

Obstacles are an interesting topic. One important thing to remember about obstacles is that they are not permanent. Sometimes people think, "Oh, this obstacle is insurmountable." But that is never the case. Everything occurs as it does because of causes and conditions coming together. What we call "karma" is simply the fact that actions have consequences. Generally speaking, negative actions bring negative effects, and positive actions bring positive effects. A person's karma is the causes and conditions that form that person's life.

There is a saying in Tibet: "To know what you were like in the past, look at what you are now. To know what you will be like in the future, look at your actions now." To have an idea about your past lives, you don't need to ask a fortune-teller; you can see for yourself by looking at your life now. What you are now is a result of your past actions. And your future will be a result of your present actions of body, speech, and mind. If your actions are positive and you are forming positive habits, then your future will be better. If you are doing things that are negative and becoming accustomed to them, then your future will be worse. This is exactly what we mean by karma. So, you need to be careful about what you do with your body, speech, and mind.

This brings up the question of free will: Are we actually free to form our own future, or are we driven by our actions from the past? Both of these are somewhat true. The fact that everything is dependent on conditions means there is freedom. Conditions can be changed. We can act in positive ways or negative ways, and whatever we do will influence our future.

Sometimes people tell me they feel disturbed when they see others doing something negative, and they don't know what to do about it. I would say that it's not really your concern how other people act; the place to put your attention is on how you act. If you can behave well, that solves a lot of problems.

We can never control other people's actions and reactions; we can only control our own. What other people are doing or not doing is not really our concern. We have not been appointed by someone to make judgments or assessments of their actions. When we get caught up in thinking about what others did and what they said, and how this was wrong and that was wrong, we lose our own stability.

If we are clear about our own intention not to cause harm, and that we are going to do the best we can in every situation, then our problems with others are basically over. We are clear, we are confident, and our whole way of being is positive. Then, if someone is unkind to us, so what? It's okay. We don't need to get upset about it. If someone is kind to us, that's very nice, but if they are not, we needn't feel hurt. That's their problem. We are okay and we are stable.

When our intention is to never cause harm, then other people tend to treat us in the same way. This doesn't always happen, but more often than not, people treat us the way we treat them. In any case, we can never make everyone happy. But by having a positive attitude, we become stronger, more integrated within ourselves, and more consistent. We are not always watching how others react. It's good to be sensitive to others' feelings and their ways of thinking, but it's not good to become too sensitive, because then we get too touchy, too easily upset. If we are oversensitive, this can make life difficult for those around us as well. So it's important to become stable and clear, and not take the games people play too seriously. Let them play their games. We know we are not going to play that way ourselves.

Sometimes I hear people say that those who do negative things become very successful, and those who act positively are not particularly successful. But this depends on how you define success. Perhaps someone who acts negatively has more money, but is that really success? Is it more important to have a big bank account, or to have the peace of mind that enables us to sleep well? If someone is anxious all the time even though they have a big bank account, what's the use? Richer people are not necessarily happier. Sometimes they are so concerned about losing their money that they try to kill themselves. It's ironic, but it happens.

Several years ago, the king of Bhutan wrote a book about his new economic policy. He said his government is no longer concerned about their Gross National Product. From now on, they are focusing on their country's Gross National Happiness. He called an international conference on Gross National Happiness: the first one was in Bhutan, the second year it was in Canada, and the third year it was in Bangkok,

Thailand. I was invited to the conference in Bangkok, and I gave a talk entitled "The Buddhist View of Gross National Happiness." About a dozen nations, as well as the United Nations, were represented at the conference.

The question this conference addresses is whether raising the Gross National Product (GNP) actually makes people happier. The reason we want to raise the GNP is to increase our well-being. But if we give the GNP too much emphasis, we become enslaved by our need to make money, we do things that destroy our planet, and in the process we destroy ourselves. Does this make any sense?

So, the basic question is: What is success? Is it about what we have, or is it about what we are? What we have is really out of our control. Today we can have many things, and tomorrow we can have nothing. What we are is much more in our control. If we are kind and joyful and intelligent, if we have a positive attitude to our life, then it doesn't matter very much what we have or don't have.

I know from personal experience that all your possessions can rapidly disappear, and you are left with nothing. When my family was in Tibet, they were regarded as quite rich. My mother came from a very well-known family. But when we fled from our country, we lost everything. We didn't even have a tent. We had a big red cloth to put over us when it rained, but it wasn't waterproof, so it didn't help much. We started out with some cooking pots carried on the back of a mule, but in crossing a rushing river, the mule fell down and the cooking pots were lost. So, we didn't even have a pot for boiling water! Losing everything can happen just like that.

But people survive and it's okay. Riches come and go. If we feel joyful and peaceful, if our life has meaning and purpose, and if we are helping others have meaningful lives as well, this seems much more an indication of success.

To return to the main point here about karma, Gampopa is saying that even the tiniest actions can ripen into big obstacles. Something can start off rather harmless, but it can ripen into something very negative. It is the same with positive actions. A positive action can be so small that there seems like no point in doing it. But if you do it again and again, it can become bigger and bigger, and generate very powerful effects.

I know a story that illustrates this. Once there was a criminal who was sentenced to death. When asked if he had a last wish before his execution, he said he wanted to meet his mother one more time. When his mother came, they were both very moved. When he hugged her, it looked like he was going to kiss her, but actually he bit her nose.

Everyone was shocked and wanted to know why he did that. The man said that he became a criminal because of his mother's behavior. When he was a child, he used to bring home pieces of chalk from school. His mother would praise him, saying he was so clever for taking the chalk. Then, he started to bring home pencils and books, and she was even more pleased. He said he knew he was stealing, but instead of rebuking and disciplining him, she encouraged him. At first he was a petty thief, but he became a bigger thief and a bigger criminal, until he reached the point where he was sentenced to death for his crimes.

When we talk about the ripening of karma, we are talking about all karmic results, not just negative ones. Even good experiences can become obstacles. For instance, you could experience a good result from meditation, like becoming clairvoyant. This could become an obstacle if you don't know how to carry it onto the path. You could fixate on it and become arrogant, thinking, "I must be almost enlightened! I can see through walls, and I know who is calling on the telephone. I must be a special person!" So, anything can be an obstacle, even an achievement.

On the other hand, if you know how to deal with things, even big problems and difficulties can become your spiritual path. The Kagyu lineage of Mahamudra specializes in using everything as part of the path. When good things happen, you can bring them onto the path, and when bad things happen, you can bring them onto the path as well.

3. The emphasis in practice should be on karmic cause and result.

This follows from the last answer. Gampopa is saying once again that we need to be cautious about karmic effects. Exactly what are we doing right now with our body, speech, and mind? If it is something positive, then we should encourage ourselves and rejoice in that. If it is something negative, then we should look at its harmfulness and let go of it.

This point has been emphasized by many lamas, including Padmasambhava, or Guru Rinpoche, who said, "Your view should descend from the vastness of the sky, but your actions should ascend like a ladder from the ground." At every moment, whatever we do affects ourselves and others, whatever we say affects ourselves and others, and whatever we think affects ourselves and others. If we ignore this, then a high view leaves us stranded in the air. Our actions need to be down-to-earth.

Another way Padmasambhava expressed this is by saying that our conduct should not be overly influenced by the view. What he meant is that according to the view of emptiness, or the teachings of Mahamudra and Dzogchen, ultimately there is no karma, there is no good or bad, and there is no personal self. Although on the ultimate level there are no results to achieve, we need to be clear that on the relative level, everything is still happening, and even the tiniest actions have consequences. When we join the ultimate view and relative conduct, then we are good practitioners.

Actually, the main reason that lamas don't teach high views like Dzogchen and Mahamudra to newer students is because they fear that people will mix up the view and the conduct. It is not because Dzogchen or Mahamudra is dangerous. What danger could there possibly be in doing Mahamudra meditation? It would be dangerous only if the students got lost in the ultimate view and neglected the ground of karmic cause and result.

There is a well-known incident connected with this involving the Third Dodrupchen Rinpoche, Jigme Tenpe Nyima. Perhaps you have heard of the Dodrupchen incarnations: the First Dodrupchen was one of the main students of Jigme Lingpa, the founder of the Longchen Nyingtik lineage. The First Dodrupchen was a great meditation master; the Tibetan title "Dodrupchen" means the "great siddha from the area of Do." The second incarnation was also a great master, but not as renowned as the first or the third. The Third Dodrupchen, Jigme Tenpe Nyima, was an especially great master, a student of Patrul Rinpoche and other lamas, and renowned for his brilliant commentaries. The current Dalai Lama greatly admires his writings; he often quotes them when he teaches, particularly Dodrupchen Tenpe Nyima's short commentary on the *Guhyasamaja Tantra*.

That was just a little background on the Third Dodrupchen. The reason I am mentioning him is that at a certain point in his life he stopped teaching Dzogchen. He was teaching Dzogchen quite a lot, and was considered a great Dzogchen master. But one day he announced, "No more Dzogchen teachings from me. I have stopped giving them."

What happened? One time when he was leading a group retreat, he was out walking and overheard some of his students talking to each other. They said, "Everything is emptiness; nothing really exists. Everything is okay just as it is. There is actually no reason to pay attention to karmic cause and effect."

When Dodrupchen heard this, he thought, "My high teaching is doing more harm than good. I will not teach Dzogchen anymore."

This is the same point Gampopa is making. No matter what spiritual practice we do, we need to be careful about our actions. It is wonderful to have a high view and see things with equanimity, but that does not negate the ground where we live. While having the ultimate view, we need to deal with things as they are now. We need to be aware of how our actions affect our life and how they affect others' lives. This must be taken into account; it is extremely important. This is why Gampopa says, "The emphasis in practice should be on karmic cause and result."

4. Among all the views, the most important view is the right view.

As for which view is the most important, Chenrezik says it is the complete view, or the right view. That is all he says. This leads to a further question: "But which view is the right view?" I think what he means is that we have to look for ourselves to find the right view. We can't simply agree, thinking, "Yes, that must be right," and consider the matter finished.

In Buddhism, the view could be a philosophy, but more than that, it is the way we see things, the way we understand reality. We find the right view by seeing things as directly and fully as possible.

The right view is broad-mindedness; it is openness. The complete view is never one-sided. It is not dogmatic, small, or narrow-minded. Rather, it is tolerance; it is being able to look at things directly and genuinely without preconceived ideas, without being controlled by old assumptions. Sometimes people think, "My tradition explains the view this way, so that must be the right view. The other views must be wrong." This is a misunderstanding. The right view is very open; it is never restricted.

This point is emphasized in a teaching by the Buddha, in which he warned his followers about two errors, which he called "holding the two as the best." The first is to hold your own conduct and character as the best, and the second is to hold your own view as the best. The Buddha said these are serious mistakes, because when you think your ethics and your view are supreme, you've closed your mind before having completely understood. You have made a decision based on hearsay. The Buddha specifically warned against this.

When you have the right view, you don't hold on to anything. You are open and accept things as they come. This is similar to Nagarjuna's well-known statement about not holding a position. He said he did not make any assertions; he only asked questions. If other people's views crumbled in the face of his questions, he couldn't help that. Nagarjuna wasn't trying to harm their views; he was simply looking for the truth.

Having the right view means making a genuine, personal search for what is true. When we analyze and reflect, or when we ask questions, we can follow the guidelines given by the Buddha and our teachers, but we needn't conform to what some teacher or scripture proclaims as the highest view. We shouldn't think that we must learn what the Buddha said and affirm that. Buddhism emphasizes debate because we must know for ourselves what is true. We can debate anything; all the Buddha's teachings are open to question.

One unique feature of the Buddhist teachings is the way they are classified according to the provisional meaning and the definitive meaning. The provisional meaning refers to something the Buddha said that is not ultimately true but was said for a purpose. Perhaps someone would benefit from the provisional meaning but wouldn't be able to understand the definitive meaning. Provisional teachings could be appropriate in some circumstances but not others. In contrast, the definitive meaning is true, exactly as it is. This is where many debates are focused: Which teachings are definitive, and which teachings are provisional? When we study, we need to examine whether the teachings convey the provisional meaning or the definitive meaning. We need to ask: Is this teaching ultimately valid or not?

Debate and questioning are valuable, but we can never find the whole truth that way. The whole truth is not bound by concepts or intellect. This is why we meditate. The real truth comes through experience. Having the right view is a process of gradually seeing ourselves and others and all things just as they are. Our seeing has to come from within, and it comes through introspection, analysis, personal experience, and meditation. This happens slowly, stage by stage. As we continue to study and practice, our understanding gets clearer and clearer.

The view is open and limitless. There is a Tibetan saying: "If grasping occurs, it is not the view." When you have the right view, you are free of fixation. The right view is total openness.

> **5. As for the number of consciousnesses, you could say there are six or you could say there are eight. Or, if they are grouped together, you could say there is one. For example, consciousness is like a monkey inside a house with many windows.**

In terms of the number of consciousnesses, Chenrezik gives a clever answer: you could say six, you could say eight, or you could say one. He gives the example of a monkey inside a house with many windows. From the point of view of the monkey, there is only one consciousness. From the point of view of the windows, there could be six or eight.

Within the Buddhist philosophical schools, the Shravakayana and Madhyamaka talk about six consciousnesses—the five sense consciousnesses and the mental consciousness. The Chittamatra and the tantras talk about eight consciousnesses—the six already mentioned, plus the afflicted consciousness and the basis of all consciousness. There are several ways of categorizing consciousness, but it doesn't matter much which way you classify them.

Of course, this doesn't mean there aren't debates on this kind of thing. Philosophical debates are sometimes important, sometimes interesting, and sometimes confusing. Usually when people debate, they play with words and twist the meaning a little bit, so their opponents end up saying something they don't agree with.

There is an old Tibetan saying about this: "If two scholars agree, one of them is not a scholar. If two saints disagree, one of them is not a saint." In other words, true realization is the same. If two saints do not have very similar experience, then one of them is not a saint. But philosophers are a different matter. If two philosophers agree, then one is not a philosopher. It is important to remember this when you study the teachings. When two great scholars debate, we tend to assume that one must be right and the other wrong. Otherwise, why would they debate? But this is not always the case.

There are stories about debates between great masters who are considered to be equally realized. Perhaps the most well-known debate involved Chandrakirti and Chandragomin, two great masters who debated for seven years. They were debating how to best express the teachings, about which words convey most clearly the way things are. One master would say to the other, "If you explain it like that, there are several ways it could be misunderstood." Then, the other one might say, "But your way could be even more confusing, and I'll show you why." Scholars and philosophers are usually trying to explain things that are difficult to describe in words, and so the debates go on.

6. The accumulations are perfected by the *paramita* of wisdom.

The last question the monk asked Chenrezik was: "What causes the perfection of the accumulations?" From one perspective, dharma practice revolves around the two accumulations: the accumulation of merit and the accumulation of wisdom. Maybe "merit" is not the best translation, since many Westerners get confused by this word. Often they think that merit refers to some sort of medal or prize, like those awarded at school. Instead, the accumulation of merit means doing positive things or developing positive habits so that our negative tendencies are reduced. When we accumulate merit, we become so accustomed to acting and reacting in positive ways that our negative emotions barely occur anymore. And once the negative emotions subside, we no longer perform negative actions with our body, speech, and mind.

The basis for accumulating merit is compassion. What we call "positive action" is something we do with the intention of benefiting others. From the Mahayana point of view, even seemingly negative actions can be positive if they are genuinely inspired and carried out with compassion.

The accumulation of wisdom does not mean gathering a lot of information or knowledge. It means understanding and realizing the way things truly are. It is learning to be completely natural. The accumulation of wisdom means that our wisdom has become so strong that we see everything fully and directly.

Someone who has developed merit and wisdom to the fullest extent is called a buddha. Basically, the question posed to Chenrezik is: "What is the best way to become enlightened? What is necessary to perfect merit and wisdom?" Chenrezik answers that the paramita of wisdom will make the two accumulations complete.

The general way we accumulate merit is by doing fewer and fewer negative actions, and more and more positive ones. In the Mahayana, this is equivalent to the first five paramitas: generosity, discipline, patience, diligence, and meditation. Reinforcing positive actions definitely helps, but it cannot cut the root of negativity. Without wisdom, the good deeds of our body, speech, and mind have positive effects, but they cannot liberate us from samsara. All they can do is contribute to having a better samsaric life. They can make our life seem better, but they cannot make us enlightened.

The sixth paramita, the paramita of wisdom, is the only thing that can liberate you. Seeing deeply what you are, the nature of your mind, frees you from grasping, attachment, and aversion. It is through seeing what is true that you cut the root of samsara.

If you can completely see yourself the way you are, then that can free you. If you can completely relax, that can free you. If you can completely be what you are, that can free you. Knowing things directly and completely, and being able to relax within that knowing, is the key to perfecting merit and wisdom.

FOUR

The Four Dharmas of Gampopa

NOW WE COME to Gampopa's most famous teaching, the Four Dharmas of Gampopa. Here they are presented in a slightly different way than you might have heard them before. Gampopa begins by discussing how to bring all our activities to the path of dharma.

> The precious guru said: Whatever good dharma practice you do—whether study, reflection, listening, teaching, keeping the precepts, accumulation, purification, or meditation—should not become just another activity. Instead, dharma practice should be transformative. If you wonder what this means, a scripture says:
>
> > *Attachment, anger, and delusion*
> > *And the actions created by them are unvirtuous.*[1]
>
> As well, even virtuous deeds are ordinary actions if they are done to obtain the happiness of gods and humans in this life, or if your intention is degraded or based on the eight worldly concerns.

Gampopa is saying that not only negative actions are karmic activity but positive actions are also karmic activity when they are done for selfish reasons. Whatever you are doing—like listening to teachings or keeping the precepts—might look like dharma practice from the outside, but if it's motivated by the eight worldly concerns, it is merely creating further karma. For example, you might make donations, like distributing money to the poor, so that people will think you are generous. The action is seemingly good, but because it is done with a gaining attitude, it isn't real dharma practice.

Real dharma practice is free from the eight worldly concerns. To review the eight worldly concerns, they are being rich or poor, which could also be described as gain or loss; being powerful or powerless; having a good reputation or a bad reputation; and having pleasure or pain. Usually, we think that happiness comes from wealth, power, popularity, and pleasure, and that these four things will give us everything that we need—we will have "made it." But from a spiritual point of view, these things are not the answer. Being rich is not a source of happiness, and being poor is not a source of happiness. Being powerful does not bring happiness, and being powerless does not bring happiness. It is the same with being well-known or unknown, and having pleasure or pain. Lasting peace and happiness do not depend on outer conditions; they come from seeing in a clear way. When your mind is focused on any of the eight worldly concerns, whether on the positive side or the negative side, your activities are not following the dharma.

Gampopa teaches four stages of practice, the Four Dharmas, through which we can realize true peace and happiness:

> (1) What we call "the dharma" is practiced as the dharma, (2) the dharma becomes the path, (3) the path dispels delusion, and (4) delusion arises as wisdom.

The First Dharma of Gampopa, the dharma being practiced as the dharma, has two aspects: worldly dharma and transcendent dharma.

> In worldly dharma practice, you know about death and impermanence, and are certain about the workings of cause and effect. Fearing the suffering of the lower realms, you do all sorts of positive actions to avoid going there in future existences. You practice in order to obtain your own peace and happiness in future lives. For instance, you practice in order to have a good human body or a divine form in the higher realms, the

comforts of a god or a human, or the pleasures of a god. This is called worldly dharma practice.

Worldly dharma practice is done with the motivation of getting something better in this life or future lives. For instance, we want peace of mind, we want things to work out well, and we want to be happy. This motivation can include others as well as ourselves. It's good to apply the teachings to our states of mind and emotional problems in order to have a better life. This approach is called worldly dharma practice.

Even the great scholar Nagarjuna talked about the value of worldly dharma. He said: "Ascending the stairs of the gods' and humans' dharma will bring one close to liberation." He suggests that we begin with worldly dharma practice and become better human beings. By applying the teachings we can become good, solid citizens of samsara. We don't need to renounce samsara right from the beginning. It is easier to start by practicing in order to have a good life.

This is similar to the approach of modern psychology, which helps you become a healthy human being. When your mind becomes healthy, there are strong emotions, but they are solid ones. There is attachment, but it is a good sort of attachment. There is attachment to this life, to the next life, to your family, to your people, but in a good way. There is a recognition that hatred and fear are not good for you or others, and so you work with your mind to go beyond them. The Buddhist teachings have this recognition as well. The sutras and tantras agree that the first step is to become a good, stable human being.

However, most of the biographies and instructions of the great Buddhist masters focus on transcendent dharma practice, not on the usefulness of worldly dharma practice. The biographies describe how the great masters had total renunciation for samsara and attained great enlightenment. This can lead students to think that having complete renunciation is the only way to practice, and that unless they are like Milarepa, they are not dharma practitioners. But this isn't true.

Worldly dharma practice comes first. We can apply the dharma in daily life in order to take responsibility, do the right thing, go to work, make money, and look after our family. It's good to create a nice life and a nice community, to do things for others, avoid extremes, and include a little meditation to bring peace of mind.

If you want a good result, you find out what brings that result and you try to make it happen. If you want more peace of mind, or you want a more comfortable life, then you create the conditions that will lead to more peace and comfort. As we discussed when talking about karma, positive actions lead to positive results. So, worldly dharma practice means doing dharma activities in order to have a better world, a better samsara. As long as you're here, why not live in a better samsara than in a worse samsara? And from another point of view, worldly dharma is fine because there are many different people with many different objectives.

Gradually we come to see that we could go further than this, which brings us to the second type of dharma practice, the transcendent dharma.

> **In the second approach, transcendent dharma practice, you have understood the faults of all of cyclic existence, so you have no attachment whatsoever to the body and the enjoyments of a god or human. Revulsion and sadness arise because you know that samsara is like a pit of fire, a prison, a dungeon, darkness, or a filthy swamp. Being convinced that samsara is an ocean of suffering, you are not attached to any of its joys or qualities, and think, "I want to be quickly liberated from samsara."**

Although there is nothing wrong with worldly dharma practice, it will not bring liberation from suffering. There's an important distinction between actions that are positive and actions that are liberating. Through positive practices, you can be born into a higher realm, like living in America with nice things and a nice car. In fact, performing positive deeds can lead to much higher states of existence than America! But positive actions in themselves cannot take you beyond samsara.

The problem is that when your peaceful and comfortable situation ends, you continue circling within the six realms of existence.[2] A good example of circling in samsara is a fly in a bottle. A fly can go up to the top of the bottle, but then it has to go back down. It is not free until it gets out of the bottle. In the same way, as long as you are controlled by passion, aggression, and ignorance, you are not free. Even the highest sort of samsaric existence will eventually lead to more suffering and pain; there is no lasting good in it. When you are determined to free yourself from the root of samsara, this is renunciation.

Real renunciation involves recognizing that as long as your mind contains attachment and aversion, you cannot be completely joyful and free of anxiety. There is always dissatisfaction, no matter how nice the situation may be. Even if everything is fine now, you know that something could happen to make you unhappy. You know the situation cannot remain this way forever.

This is why samsara is traditionally described as a pit of burning fire. No matter how high you go, there is no safe place. Once you have reached the highest state of samsaric existence, you will eventually fall to a lower level when the karma that brought you there is exhausted. No matter how good or bad it seems, cyclic existence is still a prison. Whether your chains are made of iron or made of gold, you are still chained. Samsara is like a dungeon, like darkness, like a swamp of shit. Really, this is what Gampopa is saying.

When you see that samsara is an ocean of suffering, you become certain that as long as you are chained to mental afflictions, there can be no true happiness. This loosens your attachment to samsara so that you want to get out of it as quickly as possible. This kind of intention and understanding turn your practice into transcendent dharma. You are practicing in order to reach liberation.

> While desiring liberation, you also see the shortcomings of the lesser vehicle and the enlightenment of the *shravakas*. They do all their dharma practice and pass beyond suffering into peace and bliss for themselves alone. Seeing the faults of that approach, you direct your positive accumulation and purification practices toward complete enlightenment. Having the goal of complete enlightenment sums up transcendent dharma practice, the second aspect of dharma being practiced as the dharma.

Wanting to transcend samsaric states of mind, you can practice either the path of the Shravakayana or the path of the Bodhisattvayana. The Shravakayana is the "vehicle of the listeners" who follow the fundamental teachings of the Buddha. Although shravakas aspire to be free from samsaric suffering, they do not aim for complete enlightenment in order to benefit all beings. The Shravakayana is a narrower vehicle than the Bodhisattvayana because its compassion is less inclusive. Of course, shravakas practice loving-kindness and compassion, but they don't take responsibility for helping all beings like the bodhisattvas do.

As your practice matures and your compassion increases, you see the defects of the Shravakayana and turn to the Mahayana. Both the Shravakayana and the Bodhisattvayana are part of the transcendent dharma, but the Bodhisattvayana is greater.

Now, for the second of the Four Dharmas, Gampopa goes on to say:

> The dharma that becomes the path also has two aspects: the dharma that is the basis of the path, and the dharma that is the actual path. First, in relation to the basis of the path, because of seeing the shortcomings of the lesser vehicle, you do all your practice with the motivation of love, compassion, and bodhichitta. This pertains to whatever you do in terms of accumulation and purification, whether it is a little or a lot. In order to establish all the limitless sentient beings in perfect enlightenment, you think, "I want to attain the three *kayas,* the five wisdoms, and the omniscience of a buddha." This is dharma as the basis of the path.

For the dharma to become the path, Gampopa describes two steps: practicing the dharma as the basis of the path, and practicing the dharma as the path itself. First, the basis of the path is connected with your aspiration. Understanding the narrowness of the lower *yanas,* you do all your practice, whether large or small, for the sake of all beings throughout space. With this attitude, you might think, "I want all the infinite beings to be liberated from samsara and become fully enlightened. With love and compassion, I want to attain buddhahood in order to be able to accomplish their benefit. For their sake, I want to actualize the three kayas and five wisdoms."

In distinguishing between the Mahayana and the Shravakayana, the Mahayanists say the difference is the degree of compassion. This might sound like the Shravakayana has no compassion or doesn't teach loving-kindness for all beings. This is not true. For example, the prayer of the Four Immeasurable Thoughts that we recite as the principal bodhichitta aspiration comes from the Shravakayana. It says: "May all sentient beings enjoy happiness and the root of happiness. May they be free from suffering and the root of suffering. May they not be separated from the great happiness devoid of suffering. May they dwell in great equanimity, free from passion, aggression, and prejudice." This is a general Buddhist teaching called the Four Brahmaviharas, or "Four Abodes of Brahma." It is important to realize that compassion is part of all Buddhist teachings and practices.

So, what are the Mahayanists talking about? I think it is mainly the degree of commitment, the extent of one's personal involvement. When we say, "May all beings have happiness and be free of suffering," this is a wish. We wish very strongly that the world will be filled with love, compassion, joy, and equanimity. But the distinction in the Mahayana is being personally committed to making this happen. As followers of the Mahayana, we also act on this wish. This is where the difference lies. When we actually do something about our wish, our dharma practice becomes the actual path.

> In practicing the dharma that is the actual path, you recollect that the relative truth is like an illusion or a dream. You do all your dharma practice, whether it is a little or a lot, with love, compassion, and bodhichitta, and at the same time, you see it as illusory and dreamlike. Since your practice has both skillful means and wisdom, and they are inseparable, your dharma practice is the actual path.

The actual path is mainly about practicing the six paramitas. It is not so much a matter of your doing formal practice at a certain time of day for a certain amount of time; it is more about the way you live your life. You train in meditation, discipline, generosity, and patience while trying to understand interdependence, the transient nature of things, and the dreamlike nature of all experience. The more understanding you have, the more your wisdom grows and your clinging fades away. You can let your mind be, which allows its natural qualities to shine forth. This is your wisdom and your realization.

At the same time, your dharma practice is joined with compassion, love, and bodhichitta. The practice of dharma is not something extra that you have to do. It is the way you work with your everyday life and how you connect with people and situations. With compassion as its basis, the actual path is the blending of wisdom and skillful means.

With wisdom you see what you actually are; you know the nature of your mind. Awakening wisdom is the main aim of Buddhist practice, because when this happens, liberation from samsara dawns. Samsara is based on ignorance, on not knowing what you actually are. This causes a dualistic view of self and others, which leads to anger, greed, and all sorts of emotional problems. So wisdom is the most important spiritual quality because it uproots samsaric suffering.

It usually takes time to develop wisdom, so various skillful means are used to help you along. The skillful means are methods that take you from one stage to the next. For instance, in order to make your mind more calm and clear, you do meditation, concentration, or other kinds of mental training. If your mind is habituated to negativity, then you train in making your mind more positive by practices such as visualizing the buddhas with their love and compassion. Buddhism is full of methods for working with yourself and others. Using these skillful means with wisdom and compassion is the actual path.

When you are working with your mind in this way, sometimes you put more emphasis on compassion, and sometimes you put more emphasis on wisdom. Because of compassion, you don't run away from samsara. You want to help others, and you become more courageous about doing so. Because of wisdom, you understand the true nature of things, and your attachment and grasping diminish. Only with both wisdom and compassion will you be able to reach complete enlightenment. Needing both wisdom and compassion is like a bird needing two wings to fly. When we are cultivating both compassion and wisdom, we know we are practicing the actual path.

Now, for the third of the Four Dharmas, Gampopa says:

> **The way that the path dispels delusion has two aspects. The first type of delusion is grasping at existence and non-existence, or eternalism and nihilism. This is dispelled by practice in which they are seen as a dream or an illusion.**

The Third Dharma is that the path dispels delusion. How is this done? It is done by experiencing wisdom and compassion in union. There are two main types of delusion that sentient beings have: wisdom dispels the first, and compassion dispels the second.

The first type of delusion is taking things to be either truly existent or non-existent. Instead, if we relate to everything as a dream or an illusion, and if we practice with that understanding, we come to see the inseparability of the two truths—the relative truth and the ultimate truth. Conventionally, on the relative level, there is karma, there is interdependence, there are six realms, and so on. Yet on the ultimate level, none of this exists.

Coming to understand the unity of the two truths is the actual path. The two truths are not two separate things. When we see the nature of things, we see their emptiness. Saying that the nature of things is emptiness doesn't mean that things, like a glass, are not here. On the relative level, we can accept the existence of everything we see. But when we look deeper to see exactly how they exist, we see that they arise interdependently due to causes and conditions. Nothing exists as an independent or separate thing. Understanding that the relative is merely relative is the same as understanding the ultimate. When we see this, our way of reacting to experience changes, and we are practicing the actual path.

Usually we react very strongly to relative reality. But the more we see the relative nature of things—that everything is impermanent and interrelated—the less solid our view is. This brings less fear, so there is less aversion and attachment. The main difference between being enmeshed in samsara and being liberated from samsara is whether our mind is controlled by attachment and aversion. If our mind is not controlled by our likes and dislikes, what we experience is nirvana. Although this is easy to say, it is not easy to do. We are often overwhelmed by our emotions.

So how can you be free from strong emotions? You need to be certain that there is no point in acting them out. This recognition comes from wisdom. When you know that there is nothing to fear, that there is nothing real to get or to get away from, then you don't get caught in attachment and aversion.

The key to understanding emptiness is seeing that what you are is impermanent. You are always changing, and therefore, you are emptiness. How often do you change? Do you change every year? Every month? Every hour? Minute by minute? Second by second? I have been told there is a mathematical rule that between two points—for instance, in one meter—there are an infinite number of points. Not only in one meter but in one millimeter there are countless points. This applies to time as well. We say things change second by second. But is one second an indivisible unit of time? No; within one second you can have an unlimited number of instants. So, it is never the case that now something is changing, but later it will stop. Change is unceasing.

If you are changing all the time, then there cannot be a "you" who is really there. Does this make sense? If you are not staying present as one thing, then what are "you"? You are just a flow. Anything that is changing is simply a flow. Perhaps this could become a new type of reasoning called mathematically establishing emptiness.

If you deeply understand that your mind, your body, and everything you experience is transforming in every fraction of a second, then why grasp at things? Nothing can be grasped. There is nothing you can hold on to, whether it is good or bad, right or wrong, pleasant or unpleasant. When you have the wisdom to see the empty nature of things as they are, you know there is no point in attachment or aversion. This is what liberates you. Positive deeds can make your life better, but it is wisdom that uproots samsara. Since practicing the path brings the understanding that reality is beyond existence and non-existence, the path dispels delusion.

The second delusion is acting for one's welfare alone and having a Hinayana approach. This is dispelled by meditating on love, compassion, and bodhichitta.

It's important to be clear about our main objectives in life. Our first concern is for ourselves to be free from suffering, and on top of that, we would like others to be free as well. The clearer we become about this, the more we want to be of benefit, not only in small ways but in very large ways. As our aspiration grows, we want ourselves and others to be completely and totally free, and we become inspired to work toward this goal. This is the motivation of bodhichitta. We realize that actualizing bodhichitta is the most important thing we could possibly do, and we make a commitment to do it. This is the second way that the path dispels delusion.

Next, there is the Fourth Dharma of Gampopa, which is that delusion arises as wisdom. This is the best way of dispelling delusion. From a higher point of view, delusion is not dispelled; it is transformed when its nature is recognized and experienced. With this kind of understanding, delusion arises as primordial wisdom. There are two approaches to this: the Sutrayana system of the *Prajnaparamita*, and the Vajrayana system of secret Mantrayana.

In relation to the first approach, Gampopa says:

According to the *Prajnaparamita Sutra,* the consciousness
that eliminates delusion is part of the relative truth. This
makes consciousness itself like an illusion or a dream. The
perceiving mind and its perceived objects have never been divided, and their nondual nature is inherently pure. Ultimately,
there is no perceiving and nothing to be perceived. When you
realize that the grasping and the grasped are completely at
peace, beyond any conceptual fabrications, then delusion
arises as primordial wisdom.

According to the *Prajnaparamita Sutra,* realization comes from understanding emptiness and interdependence. In particular, it arises
from seeing that the awareness that eliminates delusion is itself like an
illusion or a dream. When you are dreaming and you realize it's a
dream, you don't get caught in grasping at the pleasant things that appear, because you know they are illusory. Nor do you worry about losing
things, even your own life. Since it is only a dream, your reactions
change.

Consciousness, as well as delusion, has no inherent nature; both consciousness and delusion are pure and nondual. Ultimately, there is no
act of grasping and no object to be grasped. There is complete peace
without concepts. When experiencing things directly, there is no need
to cling or make any assertions about them. There is no need to add
concepts of good and bad, or make any judgments at all.

Once you see everything as relative and interdependent, then things
become dreamlike and your fear dissolves. Being free of fear is the key
to liberation. Without fear, there is no reason to run after things or run
away from them. All experiences can come and go, and you simply go
through them. Your awareness is very clear and your emotions occur
without grasping. Since nothing binds or traps you, every delusion
arises as wisdom. At this level, you realize there is nothing that could be
called delusion. There are no real obscurations. This is the Sutrayana
method for experiencing delusions as wisdom.

To say this in another way, it is by seeing everything as interdependent and empty that there is no more delusion. Interdependence and
emptiness apply not only to outer objects but to our consciousness as
well. Consciousness is relative, just like outer objects. It is an illusion,
like a dream. Not only are there no real objects to be grasped, there is no

real act of grasping. The perceiver and the perceived are inseparable. They are nondual and pure in their very nature. Ultimately, there is nothing to purify, nothing to get rid of, and nothing to perfect.

When you realize this, you see there is nothing more to do; there is no need to struggle. This is not a case of purifying something or doing something to get rid of delusion. There is no need to change anything, because there is nothing to be changed, and no one to do the changing. By knowing this, delusion arises as wisdom.

This is the same as enlightenment. As we discussed in the chapter on the lineage history, when you become enlightened, you become enlightened as the primordial buddha. You don't think, "Finally, I've become enlightened. Yesterday I wasn't enlightened, but today I am." It's not like that. It's more that you see there is nothing to purify, there is nothing to do; everything is already completely okay. This experience comes when you fully see the way things are.

This is similar to the Buddha's teaching on the four noble truths. First, he said there is suffering, the cause of suffering, the cessation of suffering, and the path to the cessation of suffering. Then he said it like this: there is suffering, and we must understand it. There is the cause of suffering, and we must eliminate it. There is the cessation of suffering, and we must attain it. There is the path to end suffering, and we must accomplish it. Then he explained it again, this time according to the view of the *Prajnaparamita:* there is suffering and we must understand it, and yet there is nothing to understand. There is the cause of suffering and we must eliminate it, and yet there is nothing to eliminate. There is the cessation of suffering and we must attain it, and yet there is nothing to attain. There is the path to the cessation of suffering and we must accomplish it, and yet there is nothing to accomplish. These were the Buddha's words.

In teaching about wisdom, we sometimes say that the mind poisons—greed, anger, and ignorance—are themselves wisdom. Students often think this means the afflictive emotions are somehow turned around and polished, and then they shine as wisdom. It's not quite like that. It is more that you see what is happening in a different way. You know there is nothing to grasp and no need to grasp, and so you don't grasp. A shift happens when you know the true nature of whatever appears; you see that there's nothing wrong with it. What *is* wrong is the way we grasp things. If there is no grasping, we need not do anything else. This in itself is wisdom. Gampopa is renowned for saying that enlighten-ment is simply the clearing away of misunderstanding. When mistaken thinking is gone, liberation has happened.

> The way delusion arises as primordial wisdom according to the Vajrayana is like this: all delusion and nondelusion are in-separable from your mind. Not being separate, they are the nature of the mind, the essence of the mind, and the magical display of the mind. In itself, deluded consciousness is non-conceptual clarity.

Gampopa teaches a second way that delusion arises as wisdom, which accords with the Vajrayana teachings. In this approach, you see that the state of being deluded and the state of being undeluded are both dis-plays of your mind. Whether delusion is present or not, whatever arises is still the mind. The deluded aspect is a magical display of your mind, and the undeluded aspect is a magical display of your mind.

The Vajrayana approach is to look right at the mind itself. There is no need to analyze the whole universe, because all your experience hap-pens in your own mind. Without your mind, you wouldn't experience anything. You hear whatever you hear, and you see whatever you see. Whatever you experience is nothing other than your own experience. But what is doing the experiencing? What is your mind like?

When we look, we can see that the mind is clear, conscious, and aware. But where is it? What is it like? In Mahamudra practice, we do investiga-tions to look for the mind. For example: What color is the mind? What shape is it? Where is the mind? Is it inside the body or outside the body? Sometimes people think the mind is in the brain. But in which part of the brain? Is it in one cell or many cells? If it is not found in one cell, how could it be found in many cells? When you look for the mind and exam-ine introspectively, you cannot find it. There is nothing you can hold on to and say, "This is my mind." You can look from any angle, with any instrument, from inside or from outside, and there is nothing you can find that is "my mind." We could call the inability to find anything "emptiness." What emptiness means is that there is nothing graspable.

Yet at the same time, awareness is happening. The mind is emptiness and awareness, or emptiness and clarity. Within the clarity aspect, the thoughts, emotions, and sensations arise. These are the mind's manifestations. In Vajrayana terminology, these three aspects of the mind are known as the three kayas: the mind's nature is emptiness, which is the *dharmakaya;* the mind has clarity or awareness, which is the *sambhogakaya;* and the mind is continuously manifesting and displaying, which is the *nirmanakaya.* Please don't get confused by these terms— sometimes using Sanskrit is more of a drawback than a help. Just as these three aspects describe one single mind, the kayas are merely different aspects of the mind and not three separate things.

The displays of the mind are the most important part for us. Something happens and we think, "This feels great, that felt terrible," and so on. We think we're experiencing something external that is pleasant or unpleasant. Actually, it is only our mind. What we experience is not out there; our experience is merely a display of our own mind.

This reminds me of a famous song of Milarepa, where he talks about meditation with a young woman called Palden Bum. He tells her, "Meditate like the mountain, meditate like the ocean, and meditate like the sky."

She goes away to meditate, and then comes back and asks him, "When I meditate like the ocean, there are lots of waves. When I meditate like the sky, many clouds appear. When I meditate on my mind, many thoughts and emotions arise. What should I do?"

Milarepa told her, "If you can meditate like the ocean, then waves do not matter, because they are part of the ocean. Waves come out of the ocean and dissolve back into the ocean. They do not harm the ocean; they themselves are the ocean. It is the same with the clouds. They appear in the sky and disappear in the sky. Similarly, thoughts are just displays of the mind, and they do not harm the mind."

In this way, deluded consciousness, by its very nature, is luminous, aware, and nonconceptual. It displays as thoughts and emotions, but if you look deeply, you see that consciousness is nonconceptual clarity or nonconceptual awareness.

> **Clarity-emptiness cannot be pinpointed. Clarity-emptiness is uninterrupted. Clarity-emptiness is without a center or boundary. Awareness is baseless and naked.**

Although consciousness is considered to be deluded, its nature is undeluded because it is inseparable clarity-emptiness. Clarity-emptiness is continuous. It has no boundaries and it has no basis. Its nature is naked awareness, even when it appears deluded. When you understand and experience this, then your mind is undeluded, and whatever could be considered a delusion arises instead as wisdom.

There is no solid delusion in the mind that needs to be removed. There is no separate confusion that could be taken out so that wisdom could appear. The nature of the deluded mind itself is wisdom; this is what we need to see. This is similar to the well-known verse in the *Uttaratantra Shastra,* or the *Sublime Continuum:*

> *There is nothing at all to be removed,*
> *And not the slightest thing to be added.*
> *Look genuinely at what is genuine.*
> *When genuinely seen, there is total liberation.*[3]

When you compare the Vajrayana approach with the Sutrayana approach, you see there is no real difference between them. The Sutrayana way is to look at the deluded mind and see it as relative rather than real; the mind is like a dream or an illusion. Then, this understanding is applied to all phenomena so that everything is recognized as illusory.

The Vajrayana approach is to see that the deluded mind has the nature of wisdom. Because the Vajrayana way is to look at the mind itself, it is possible to become enlightened in one moment. This is the claim of the Vajrayana: samsara could be over in an instant. All it takes is truly knowing the wisdom nature. It sometimes happens that people don't have to go through a long training to realize the wisdom within the delusion. But I must say, one has to be very, very lucky for that to happen. Sorry to say, very few people are that lucky. Although it is rare, it can happen that the guru introduces the nature of mind, and the student immediately experiences it fully. However, even that glimpse needs to be practiced and stabilized.

This is why the great Vajrayana masters say there is no reason to be afraid of samsara. In its ultimate nature, samsara is relaxed and free. Since the nature of the deluded mind is wisdom, where could samsara be? Actually, there is no samsara. Many of the great songs of realization come from this understanding.

We need to realize directly and vividly that this is the dharma-
kaya. The coemergent nature of the mind is the essence of the

**dharmakaya. The coemergent appearances are the radiance of
the dharmakaya.**

The dharmakaya is not something other than the nature of the deluded mind at this very moment. This is sometimes called the coemergent essence of the mind. The word "coemergent" or "connate" is
Mahamudra terminology. It means that the dharmakaya is always here,
no matter what we may be experiencing. The nature, or essence, of our
mind is the coemergent wisdom of the dharmakaya.

After describing the coemergent essence of the mind, Gampopa
adds a further point: coemergent appearances are the radiance of the
dharmakaya. This is a key teaching of Mahamudra. The arisings or
manifestations of the mind, which are everything we perceive around
us and all our thoughts and emotions, are nothing but the radiance of
the dharmakaya. Gampopa says:

> **All objects perceived externally as apparent existence, all as-
> pects of samsara and nirvana, are indivisible from the nature
> of the mind. They are nondual equality and simplicity, which
> arise as great bliss.**

All our consciousnesses and manifestations arise from the dharmakaya, just like waves arise from the ocean. They are not separate from
the dharmakaya; they are its radiance. This is similar to the rays of the
sun. When the sun is present, its rays are naturally there as well. One
cannot separate the rays from the sun. One can't say that one ray is good
and another ray is bad. It is simply the nature of the sun to have rays.

Similarly, our thoughts and emotions are the radiance of the dharmakaya. Just as there is no problem with the rays coming from the sun,
there is no problem with the thoughts and emotions that radiate from
the dharmakaya. Problems arise when we form judgments that generate
fear or attraction.

In terms of not making judgments, my favorite example is a shadow.
When you are in the sunshine, your body casts a dark shadow. You cannot get rid of your shadow, and if you judge your shadow as bad, and
decide you want a different shadow, then you have a problem. The
shadow is not the problem; the problem is the way you are relating to the
shadow. When you see that the shadow is simply your shadow, then it's

no problem. But when you think there is something big and dark following you, then you have a problem. In the same way, when you understand that all appearances are the radiance of your mind, there is no reason to be afraid. All appearances come, and all appearances go. When you understand this deeply, you are liberated.

We don't need to clear away each delusion individually to cultivate pure vision. The only thing needed is a shift in the way we grasp things. To no longer be afraid of your shadow, you don't need to get rid of your shadow; you just realize that it's nothing but your shadow. This is analogous to delusion arising as wisdom. Once you know the nature of delusion, then liberation is not far away or somewhere else.

To do this, we need much more than intellectual understanding. It is very easy to say these words and think they are true. For liberation to occur, this must be a personal experience that affects us deeply enough to change the way we behave. What makes this difficult is that our habitual tendencies take over because they are very deep-rooted. Over and over, lifetime after lifetime, we have reacted with aversion and attachment. To truly change the way we act takes time and familiarization, and it happens only gradually. Sometimes a deep understanding can occur, but then it passes because it was only a glimpse.

To bring our understanding to a deeper level of experience, spiritual practice is necessary. We begin by experiencing this occasionally during meditation. An experience of wisdom comes, but then it goes away. Slowly, slowly, we can experience this in meditation, but not outside of meditation. Eventually, it is happening all the time, and this is realization.

> **To condense this into one point: delusion is unawareness, and once awareness has arisen as wisdom, then delusion arises as wisdom.**

Gampopa concludes by equating delusion and unawareness. Unawareness means that we lack understanding of the nature of our consciousness. When we react without genuine understanding, we are caught in delusion. Once we know the true nature of the deluded mind—that awareness itself is pristine wisdom—and once our awareness is fully experienced, then delusions are recognized as wisdom.

FIVE

The Application of Coemergence

BEFORE WE DISCUSS how to apply coemergence, I should mention, in case you don't remember, that the notion of coemergence was explained near the end of the previous chapter. As a brief review, coemergence means the dharmakaya is always present, no matter what we are experiencing. Coemergence doesn't mean that two things are joined into one. It is the recognition of inseparability, or the experience of nonduality. In the previous chapter, as part of Gampopa's explanation of the Fourth Dharma, "Delusion arises as wisdom," he says: "The coemergent nature of the mind is the essence of the dharmakaya. The coemergent appearances are the radiance of the dharmakaya."

Now, in this chapter Gampopa is going to discuss how we can apply coemergent wisdom in our experience within meditation and outside of meditation.

> Lama Rinpoche said: Here are the lama's instructions for applying coemergence in your practice.[1] Coemergence needs to be carried onto the path with two armors: the outer armor of the view and the inner armor of wisdom.

The view of coemergence needs to become the path; we need to apply this understanding until our way of being is completely transformed. Merely having a conceptual understanding or a little bit of experience will not transform us. We have to practice; there is no other way. The practice is applied on both outer and inner levels. The outer level is called the armor of the view, and the inner level is called the armor of wisdom.

> **Wearing the outer armor of the view means that you do not commit any negative actions, even to save your life. You constantly act in positive ways.**

Acting in positive ways is repeatedly emphasized throughout the Buddhist path. Sometimes when people hear advanced teachings, they develop a wrong view. Instead of understanding the nature of things in a nonconceptual way, they treat the nature as a concept and become very confused. Someone might think, "There is nothing wrong with samsara; everything is okay. There's no problem with negative deeds. What are negative deeds, anyway? They are delusion arising as wisdom. What are positive deeds? There are no real positive deeds. It's all co-emergent wisdom. There is nothing called karma. All I need to do is realize the view, and that's it." This kind of thinking is a big mistake. It's very important not to misuse the view. Ultimately everything is equal, but if you hold this view as a concept, then it becomes nihilism, which is a wrong view.

On the relative level, interdependence continues to operate, and the effects of your actions will ripen on you. As long as you don't have a deep experience of the ultimate truth, you will suffer. Even if intellectually you think there is nothing called samsara, you will still be in samsara and you will still be suffering. Our understanding of the two truths must be balanced. Guru Padmasambhava always warned that even when our view is very high, our actions need to be low to the ground.

In Tibet, all four Buddhist schools adopted the Vinaya as the code of moral ethics, and the Anuttarayoga-tantra as the essential practice. The Vinaya is as important as the Anuttarayoga-tantra. Even while doing the highest practices, there must be strong moral conduct. As long as we are in society, in this samsaric state of being, we have to be careful about what we do, what we say, and what we think. We cannot dismiss it all as being the dharmakaya, because our actions affect others, and they affect ourselves as well. Since we are not completely realized, without ethical conduct we will have all kinds of problems. So we need the outer armor of the view.

In fact, this is the main reason why the Mahamudra and Dzogchen teachings have always been kept rather secret. Generally, one doesn't teach Mahamudra or Dzogchen until the students are stable enough. It is not because teachers wants to keep these teachings to themselves and won't give them unless the students are very devoted and generous. It's more that if the ultimate view is misunderstood, it might not help the students, and in fact it might harm them.

Students need to develop complete confidence in karma and the causes of samsara. This is why the Ngöndro practice includes the four thoughts that turn the mind toward the dharma. When this understanding is firm, then one can hear teachings on Mahamudra and Dzogchen, and the teachings won't do any harm. But without this foundation, students can develop wrong ideas that bring suffering.

Armor is something that protects you. Gampopa says: "Wearing the outer armor of the view means that you do not commit any negative actions, even to save your life." This is a very strong statement. In all honesty, it is very difficult to never do a negative thing. We are samsaric beings, so we act in negative as well as positive ways. What is most important is to see very clearly that negative deeds bring negative results, and positive deeds bring positive results. When you recognize that good actions bring pleasant results for everyone, then you act accordingly. This basic law of karma applies, no matter what your view or understanding may be.

On the basis of personal experience, if your understanding goes deeper, there is no reason why you would choose to do anything negative. If you are no longer driven by fear and attachment, why would you act in a negative way? However, as long as you have fear and attachment, you need to be very careful.

I expect you have heard of crazy wisdom yogis, who can do things that are seemingly wrong but turn out to be perfectly appropriate, but that is something else. Those people have complete realization; they are not affected by karma, and they can act in strange ways to benefit beings. It is possible. But we mustn't try acting that way at our level. Also, we cannot tell who is a crazy wisdom person and who is just crazy, so we shouldn't imitate them. We know ourselves much better than we know others, and if we know that we still have our share of samsaric emotions, then we have to be very careful about what we do, and try to avoid anything negative.

Wearing the inner armor of wisdom has two aspects: the outer aspect is that you do not reject the sickness in your body, and the inner aspect is that you do not reject the thoughts and emotions in your mind.

In terms of not rejecting the sickness and pain that arise outwardly, there are three approaches: thinking that it could be much worse, getting to the root of it through investigation, and carrying it onto the path.

As for the first way of not rejecting sickness, previously you did not consider your pain to be a small problem, but after you imagine how much worse it could be, you feel better.

This section on the inner armor contains some very practical instructions on bringing negative experiences onto the path. First, Gampopa talks about the pain and sickness that arises outwardly. "Outwardly" refers to physical experiences rather than mental experiences. The first way of working with physical pain is to use our ability to see things as relative. For example, if you expect something terrible to happen and it turns out to be relatively small, then it's not too bad. If you were about to lose your life, but instead you lost your finger, you might think, "Oh, this is great! It's only my finger." Otherwise, if you lost your finger you could get very distressed: "Oh no, I've lost my finger! How terrible!" This is the way our mind works, so imagining how much worse it could be is one way of reducing our pain.

Another example of this comes from my personal experience. When we first came out of Tibet, everything was very difficult. We didn't know anything about India, and India was so hot and full of mosquitoes that almost everybody got sick, and many people died. But we used to say to each other, "This isn't so bad! At least we could die in a warm bed." Compared to dying in prison in Tibet, dying in a warm bed in India didn't seem so bad. Of course, in India it was not only the bed that was warm—everything was very, very warm!

This principle can be applied in many ways, and it is a very helpful method of thinking. How we feel is very much a matter of how we conceptualize what is happening. Our concepts are so important. In fact, our life is run by concepts.

Recently I was traveling by plane from Brussels to Bhutan, and two African men offered to switch seats so that my uncle and I could sit together. I started talking to the African I was sitting beside, and he was a very nice person. He told me he had been orphaned in Rwanda. You know, I have met other Rwandans, and they are a kind and gentle people. But if you remember, there was a civil war there between two tribes, the Tutsis and the Hutus, and a million people were killed. They were chopping up each other with machetes. If you think about it, killing someone with a gun is easy, but hacking a person up with a knife is very intense. One wonders, how could they do that? How could one human being kill another human being so mercilessly? It was not only the army that was being killed with machetes but even little children.

After I had met the man on the plane, I happened to see a film on the civil war in Rwanda, and it showed the fighters yelling, "Where are you, cockroaches? Come out, you cockroaches! You are going to die!" The killers were slaughtering men, women, and children. The killers thought of the people in the other tribe as cockroaches, which are insignificant and disgusting. They treated the other tribe as if they were mere insects.

When we name or conceptualize something in a certain way, then it becomes that way. We could decide that some action doesn't matter, and then we don't feel bad about it. Most of our experience is our concepts. We can call someone a cockroach or a human being or a loved one, and that's the way we relate to them.

An important aspect of concepts is that concepts can be changed. We can see in our own experience how we relate differently to things depending upon our ideas about them. It's like the proverb: "Beauty is in the eye of the beholder." For example, you can go through a very painful situation, and afterward think, "Thank goodness, that's over! I'm so glad it's finished." You can feel so happy when this painful experience has passed that it no longer seems problematic; it almost becomes a source of happiness. You appreciate the current situation more because of how miserable you were before. Or you could think, "That was absolutely terrible! It shouldn't have happened to me." You carry that memory for the rest of your life, reinforcing it every time you think of it, which makes the event seem worse and worse as the years go by. The situation you went through is exactly the same, but because of the way you choose to recall it, it has a totally different effect on you.

So, Gampopa's first suggestion is that we relate to our pain by comparing it with something much worse, and then we will feel better.

The second way gets to the root of the pain by looking for it. To start with, where did it come from? Where does it abide? Where does it go? You find that it does not come from anywhere, it does not abide in any place, and there is no place where it goes. When you see this very clearly, your thoughts subside.

This way is based on investigating and analyzing to see the emptiness of the pain. When you look directly at the pain and your feeling about it, you begin to see it as the mind's grasping. To actually see your pain this way takes a lot of experience. Just having a concept of emptiness, and just saying there is no pain, will not make the pain go away. When you have a toothache, you will find that the concept of emptiness doesn't help very much.

You can apply this in your experience. When you go to the dentist, the more fear you have, the more pain you feel. The more you relax, the less pain you have. There have even been lamas like Tulku Urgyen Rinpoche who had operations without anesthesia. There was a doctor in Germany who was so impressed with Tulku Urgyen's ability to endure pain that he took on Tulku Urgyen's health care for the rest of his life. Having surgery without an anesthetic shows a very high level of realization.

On our own level, we can start with small pains, and look for where they come from, where they abide, and where they go. Practicing with small pain is not unimportant, especially where emotions are concerned. In a way, physical pain is also an emotional experience. If we start with small amounts of pain, this approach can already be useful.

One way of doing this is to look for the exact location of the pain. You feel the pain and try to pinpoint it precisely, but it doesn't stay on one point; it seems to move around. You can't exactly find it. This can be done in mindfulness meditation, and there are people who have been totally cured of their illness by doing this. For instance, the Indian businessman, S. N. Goenka, did this. He was a wealthy man living in Burma who had terrible migraine headaches. He went to all sorts of doctors in Asia and the West, but no one could cure his headaches. Finally, he met a Vipassana meditation master who taught him the practice of mindfulness of feelings. Goenka applied this technique, and his headaches went away.

Goenka got very excited about the technique and asked his master what he could do to show his gratitude. His teacher told Goenka to teach this technique to people like himself with similar problems. This is what Goenka has done; he developed a program of rigorous ten-day retreats, which are still offered all over the world.

Going back to Gampopa's second point, we can use a technique like mindfulness of feelings to look at the nature of the pain or the sickness, and when we do not find anything concrete, this allows us to relax.

> To carry sickness onto the path, see that all good feelings and all bad feelings are inseparable. It is the mind that feels sick, and it is the mind that holds on to the idea of being sick. Seeing this, you think, "I will use this sickness to accomplish something beneficial."

This third approach is like *tonglen* practice, in which you take on the suffering of others and give your happiness to them. If you are sick or in pain, then you develop a sincere longing to take on all similar pain that others are experiencing. You might think, "May all beings be free from sickness. May their sickness ripen on me, so they need not experience this pain anymore."

With this approach, you use your sickness as a means to purify and heal the sickness of other beings, and in a way, this heals your own sickness. If you have a headache, then you bring everyone's headache into your headache, and purify that. Then you radiate to everyone else the experience of a pain-free head, a head that feels relaxed and comfortable. You can turn your pain into a path to freedom. Pain can be a way to purify your mind, and a means for working with your aversion and fear. It can also be a vehicle for you to send healing energy to others.

Gampopa has just given us three ways of bringing physical pain onto the path. Now he goes on to address how we can apply coemergence to the mind.

> In terms of not rejecting the thoughts and emotions that arise inwardly, you could view your thoughts with gratitude. It would be impossible not to have thoughts. Thoughts, emotions, perceptions, and sensations are quite necessary. Thoughts and emotions are beautiful! It is natural for

thoughts to arise. Thoughts are our friends; thoughts are the
path; thoughts are fuel for the fire of wisdom.

To start with, do not deliberately focus on thoughts or cultivate them. As your practice progresses, do not let any states
of mind linger. Finally, do not hold on to them.

First, in order to not deliberately focus on thoughts or cultivate them, come to the conclusion that whatever occurs in
your mind is a thought. View thoughts and emotions as the
mind, and view the mind as the unborn dharmakaya.

The second part of the inner armor is not rejecting the thoughts and
emotions that arise in our mind. If we want to have good meditation, we
must make friends with our thoughts and emotions. It's impossible to
get rid of them, anyway. Instead, we need to learn how to relax with
them, to live with them in a friendly way.

It's completely natural to have thoughts, emotions, and sensations
when we meditate. They are not a problem unless we have aversion or
attachment to them. Working with our thoughts is always a matter of
balance. We can liberate our thoughts in meditation by realizing that
they are merely a display of our true nature. They are manifestations of
the dharmakaya, or empty awareness.

There will never be a time when no more thoughts or emotions arise.
Thoughts are temporary and fleeting, even though they continue to appear. Whether it is a good thought or a bad thought, whether it is a
positive emotion or a negative emotion, it is insubstantial. Although
you have to be careful about negative emotions, you don't have to take
them too seriously. This is where the balance comes in.

This doesn't mean there are no good thoughts or bad thoughts, no
positive emotions or negative emotions. Please don't misunderstand
this teaching to say that you don't need to work on transforming your
afflictive emotions. You definitely need to work on them. Afflictive
emotions bring problems for yourself as well as everyone else.

Keep in mind that negative thoughts have negative results. Afflictive
emotions make us uncomfortable inside, and when we express them,
they bring suffering to those around us, too. We can witness this in our
own life; not only in the long run but at the very moment the emotion
appears, we can feel its poison. Clearly, we need to be aware of this and
act accordingly.

We need to be aware, but we don't need to panic when a negative emotion appears in our mind. Certainly, negative emotions are not good, and we need to learn how to let them go. But it is not like the sky is falling on us. We mustn't take them too seriously and solidify them into problems. Sometimes people think, "I shouldn't feel like this. I shouldn't be angry; I shouldn't feel jealous. I need to get rid of this feeling." When the emotion becomes too important, it seems like a big problem.

> For beginners, it is necessary to use positive thoughts to clear away negative thoughts. However, a meditator is just as constricted by good thoughts as by bad thoughts. It is similar to the sun being just as obscured by white clouds as by black clouds, or a person being just as restricted by gold chains as by iron chains.

As beginners, it's good to replace negative thoughts with positive thoughts. But eventually, the path is not about being positive instead of negative. It is about becoming liberated from both positive and negative, since both of them are concepts. As Gampopa says, if you are chained, it doesn't matter if you are bound by a gold chain or an iron chain. Either way, you are still chained.

It is similar with positive and negative deeds. Acting positively is much better, but being good does not free you from being samsaric. The point is to become totally free, not merely to improve the quality of your chains.

> Here, negative thoughts and emotions are seen to be the mind, and positive thoughts and emotions are seen to be the mind. The mind itself is seen as the unborn dharmakaya. This seeing is called the emptiness of cutting through.

In Mahamudra, the main approach to not rejecting or cultivating our thoughts is to see them as the mind's manifestations, which simply come and go. Instead of reacting, we can allow whatever arises to dissolve by itself. It's like having a bad smell in your room. What do you do to get rid of it? You just open your doors and windows, and the smell goes away.

This is similar to the famous advice that Tilopa gave Naropa: "My son, it is not the appearances that bind you; it is the grasping that binds you." We need to cut the grasping, that's all. When any kind of emotion arises, whether positive or negative, if you don't hold on to it, then it's not a problem. As you become more familiar with this approach, you don't have to react at all. When you let emotions come and let them go, they pass right through you. Even if you do react, they will immediately disappear if you don't hold on. The emotions liberate themselves.

An example of this in the Kagyu lineage is Marpa the Translator. Marpa was a very emotional person; he was short-tempered and difficult to get along with. When he was young, he was always fighting with the other children, and his parents thought he was useless. Actually, they thought he was not only useless, but dangerous. He might kill someone, or someone might kill him, and either way it would cause big trouble. They decided to send Marpa away, so that whatever he did would happen somewhere else. Marpa's parents gave him his share of the mules and yaks, and then they asked him to leave.

Marpa was happy to go, and he went away and met the famous translator Drokmi Lotsawa. He was very impressed with Drokmi, and he studied Sanskrit with him. I expect Marpa had some little fights with Drokmi as well. Then he decided to go to India rather than continue studying with Tibetans. In India he met Naropa and went through his training.

Marpa became a great master, but even after that, he still had a bad temper. He would shout at people, but because of his realization, he had changed inside. He shouted in the same way as before, but now his anger did not last; it was gone very quickly. He would get red in the face and run after someone with a stick, but then he would stop, and be kind and gentle. He had learned how to let go.

> At the intermediate level, the practice is to not abide in mental states. Having cut through all positive thoughts as just described, if your mind becomes fatigued and then becomes peaceful, do not dwell in that peaceful feeling. If an experience of nonthought happens, do not abide in that. If there is a perception of emptiness, do not allow that to remain. Cut through these experiences as mental states. See the mental states as primordial wisdom. See the mind as the unborn dharmakaya.

The point here is that you don't hold on to anything, even good meditative experiences. Ordinarily, when the mind becomes stable and peaceful in meditation, we tend to remain that way and think we are meditating well. When our meditation feels successful, it is very easy to become attached to those feelings. However, from the perspective of thoughts liberating themselves, the training is to be unconcerned when good experiences arise. Although you might not be clinging consciously, you can find yourself not wanting to lose the peaceful feeling, and trying to prevent discursive thoughts from arising.

From the Mahamudra point of view, having a calm, quiet mind rather than an active, moving mind is not the point. You must dare to cut through all positive states of mind. Dare to let them go. It doesn't matter if the state of mind seems clear and blissful. Disrupt positive experiences as much as you can. The instruction is to cut through all states of mind.

When Gampopa says we should disrupt our meditation, he doesn't mean we should stand up and go do something else. Although there are techniques, like saying a loud "PHET" to scatter your thoughts or experiences, you don't need to do that. It is fine to do that if it works for you, but the point of disruption is to stop clinging. When you realize that you are dwelling on something, immediately stop, and then start the main practice again.

As well as pleasant or peaceful feelings, you can have an experience of nonthought, or a perception of emptiness. You might think, "Now I am going beyond concepts. Maybe I am transcending duality. Maybe I'm about to become enlightened. How exciting!" Actually, there is nothing to get excited about. This is just another experience. It is just another concept, which needs to be released.

At this higher level of practice, it is extremely important not to hold on to any arising or any experience. No matter how good an experience is, it is still a mental arising. It doesn't matter whether it is nonthought, peace, emptiness, or whatever. The moment you cling to it, it is samsara. Actual wisdom is being able to free yourself from anything. This is what the higher teachings call cutting through.

There is a well-known quotation, possibly from Machik Labdrön, that when a stream runs down a steep mountain, the more it hits the rocks, the better the quality of the water. I once talked to some scientists about this. They said it's true that when water hits the rocks, it becomes

more oxygenated. This is analogous to meditation: the more you break
it up, the better the meditation becomes.

It is problematic if meditation becomes a cocoon where you remain
comfortable. Good *shamatha* meditation cools your mind and makes it
tranquil, but it does not bring liberation. You could remain tranquil
for a long time, but find that you are not making any progress; you are
not uprooting ignorance at all. Shamatha is a good stepping-stone, but
it is not real wisdom. Even in shamatha, we train in the quality of *shin-
jang,* or "pliancy," in which the mind is fully trained or under control.
With pliancy, we can easily go into meditation and easily come out of
meditation.

Another reason that comfortable meditation binds us in samsara is
that once we long for positive feelings, then we dread negative feelings.
As long as we are caught in hope and fear, we will have problems. This is
very important to understand. The main goal of Mahamudra practice is
to free ourselves from fear. The practice is to cut through attachment
and see that whatever happens is okay. If blissful or stable feelings arise,
that is no problem. If negative, tumultuous feelings arise, that is equally
no problem. When whatever happens is seen as okay, then there's no
reason for fear. Being uncontrived without hope and fear is real meditation. This is Mahamudra. Learning to let all experiences come and go,
without holding on to anything, is what Gampopa calls not remaining.

> As for not clinging at the end, having cut through all mental
> states, do not hold on to the cutting, either. Do not cling to it
> as the path, do not cling to it as the result, and do not cling to
> it as the view, meditation, or conduct.

In other words, don't form any concepts about what is happening in
your mind. However, it's very difficult to free ourselves from concepts
because everything about ourselves and our existence is conceptual.
The actual practice of meditation comes down to not doing anything.
The best meditation is nonmeditation; we are simply being completely
relaxed, completely aware, and not holding on to anything. Sometimes
this is called "resting in natural great bliss" or "resting in natural peace."
We just relax in the most natural state of being. Because there is no dis-
turbance, there is peace, and this peace is joyful. It is simply a state of
being without anything to be done.

In terms of how various states of mind are mingled with emptiness, there are three analogies: dissolving upon contact, going back, and fire and snakes. First, the analogy for dissolving upon contact is like meeting someone you knew before. As soon as thoughts and emotions arise, you recognize them as the dharmakaya.

This is a key Mahamudra instruction on how to realize coemergent wisdom. "Dissolving upon contact" means that as soon as a thought or emotion arises, you recognize it as the radiance of the dharmakaya, and the thought or emotion is liberated. Thoughts and emotions are simply manifestations of your natural awareness, which, in a way, is actually nothing.

It is like seeing your shadow. When you recognize that what you see is your shadow, you don't have to do anything about it. It doesn't matter whether your shadow is there or not. Similarly, when you recognize that your thoughts and emotions are the dharmakaya, then you are not bound by them. It doesn't matter if they appear or not. Gampopa uses the analogy of meeting someone you already know. You know who the person is, and you are not suspicious or fearful. I think the shadow is a better analogy, because as soon as you recognize the darkness as your shadow, that's all there is to it. There is no need to relate to it at all.

The analogy for going back is like meeting someone you had not known before, or like snow falling on a lake. The snow does not dissolve instantly, but it dissolves in a moment. In the same way, you may not immediately recognize the nature of the thoughts, but then understanding dawns because of having previously seen and contemplated this.

With this approach, when a thought arises, you look at it and see that it is simply a mental arising. It is nothing separate that you need to be afraid of or attached to. We need to apply this in a very personal way. For instance, if a feeling of strong desire comes up—or fear, sadness, compassion, or whatever it may be—at the moment it arises, you see it as a display of the nature of your mind. When you can see your feelings and thoughts in this way, then you can relax with them.

One analogy for this approach is meeting someone you didn't know before. Once you get to know people, then you recognize them. A second analogy is snow falling on a lake. When snow falls on a lake, it merges into the water, but this doesn't happen the instant the snow touches the lake. It takes a moment for the snow to melt into the water. It is the same with thoughts and emotions at this stage. You experience them with awareness, and they don't last long. They dissolve and don't become a problem.

Usually when a feeling comes up, we create a whole story around it. Our emotion is not seen as a passing mental arising but as something separate that is happening to us. This is what we call duality. We think we have to do something about the feeling, or else we won't be able to get rid of it. But that's not so. Even if we get rid of that particular feeling, there are always more feelings coming up.

If you can see the empty nature of the emotions, then you can free yourself. The Mahamudra approach is to allow the emotion to self-liberate. Ideally, you immediately see that whatever appears is your mind's manifestation, and then the emotion disappears. If this doesn't happen immediately, then you may have to look at it, examine it, and then it can dissolve.

> The third analogy is fire and snakes. When a fire is small, the wind can extinguish it. But when a fire is big, wind helps the fire to spread. So, when serious accusations are made against you, or you get leprosy, or any terrible situation occurs, and you meditate, you cut through them as mental states. Mental states are decisively seen to be the mind, and the mind is seen and meditated upon as the unborn dharmakaya.

Here, the fire is analogous to our emotions. When you catch your emotions at an early stage, it takes only a little effort to dissolve them. But if the emotions are already strong, the more force you apply to dissolve them, the stronger they grow.

This principle also applies to our inherent wisdom. If your wisdom is weak, then even a small negative emotion can overpower your awareness. On the other hand, if your wisdom is strong, then the bigger the negative emotion, the stronger the wisdom can become. With a deep experience of wisdom, a big problem—like leprosy or AIDS or serious allegations of wrongdoing—can make you even stronger. The problem, like the wind, does not kill the fire of wisdom but makes it burn much brighter.

This is similar to what is called transforming emotions into wisdom. This does not mean that there is a solid emotion that somehow turns into wisdom. It means that when you understand the nature of the emotion and simply let it be, that in itself is wisdom. It is not that wisdom comes and destroys the emotion. Even while an emotion is being felt, if you can catch the experience with wisdom, then the emotion is no longer deluded. This is because you are no longer immersed in it. Wisdom cuts through the clinging, which frees the emotion from attachment and aversion. And without attachment or aversion, the emotion is no longer there.

The way that snakes uncoil themselves provides another analogy. Their bodies might appear to be tied in knots, but no manipulation is needed for them to unwind and move on. Similarly, our thoughts and emotions liberate themselves when they are not manipulated. They simply appear and then disappear without leaving a trace.

Training in meditation is what enables us to understand this deeply. When we experience this for ourselves, we find that whatever happens is self-liberated. We see everything as a manifestation of the unborn dharmakaya, the nature of our mind.

> **There are four remaining points about applying coemergence in your practice: (1) being able to reconstitute your understanding, (2) being able to transform adverse conditions, (3) being undeluded, and (4) using wisdom to open the door of the dharma.**
>
> **First, for the ability to reconstitute your understanding, by knowing that one thought or emotion is the dharmakaya, you know that all thoughts and emotions are the dharmakaya.**

The Mahamudra instructions say, "Look at your mind," but there is no whole mind to be found. The mind is a succession of thoughts and emotions, instant by instant. Each perception is your mind, each feeling is your mind. If your wisdom can catch one thought and liberate it, then all other thoughts can be liberated in the same way. By knowing the nature of one thought, you know the nature of all thoughts. Gampopa gives some analogies for this.

For example, when you drink the water in one area of the ocean, you know the taste of the whole ocean. Similarly, when you see that one straw is hollow inside, then you know that all straws are hollow inside. When you see the way the roots grow on one *tsarbu* plant, then you understand how the roots grow on all tsarbu plants.[2]

Then, he goes on to the second additional point:

Second, the ability to transform adverse conditions means that by training your mind, all negative conditions become supports for your realization. This is like the wind helping the fire in the previous analogy.

This is just what we were discussing above. When wisdom is strong, then negative emotions make it shine even brighter.

Third, in terms of being undeluded, previously there was delusion because the nature of the thoughts and emotions was not recognized. But when you cut to the root of the various states of mind, you recognize them as the dharmakaya, so there is no cause for delusion.

In other words, when a feeling of confusion arises, and you look into the nature of the confusion, you cannot find the presence of anything that could be confused. When you know this for yourself, there is no more confusion, and the misunderstanding is cleared away.

Fourth, for opening the door through wisdom, the analogy is twirling a spear in the sky. This is the realization that everything is in the state of equality.

This refers to an Indian martial art in which a warrior turns a stick very fast in a circle overhead. It makes a very loud sound, and no one can get close to the warrior. It is not clear to me how this applies to seeing wisdom and equality in everything. Perhaps it is a matter of the mind being unobstructed or being protected equally in every direction.

In any case, the key to all these points about coemergent wisdom is to recognize all your states of mind as the dharmakaya. To be able to apply this recognition as soon as thoughts arise, your understanding must come from your own investigation and your own meditation practice.

It can seem difficult to have this experience, but that is because it must be learned. We learn by doing it, and then we know how to experience it. Any practical knowledge has to be learned through training; there's no other way. To learn how to speak a foreign language, we have to practice speaking it again and again. It's the same with learning to play a musical instrument or drive a car. Just knowing the theory doesn't give us the skill. To know the nature of the mind, we have to meditate without being distracted. We have to keep working on it with joy and devotion.

The Nature of the Mind

The lama Jetsun Rinpoche said: According to the approach of the paramitas, you start by cutting through objects perceived externally. The analogy is a fire made by vigorously rubbing together a horizontal stick and a vertical stick. That fire can burn the whole forest, so that not even ashes remain. Likewise, one can use reasoning, such as "neither one nor many," to investigate phenomena and reach a definite conclusion about them. When one cuts through objects perceived externally, then the mind that perceives them is naturally loosened as well.

THIS DESCRIBES THE Madhyamaka way of reasoning. According to the approach of the paramitas, you begin by fully understanding the nature of objects seen outside yourself. For example, we can take any object—anything we can see or hear or touch or taste—and see how it exists. It is singular? Is it permanent? Singular things cannot have any parts or elements; they cannot be taken apart. When we investigate, we find that everything has parts, everything is changing, and everything appears due to various causes and conditions. Since the causes and conditions change in each moment, the thing itself changes in each moment. Therefore, it cannot be a single thing or a permanent thing; it is a continuum of causes and conditions. Everything we experience is dependently arisen and dependently designated.

If we cannot find a single thing, it follows that we cannot find many things, since "many" is made up of numerous "ones." This is the philosophy of interrelationship. Everything exists in relation to something else. For instance, we can call something "short" because there is "long," and we designate "left" on the basis of "right." There is always something an object is related to, something it is interdependent with. Even how fast something is moving is measured in relation to something else. In relation to a person standing on a platform, a train might be moving 100 kilometers per hour. But if measured in relation to another moving object, the speed will be different. Everything is in relationship.

Gampopa uses the example of starting a fire by rubbing one stick against another. Exactly where does the fire come from? Is it from the first stick, the second stick, or the rubbing hands? It's not any one of them; it's all of them. When the right conditions come together, fire occurs. The fire can burn the bottom stick, the top stick, and even the whole forest so that not even ashes remain.

The reason for this kind of analysis is that if you understand the interdependent nature of everything, then your clinging to things is transformed. We usually think things are separate and real. If we perceive something negative, we think it is very much there. If we perceive something positive, we think it is very much there. Things look very solid, and we think, "I want this, but I don't want that." All our struggles and problems come from seeing things as truly existent. With a thought like "I need that," the "I" is already assumed to be there, very solid and independent. This kind of thinking is what we call duality.

It's important to see things as the coming together of causes and conditions. Things are not merely formed through causes and conditions; they actually *are* causes and conditions. These are two different statements. If we say a glass is produced by causes and conditions, it sounds like the glass is really there and it came about due to various conditions. But if we say, "This glass *is* causes and conditions," then that is just what it is. As the conditions change, the glass also changes. The glass is a continuum; it is a changing phenomenon. It is dependently arising and dependently designated; it is a fluctuating continuum.

This is the Madhyamaka approach. Because of understanding emptiness on the outer level, the ties that bind the inner perceiving mind are loosened as well. Once you see that outer things are interdependent, you can apply the same reasoning to your inner experience and see that your mind and perceptions are interdependent as well.

The implication of seeing interdependence is that you realize you have nothing to lose, since nothing truly exists that could be destroyed. Similarly, since nothing exists that could be possessed, you have nothing to gain. Taking this a step further, when you recognize that emptiness and interdependence are themselves empty, your grasping is completely loosened, and you are free to relax and let be.

> In the Mahamudra approach, when one cuts through the perceiving mind, then the perceived objects are naturally loosened. In relation to cutting through the perceiving mind, Rinpoche taught three aspects: the mind's characteristics, essence, and nature.

The Mahamudra approach works from the other side. Rather than examining the external world, it begins by examining the mind, and once the nature of the mind is realized, then the ties that bind us to outer objects are freed as well. In Mahamudra, you start with the mind because everything is experienced through the mind. You do not perceive anything without your mind. If you see something, that is your mind; if you hear something, that is your mind. All your ideas and experiences and feelings are nothing but your own mind.

Then the question becomes: What is your mind? When you thoroughly understand the nature of your mind, that understanding liberates everything. This is the Mahamudra approach, which begins by introducing the nature of the mind. Gampopa does this by pointing out three main aspects of the mind: its characteristics, its essence, and its nature.

> The mind has two characteristics: it appears as various colorful, outer forms, and it emits various positive and negative mental states. In other words, there is the mind's essence and its two characteristics. These are equivalent to the mind itself and what arises from the mind. In the sky there are various colorful appearances, like thick and thin clouds, which arise from the sky and dissolve back into the sky. In the same way, the radiation of various thoughts and emotions, as well as the appearances of various sense objects—like form, sound, smell, taste, and touch—come from the mind. In this way, appearances are the characteristics of the mind.

The mind is essentially the union of clarity and emptiness. Because the mind is aware, we have experience, but since the mind is nothing at all, it is emptiness. We cannot pinpoint the mind and say where it is, and yet the mind is present because we experience its characteristics. When Gampopa speaks of the mind's characteristics, he means the mental factors or mental events that arise from the mind. There are two types of these: the various colorful appearances perceived externally, and the various positive and negative states perceived internally.

The mind has the capacity for limitless manifestations, which seem to be outside us or seem to be inside us. But all of these manifestations are part of the mind. We can feel good, we can feel bad, we can have all kinds of feelings and thoughts. Anything is possible because that's the way the mind is. That is the way the Buddha's mind is, and that is the way everyone's mind is.

Usually, when some characteristic or manifestation of the mind appears, we think it is outside us. But if we understand that whatever appears is merely a mind manifestation, then anything can manifest and it's no problem. It is very important to know this and to be able to experience the mind in this way.

This reminds me of something that students talk to me about. Some of us feel very uncomfortable around other people. Some of us want to be left alone; we want privacy, we "need our space" apart from others. Why would we feel that way? Actually, it's not because of them; it's because of us. The discomfort is in our own mind. We feel unable to simply be who we are when other people are around. We need to lock the door and be alone so we can relax. When this attitude takes over, we get stressed and can't be natural.

The problem is not outside our mind. If we can allow ourselves to relax and be natural, then whatever is going on is fine. We can learn to be natural with a hundred people around us. What difference does it make if people are looking at us? Recently I went to a spa where everyone was totally naked. It was no problem. If we were naked on the street, people might get upset, but everyone can be naked in the spa; it doesn't matter if someone is looking at us.

If we don't let ourselves relax, if we don't know how to relax, then all kinds of things disturb us. We think the disturbances are outside us. For instance, some people get disturbed by little noises. However, we could feel totally natural with tremendous noise and turmoil around us. How disturbed we are does not depend on how chaotic the environment is; it depends on how much we understand our own mind.

Our suffering and problems are manifestations of the mind. At the same time, our mind is completely flexible. We don't feel bad all the time; sometimes we feel very happy. This is because there is nothing concrete about the mind. The mind changes in each instant. Everything is arising and forming like bubbles.

The manifestations of the mind are like reflections in a mirror. When you look in a mirror and you grimace or frown, you might feel alarmed or afraid. And then when you see yourself smiling, you might feel enchanted. You have various reactions to what you see, but all of them are your own reflection. It's the same with the reflections of the mind.

Gampopa uses the analogy of the sky and what appears in the sky. All sorts of colorful displays arise from the sky and dissolve back into the sky. Likewise, everything comes out of the mind, and everything dissolves back into the mind. There is nothing outside the mind as far as your personal experience is concerned. Your mind is your experience, and your experience is your world.

Next, Gampopa goes into more detail about the essence of the mind.

> What is meant by the "essence of the mind" is your own awareness, that which you think of as "I" or "me." The essence of the mind is clarity-emptiness. It cannot be pinpointed, yet it never ends. Awareness is baseless, fresh, naked, and spontaneous.

Exactly what is the nature of your mind? What is the mind's very essence? When you look for the mind, the only thing you can find is awareness. The mind is nothing more than that. Sometimes awareness is called clarity; it is that which experiences.

We need to look at the mind experientially. We can approach this in two ways: an outer way and an inner way. The outer way is to look for the mind in terms of its aspects: What is its texture? Does it have a color? Does it have a shape? We can try to find the mind's location: Is it inside the body or outside the body? Where is it? Although you look and look in this way, you cannot find the mind.

Even if you were to believe that you had found the mind, it would only be your mind saying that. Or if you were to answer that the mind must be in the brain, what is saying that? This is just another thought, another concept, another display of your mind. This is nothing more than any other experience you have of the outer world, like saying that the weather is nice today, or the grass is green. This is simply another thought.

The inner way of looking at the mind is to look at experience itself. Then, what is the mind? It is just awareness. We could call the mind "clarity" because it is not a dark thing; it is aware. We experience our mind as one experience after another. The Mahamudra teachings usually describe this as clarity, luminosity, or awareness. This is the essence of the mind.

But where is that clarity? What exactly is it? We cannot find it anywhere. We cannot say, "Here is my awareness." This clarity cannot be pinpointed. It is not something we can pick up and show someone; it cannot be put in a box. This is the mind's empty aspect. From the point of view of meditative experience, the nature of the mind is nothing but awareness-emptiness.

Although awareness cannot be pinpointed, at the same time, its nature is such that it never ends. You can never find a beginning or an end to awareness. Awareness is baseless, fresh, naked, and spontaneous. We are using all these words to point toward something that must be directly experienced. The nature of the mind is something we have to see for ourselves. To do Mahamudra meditation, we have to individually and genuinely look at our own consciousness.

Traditionally, Mahamudra teachings are not presented in this way, where you are told beforehand what the essence of the mind is. Usually, students are told to look at their mind, analyze their experience, and then try to express their experience to their teacher. If you have been told about the nature of the mind beforehand, then when it is time to look at your mind, you might think, "Well, the Mahamudra texts say the mind is clarity-emptiness, so that must be what it is." It is of no help for you to simply copy and repeat what you have read. That won't bring realization or liberation. Nevertheless, in this context, I'm still going through the rest of Gampopa's book!

> **What is the essence of the mind like? It is not existent, and yet it is not non-existent. It is neither eternal nor nothing. Free of the two extremes, it is not found in the middle, either. In relation to cutting it, it cannot be cut. In terms of destroying it, it**

cannot be destroyed. The essence cannot be changed. As for stopping it, it cannot be stopped. At all times, it is free of coming and going.

Since the essence is unbroken throughout the past, present, and future, it cannot be cut. It is uncompounded. It is primordially and spontaneously present, so it cannot be destroyed. It is devoid of form or color. It is not a substance or a thing, which is why it is unstoppable. When you understand what this means, it is called the essence. It is called great bliss. It is called coemergent wisdom. It is called nonduality.

How can you describe the essence of the mind? You cannot say it exists, and you cannot say it doesn't exist. You cannot say it is always there, and you cannot say it is never there. Since it is not interrupted in the past, present, and future, it cannot be cut, even if you want to cut it. It is not compounded but spontaneously present from the very beginning. Therefore, the essence of the mind cannot be destroyed, even if you want to destroy it. Not having form or color or substance, it cannot be stopped, even if you want to stop it. It is great bliss, it is coemergent wisdom, it is nonduality.

When you become aware of the essence of the mind, it is the clear light experience. When someone has the clear light experience, they have very subtle awareness, even in deep sleep. For instance, a friend of mine has a friend in Tibet who is a master meditator. He lives like Milarepa— he doesn't need to wear clothes, he doesn't need to eat, he doesn't need to sleep; he just sits there and goes into the clear light meditation.

These two men have been friends since childhood, and recently they were together again in Tibet. When it was time to sleep, the great meditator said, "Now I am going into the state of clear light. Please see whether or not I do it right. You will know because if I go to sleep and don't snore, it means I have entered the clear light. In the clear light, you know everything that is going on around you. You see as if you were not sleeping. However, you get as much rest as you would get from deep sleep."

As this meditator reported, in the clear light nature of the mind, there is awareness, very clear like daylight, but no stress. This state is completely at rest, completely joyful. This kind of awareness is the essence of the mind, so it can be called great bliss. Great bliss is a natural quality of the mind when it is undisturbed. It is not something cultivated.

The essence of the mind is also characterized as nondual. Not in the sense of not knowing what is what but in the sense of being so clear that there is no differentiation. There is no feeling of being a self that is separate from others, or of there being separate objects that are wanted or unwanted.

When you analyze your experiences, you find that they come from awareness and nothing more. There is no boundary or limitation to the mind. Because the essence of the mind is nothing but awareness, and because it has no shape or form, it is not something tangible. If the mind was something tangible, you could cut it into pieces, but there is nothing that could be cut.

The clarity nature of the mind is what makes it possible for us to see things and have all kinds of experience. The mind is not subject to any limitations; it can go through anything. Because of clarity, the mind has the capacity for clairvoyance and the capacity for omniscience. As your mind becomes calm, clear, and completely undisturbed, it can see through time and space. It has the capacity to know much more than you might think.

When you have a deeper understanding of this, and when you can experience consciousness itself, you see that consciousness is bigger than the body. The mind is not contained in the body; it is beyond the body. For example, people who have had near-death experiences have had their bodies declared clinically dead. But their minds could see; they could not only see their body lying on the bed or the ground, but they could also see what was happening all around them, like in the parking lot of the hospital, or things like that. So, the body is not the mind, because in those situations the body is dead, or the body is inside a room and can't see outside.

The essence of the mind is not something that can die. It cannot be killed. Although the body dies, the mind continues. Particularly where death is concerned, it's important to have a clear sense of how the body and mind are different. The body and mind are together, they are interdependent, but they are not totally one. Of course, the body and the mind affect each other. When the body has pain, it affects the mind. Nerves can get damaged, and then you can't think clearly or you can't remember things. Body and mind are closely related, but they are not exactly the same.

The mind has its own continuum, its own essence, nature, and characteristics. The mind is aware and knowing, it is conscious and clear. The mind is the continuum of consciousness. It is not made of matter. The body, on the other hand, is made of earth, water, wind, and fire, and it comes from the father and mother's essence elements. The mind has different levels of consciousness: gross, less gross, subtle, and very subtle. The essence of the mind that we are talking about is the very subtle level of consciousness. It doesn't dissolve in deep sleep; it doesn't dissolve when you die. Although the body dissolves, the mind does not dissolve.

All these statements must be known through personal experience, rather than just repeating words. To truly know this, you have to examine your mind for a long time. Examine it repeatedly in meditation. But even though this is a process of investigation, the process itself is not particularly intellectual. You look, and then you relax and let be in original naturalness. When you cannot find a thing that is your mind, you simply let be in your natural state. Feel this gradually, and let its inherent clarity become apparent.

As you become calmer, you become clearer. The fewer concepts you have, the more clear you become. This is a very important part of practicing meditation. Intellectually, you can say whatever you like; it doesn't make any real difference. You can be 100 percent correct in your intellectual understanding, but if your understanding remains intellectual, it doesn't do much good. It is easy to grasp the concepts, but it is not easy to have the experience. This experience is sometimes called awakening, and it must be realized within yourself. You cannot force it; you let it arise. The way to do this is by relaxing. In a way, the only thing we can do to make realization dawn is to relax in meditation and do nothing. This is how we will come to know the nature of the mind.

Sometimes people come to their teacher and tell all kinds of experiences, but the teacher usually says, "No, sorry, it's not like that." For example, I was told that Jamgön Kongtrul of Shechen used to come to my monastery at Rigul every year, and many people would meet with him to discuss their meditation. There was one very good monk who always came. He was like Milarepa and always stayed in caves; he had renounced all comfort and devoted his life to meditation. But Jamgön Kongtrul was never happy with what this monk told him. One day Kongtrul Rinpoche even beat him! I heard that later on the monk's meditation got a little better. However, there was another monk, who was crippled and considered not very bright. Whenever he came to see Shechen Kongtrul, their discussion would go very well.

Realizing the nature of the mind has nothing to do with how clever you are. Sometimes, having a great deal of theoretical understanding is not the best thing. The only quality that is always stressed is devotion. Meditative experience can arise through devotion. The more you are able to let be and free yourself from concepts, the more you are able to open your heart. And the more you open your heart, the more you can relax in the nature of the mind.

Another story along these lines is about a student who went to see a famous master to offer his meditative experience. The student thought he had very good experiences, and he was hoping the master would confirm that. This master was a crazy yogi, and after the student related his experiences, the master became very stern and irritated and said that the student lacked genuine experience.

When the student heard that, he felt very sad and gave up on getting confirmation from the yogi. He just sat there for a while, remembering his root teacher, the one who had given him the instructions he had practiced for so long. A feeling of strong devotion welled up inside the student, and he just sat there without doing anything in particular, just thinking of his guru.

When the student looked up, the master was smiling at him. The master said, "That's it! Now you've got it!"

So, the student's experience of the natural state arose when he was not thinking about it or doing anything. It arose as a result of devotion.

> You need to understand that the essence of the mind and its radiance as various thoughts and emotions are not two different things. When you understand that the essence and characteristics of the mind are naturally inseparable, this is called the nature. When you realize what this means, it is the heart essence of all the buddhas of the three times. This nature is present within all beings. A sutra states:

The buddha nature pervades all beings.
There is not even one sentient being who is unsuitable.
Generate bodhichitta to the greatest possible extent,
Since all beings have the cause of buddhahood.[1]

The heart essence of the buddhas of the three times is the experience of knowing the mind itself. Buddha nature means that every being has an enlightened nature. The nature of the mind is exactly the same in everyone. This is not to say that we are all great, with lots of compassion and lots of wisdom. In fact, most of us have very little compassion and very little wisdom. But this is just the result of habitual patterns. The very essence of our consciousness and the Buddha's consciousness is exactly the same.

To understand what this means, practice with diligence and devotion, free from distraction. When practicing meditation with characteristics, do not practice formless meditation, and conversely, when doing formless practice, do not have any reference points. It is said that one should tie the elephant of the mind to the pillar of the meditation object with the rope of mindfulness, and then practice with alertness.

Clear light, the essence of mind, needs to be experienced again and again. But sometimes our mind is so distracted and so busy thinking that it cannot stay focused for even one or two minutes. As soon as we relax, it goes here and there. Our untrained mind is like a wild and drunken elephant led by a wild and drunken monkey. It's very active, like a monkey who can't stay still for a moment, and it's very forceful, like an elephant, so heavy that it tramples everything underfoot. The mind needs to be trained, and the only way to train it is through mindfulness and alertness. These are the only tools we have. We need to apply them to our own awareness.

One way of training is the Mahamudra way: you don't reject the inner or outer arisings because you know they are the radiance of your mind. You don't have to get rid of them or push them out of your mind. On the other hand, you don't want to be overwhelmed and carried away by them. The thing to do is relax and allow the radiance to radiate but not overpower you. If you can relax this way and simply be in the clarity and emptiness of the essence of the mind, then there's no need for any particular reference point. There is no need of an object to meditate on.

In Mahamudra, we just let things be, and this transforms our emotions. We allow whatever happens in our meditation to happen, and we just experience the naturalness, our own natural joy and peace. Directly relaxing into the nature of the mind is the highest and most profound way of meditating.

However, most of us are beginners, so it's not easy to meditate like that. It's not necessarily a difficult thing to do; the problem is that we don't know how to do it. If we don't know how to go about it, then we should start by using reference points in our meditation. Having a focus for meditation is especially helpful when our mind is turbulent and won't stay still. When we can't bring our mind home, it's good to focus on something. The focus is like the pillar where you tie up your elephant. A wild elephant needs to be tied up, or else it creates havoc.

The focus could be your breathing—many meditation practices focus on being aware of breathing in and out. Or the focus could be on some substantial object like a flower or a painting or a sculpture of a buddha, or it could be an imagined object like a light, a letter, or a mental image of an enlightened being like Tara or Chenrezik. The main technique is to come back to this reference point whenever you realize that your mind has wandered away. Focus lightly on the object of meditation. Focus just enough to not forget the object, but don't focus enough to be totally concentrated or feel any stress.

As you sit there meditating, suddenly you will find your mind somewhere else—New York, Bodhgaya, downtown, or wherever. Then you remember the focus, which brings your mind home. You don't have to struggle because the mind has gone far away. You don't need to get into the car and go to the airport and take a plane to get back home. Just remember the focus, and here you are. This is how you learn to focus and let the mind be present.

Gampopa's next main point is that we need to practice with alertness. It's very important to remain aware and alert in meditation. Meditation is not semi-sleep or a dull state of mind. Sometimes we give too much emphasis to feeling peaceful in meditation. We think we need to be quiet with not much thinking going on, so we let our mind be dull and quiet and not so alert. We enjoy the cozy, warm, snuggly dullness. Like when the weather outside is windy and cold, it feels very nice to sit comfortably inside with a little fire or the heater going. However, that is not meditation; that's just being dull and quiet. In meditation, more than being peaceful, the mind must be fresh and aware.

Being without thoughts or sensory awareness is not the point. The point is to be undisturbed by whatever sense experiences or thoughts appear. Whatever you are seeing—just let yourself see it. Whatever you hear doesn't matter—just let yourself hear it. Your ears are open, so you hear, and then you hear again, and then you hear again. The training is in not grasping at the sounds. Of course, you also smell, your body feels whatever it's touching, and so on. You are aware but not grasping. The technique is to be relaxed, yet very aware.

It's the same when focusing on an object of meditation. Lightly remember the focus. Engage the object of focus, but not too much. You still need to know what's going on around you. The main thing is that your mind is undisturbed. When there is a loud sound, you don't think, "Oh, there shouldn't be any noise now. I'm meditating. Those people should stop making so much noise!" Rather, our attitude should be, "Yes, there is a sound, and so what? It doesn't matter." There are sounds even in the most secluded forests. Often the forests are much noisier than the cities in northern Europe!

> No matter what type of practice you are doing, try not to get distracted. Whatever the type of practice, apply whichever of the lama's instructions are appropriate at that time. The meditation will never happen if your mind is moving all over, up and down. Understand this to be an obstacle.

Gampopa goes on to say that you should practice with alertness, no matter what type of practice you are doing. Follow the lama's instructions and do the practice that fits the level where you are. It is a mistake to think that you should be practicing Mahamudra or Dzogchen since those are the highest types of practice. It's not a matter of high or low, or profound or simple. We need to practice what is most useful for us at this time. We have to start where we are; we cannot start at the top. Sometimes the simplest practice is the best practice. Your practice does not need to be special or complicated.

I strongly believe that the best practice for you is the practice you understand most. If you don't understand it, no matter how deep or profound it is, you cannot do it. What's the use of that? The meditation won't happen. If you understand the technique, and know what to do to get results, then start with that practice and stick with it. It is not a matter of progressing through a series of practices, trying to climb a ladder of higher and higher practices. Recognize what level you are on, see what is most needed at that level, and do that. This is where having a living teacher is very helpful. Otherwise, if your mind is moving all around, comparing this and that, the meditation will never happen.

Gampopa ends by saying we should be clear that distraction is an obstacle. Of course, distraction is an obstacle! I certainly hope this is obvious.

If you find that your mind is distracted, do meditation with reference points and apply mindfulness. This will make the mind more focused. Then, you can go on to formless Mahamudra, or meditation without reference points. At that time you can completely let be, and allow your natural understanding and experience to shine through without further effort.

SEVEN

The Meaning of Mahamudra

> Lama Rinpoche said: For a person to become enlightened in one lifetime, it is important to meditate on Mahamudra. Mahamudra is the nondual wisdom mind of all the buddhas of the three times. If you wonder where to look for it, look at your mind.

BECOMING ENLIGHTENED in one lifetime is extremely fast. A lifetime is not limited to the time you are alive; if you become enlightened when you die, that is also considered to be within one lifetime. Even by following the Mahayana path, which is generally considered a quick path, enlightenment is said to take three countless aeons.

I must say, there is some debate about what "countless" means. Some people say that "countless" means that the aeons are numberless. But if the aeons cannot be counted, how could there be three of them?

In the Indian system, a "countless aeon" is a way of indicating the number one followed by sixty zeros. It was the Indian mathematicians who invented the zero, and they gave a name to each number according to how many zeros followed the number one. For example, the number one followed by one zero is ten, the number one followed by two zeros is a hundred, the number one followed by three zeros is a thousand, and so on. When they arrived at the number one followed by sixty zeros, they called that number "countless" or "numberless," because that is where they stopped naming them. In any case, three countless aeons is a very, very long time. It's good to know this, because it shows how long it takes to exhaust our habitual tendencies, and how strong ignorance is.

Of all the practices, the strongest ones focus on wisdom, because wisdom is the antidote for ignorance, which is the main cause of suffering. Mahamudra is one of the strongest practices because it goes directly to the root of our ignorance. It does not use the wisdom of the intellect, but it uses coemergent wisdom to directly realize the buddha nature. This is what makes Mahamudra so effective and so quick. Mahamudra means directly experiencing the wisdom of the enlightened mind.

As Gampopa points out, wisdom is not found anywhere else but in your own consciousness. This is where you look for it.

> Mahamudra is translated as *chagya chenpo* in Tibetan, and it can be understood through the meaning of the Tibetan word. The master Nagarjuna explained the first syllable, *chag*, in this way:[1]

> > *Like putting water into water,*
> > *Like putting butter into butter,*
> > *Chag is one's primordial wisdom*
> > *Fully seeing itself.*

> The second syllable, *gya* or "seal," has three aspects: the seal of the nature, the seal of experience, and the seal of realization. For the seal of the nature, it is said: "The buddha nature completely pervades all beings."
> The seal of the nature refers to the mind's natural state. There are no beings without this nature, even the beings in the lowest hell and the tiniest microbes. The *Hevajra Tantra* states: "Intestinal bacteria, and so on, possess this essential nature."

This chapter focuses on the three seals. In relation to the seal of the nature, the nature of a buddha's mind and the nature of a sentient being's mind are the same. All minds are sealed with this nature. What distinguishes ordinary beings from buddhas is how the mind is experienced.

> One might ask, is it sufficient simply to have this nature? No, it is not enough. You also need the experience that comes from

meditative wisdom. This is the direct experience of the nature
of the mind, the clear light beyond arising and ceasing.

This is the second seal, the seal of experience. The nature has to be
directly seen as the clear light beyond arising and ceasing. Although we
always have this nature, until we experience it directly, we won't become
enlightened.

> The mind has two characteristics: its radiance as various
> thoughts and emotions, and its appearance as various color-
> ful, outer objects. These characteristics are not separable from
> the essence of the mind; they are the magical display of the
> mind.

We discussed this at length in the previous chapter. The characteristics of the mind are the various thoughts and emotions that make up
our experience, and all the colorful appearances that we experience as
outer objects. These characteristics are also called the radiance of the
mind. The displays of the mind that we experience are not something
separate from the essence or nature of our mind.

> To condense this into one point: the coemergent mind itself is
> the dharmakaya, and the coemergent appearances are the ra-
> diance of the dharmakaya.

The dharmakaya, which is clarity-emptiness, is the nature of the
mind. What radiates from this is the magical display of the mind; it is
everything we experience. The radiance appears as both samsara and
nirvana. Samsara is the radiance of the dharmakaya nature of the mind,
and nirvana is the radiance of the dharmakaya nature of the mind.
Purely from this point of view, samsara is not worse and nirvana is not
better. Both of them are the radiance of coemergent wisdom.

> All possible appearances of samsara and nirvana, without ex-
> ception, are completely pure in their essential nature. They are
> completely accomplished, and free from arising, dwelling, and
> ceasing. They are beyond any words, thoughts, or concepts.
> This describes the seal of experience.

If you truly understand that the dharmakaya is the true nature of the mind, you will know that all positive experiences and all negative experiences are merely its radiance. If something frightening happens or something wonderful happens, no matter what it may be, it is a display of your own pure nature.

Speaking of purity, it is very important to understand that at this level of the teachings, the purity of the nature does not mean that the nature has become purified, like something that has been cleaned or polished. At this level, nothing is impure, and there never has been anything impure. Everything is inseparable appearance-emptiness. Every appearance is a display of our own consciousness, and there is nothing impure about its nature, which is unreal, like a dream. If nothing is impure, then everything must be pure.

There is a story about Milarepa's realization of this. It is similar to the story of the Buddha being attacked by Mara right before he became enlightened. One time when Milarepa was practicing in a cave in the mountains, all the strong and powerful spirits of the world came to attack him. There were thunderstorms and lightning, with overflowing rivers and landslides coming down the mountainside. All sorts of frightening things were coming toward him.

So Milarepa sang to the buddhas and bodhisattvas and dharma protectors to help him get rid of these obstacles, but the more he sang, the stronger the negative forces became. Suddenly he thought, "Why am I doing this? These are all displays of my mind. My body is made of the five elements, so it is a perishable thing. It is going to die, whether or not evil spirits attack me. Nobody knows when death will come, and this body will perish in any case. But my awareness cannot die, since awareness is nothing whatsoever. There is nothing solid here, so why be afraid?"

Then Milarepa said aloud, "Okay, all you spirits, you can do whatever you like. You can eat me, or cut me to pieces and distribute my flesh and bones among yourselves. However, you can do this only to my body; you cannot do this to my awareness. Go ahead, do whatever you like. It's no problem." When he sincerely felt this, all the negative forces vanished. They were completely gone.

As this story illustrates, the true nature of your consciousness is indestructible. The more you realize this, the more you realize that there is nothing to fear. There is no need for grasping because there is no one to be attached and nothing to be attached to. When this understanding dawns, you become fearless. If what appears is very nice, that is a display. If what happens is tumultuous, that is also a display.

You could think of your mind as being like the sky. The sky doesn't say, "Oh, I'm so happy today! The light is so clear, and there are no clouds. Oh, no! Here come some clouds. How terrible! Look at all those clouds!" That attitude is useless. Either the clouds are there or they are not there. In the same way, the Mahamudra understanding is that whatever happens is okay; there is nothing wrong with it. Genuinely having this attitude is the sign, or the seal, of the experience of Mahamudra.

> Third, for the seal of realization, the reality just described is not produced from causes and conditions. It is not established as a thing or a substance. It is without color or form. It is beyond any kind of assertion or negation, such as being existent or non-existent. It is uncompounded and spontaneously present. To realize this very nature is the seal of realization.

Realization comes about in three stages: first there is a correct understanding, then direct experience, then stable realization. You begin by developing a correct understanding from hearing good teachings on Mahamudra, studying them, and conducting your own investigation into the nature of the mind. At this stage, you look and analyze from many angles, and become almost 100 percent sure of what the nature is like.

It can happen that your understanding becomes so clear and strong that you mistake it for actual experience. However, once you have the real experience, you know the nature in a different way, and you don't react to things as you did before you had the experience. Another way of distinguishing understanding from experience is whether you forget it. If you can't recall it in difficult circumstances, then it was just a good understanding. But understanding is not enough; it must be assimilated through practice.

There are several ways that real experience manifests. For instance, there's the experience of deeply knowing that everything is completely okay, that there is nothing wrong and nothing to be afraid of. Another type of experience is truly knowing that everything is in the state of equality, and there is no samsara or nirvana. Or you might have a feeling of oneness with everything. At other times, you might experience pervasive clarity, emptiness, or great bliss.

These experiences are similar to realization, but the difference is that they go away; they are only temporary. If you have these types of experiences only some of the time, it means that you have not reached realization.

Once you reach realization, the dramatic experiences are over. Your experience becomes very stable and nondramatic. In every situation, you know that there is absolutely nothing wrong. You are completely relaxed with whatever happens. Realization brings a deep sense of relief. There is nothing further you need to do. In this kind of deep personal experience, there are no qualifying causes or conditions left. You see very clearly and you are completely down-to-earth. You have no special experiences, but there is absolutely nothing wrong.

Another way of talking about realization is that there are no more desires to be fulfilled. Being free from desire brings the greatest peace. Often people find desire very interesting. We usually enjoy having desire, and we enjoy fulfilling our desire. But if you look closely, desire is actually painful because it is linked with dissatisfaction. There is something you want to be different from the way it is; you are not content with the way things are.

But once you have no more desire, you are free, and freedom brings the greatest joy. Realization brings relief from the need to do something or have something or go somewhere. This kind of great joy makes your mind very compassionate. Not compassionate in the sense of feeling bad because people suffer, but compassionate in terms of manifesting a joyful, radiant kindness toward everyone. You spontaneously radiate joy and kindness. This is a sign that experience has turned into realization. This is the seal of realization.

When these three seals are accomplished, then there is the "great seal," which is the translation of the Sanskrit word *Mahamudra.*

> There is nothing superior to this, there is nothing higher, so it is called *chenpo,* which means "great."

The main point of Mahamudra practice is to see your true nature in a direct and experiential way. There is nothing greater than this, so it is called *chenpo,* or "great."

In the instructions for realizing chagya chenpo, or Mahamudra, there are four wisdoms that arise in postmeditation.

1. There is greater compassion for sentient beings.
2. There is greater devotion for the lama and the three jewels.
3. One is more careful about karmic cause and effect.
4. All attachment to this life fades away.

These four types of wisdom are not things you deliberately do, but
they naturally occur as your practice grows. If you are practicing Mahamudra and see yourself changing in these ways, then you are making
progress.

Let's begin with the first type of wisdom, which is greater compassion for sentient beings. When we have cultivated wisdom through
meditation, we can have all sorts of experiences, such as clairvoyance,
great joy, feelings of emptiness and nonduality, being able to manifest
miracles, or heal the sick. These feelings and powers are sometimes
good and sometimes not so good; they can become obstacles for us.
There is only one definite sign of progress: the increase of compassion.
So, when your compassion for all beings is getting stronger and more
genuine, this means your practice is going well. The compassion could
be coming from the practice of Mahamudra or from another type of
practice. Either way, compassion is the main sign of progress.

Generally, everybody has compassion and love. There are no sentient
beings without some love and compassion, since all of us want to be
happy and free of suffering. In general, people don't like seeing someone
else suffer; they find it very hard to witness another person's pain. Most
of us have at least one or two people whom we love, but this kind of love
is infested with attachment. As samsaric beings, it's a fact that whenever
we have love, we also have attachment. However, these are two different
things. Attachment is about yourself; love is about others.

Love is a benevolent radiance of the mind. With love, you wish someone well; you care about their welfare. On the other hand, attachment is
all about you. You want this thing, or you want him or her, and you feel
unhappy if you can't have what you want. Whenever there is attachment, the feeling of love can turn into a feeling of hate in one second,
because that love is conditional. You might think, "I love you, but if you
don't love me back, I will hate you." Or "I like you very much, but if you

don't do what I want, I will hate you." Because the feeling is conditional, there is very little real connection with the other person.

At the other extreme, people sometimes misunderstand selflessness, and think that their own welfare is unimportant. They hear that they should be compassionate and work for the benefit of others, but they misinterpret this to mean that they should never do anything for themselves. This is a misunderstanding. The teachings of the Bodhisattva-yana repeatedly speak of the two benefits: you work for your own benefit as well as for the benefit of others. Beginning bodhisattvas in particular must protect themselves and take care of themselves.

If there is something that is good for yourself and good for others, both now and in the long run, then try to do it as much as you can. If you can see that although an action might be good for others, it is not good for yourself, then you have to look closely and ask, "How good is this for others, and how bad is this for me?" If you find that the action is extremely beneficial for many people but bad for you, then you have to check whether it is too much sacrifice or not. If the sacrifice is more than you can bear, then it is fine to say "No." You don't need to do it, even if it would help many people.

Another variation is seeing that an action would be very beneficial for others and not much sacrifice for yourself, and yet you feel you would regret it later. In that case, the Mahayana teachings say that you shouldn't do it. If an action would be very good for others and only a small sacrifice for you, and it is nothing you would regret, then of course, do it. But if it is not very good for others, do not sacrifice yourself.

Going back to the four wisdoms that arise in postmeditation as a result of Mahamudra practice, the second is having more devotion to the lama and the three jewels. As our realization of Mahamudra increases, our devotion to the teacher, the Buddha, the dharma, and the sangha naturally grows stronger as well.

The third wisdom is that one becomes more attentive to karmic cause and effect. Here, it's important to remember that karma is completely dependent upon intention. Two people could perform the same activity, and based on their intentions, one action would be positive and the other would not. The Buddhist view is that if the motivation in your heart is pure, then the action is positive, even if the situation seems to go all wrong. Whether the situation goes right or wrong, it does not depend solely on you. There are always many factors involved. Even with a good intention, if you don't have the wisdom to know how to do something, the situation can easily go wrong. But it is important to know that in terms of karma, if the intention is positive, then the karma is positive.

This doesn't mean that you can simply have a good intention and forget about the consequences. Of course, you need to think about the consequences. If your intention is genuine and you try your best, that's the most you can do. If things don't go well, at least you know that you did your best.

In a way, we could say that the whole purpose of practice is to transform our karma. Karma, habitual tendencies, and personality are all the same thing. Karma can be changed, and karma has to be changed. Otherwise, if we carry the same karma and go on in the same way, we just repeat the same patterns again and again, and get nowhere. If we react in a certain way throughout this lifetime, we will die in the same way and continue to react in the same way in the next lifetime. We need to change our karma.

Of course, the better our karma, the easier it is to change. People who have more negative states of mind will need to work harder. If we use skillful means, it can be much easier to change our karma. This is why we have so many different practices; they make it easier to change our karma. The transformation that happens through practice is a transformation of karma. To change our habitual patterns is very difficult, because we have been acting in certain ways for a very long time. And a lot of our tendencies are unconscious. To transform at this deep level is not easy, but it is certainly possible. It will have to be done at some point.

Another important point about karma is connected with regret. When you do something wrong, regret is the most important aspect for purification. But sometimes students confuse regret with being hard on themselves. It is important to recognize that what you did was wrong, and clearly see that you shouldn't do it again. But punishing yourself does not purify anything. Rather than being focused on negativity, purification happens from doing positive things, from creating positive karma. This is a much better approach.

The instruction is this: recognize what you have done wrong, make a resolution not to do it again, and then do something positive to purify the wrongdoing. You need to let go of the negativity. Just as in Vajrasattva practice, letting go of negative deeds and negative feelings becomes a strong purification.

There is a story about this from the time of Atisha Dipankara. When Atisha came to Tibet, he was asked by one of the monks, "If I do something wrong and break one of my vows, what should I do?"

Atisha asked him, "Where are you living now?"

The monk said he was living in retreat in a cave.

Atisha said, "Okay, if you break a vow, go to Sangphu Monastery and publicly say, 'I have broken this vow.' Then go to Samye Monastery and again say to everyone, 'I have broken this vow.' Then go to Lhasa and say, 'I have broken this vow.' After that, go back to your retreat place and act as if you had never broken the vow."

In other words, when you have done something wrong, you shouldn't agonize over it for the rest of your life. Dwelling on it doesn't help. This can make you uptight and worried about doing every little thing wrong. This makes it difficult to practice. Practice should not be a burden; practice should be a joy. If you get distressed about making a mistake, your practice will never be a joy. So you need to make a confession, then let it go and act as if it never happened.

We need to be realistic and keep our feet on the ground. It's important to form the resolve not to do a negative deed again, but it's also important to recognize that everyone makes mistakes. This doesn't mean that what you do is inconsequential. It's important to recognize that negative deeds are not good for yourself and not good for others. So, do take care. But when a negative thought comes into your mind, you don't need to panic. It can't be the first negative thought you ever had! Okay, it appeared. So what? Let it come and let it go. Let it go as quickly as possible. Then, it's okay.

The fourth wisdom that arises from Mahamudra practice is that all attachment to this life falls apart. Attachment and aversion always come together; they are two sides of the same coin. So, the more we are free from aversion and fear, the more we are free from attachment. For example, we might fear loneliness and want someone to be with. But the more we let go of the aversion to loneliness, the less attached we are to having someone with us, and the more contented we feel on our own. And further, the more we are free from attachment, the more genuine our love and fearlessness become.

The more fearless you are, the freer you become. This is how liberation happens. For this to occur, you need to truly know yourself and know your awareness. This knowing can be done only by you. This is what makes it difficult—it cannot be taught. Actually, no one can teach you how to practice, either. All a teacher can do is show you how to learn for yourself. You have to come to understand what you are—what your true nature or the coemergent wisdom is. The more you understand the nature of your mind, the more you understand the nature of everything. This is what we call wisdom, and it is what Mahamudra practice is all about.

EIGHT

Six Points Concerning the Creation Stage Practice

Lama Rinpoche said: In order to bring your practice into experience, keep in mind impermanence and death. Be mindful
of karmic cause and effect. Keep in mind the shortcomings of
samsara. Remember the shortcomings of the Hinayana, and
go beyond that by cultivating love, compassion, and bodhichitta.

NOW WE COME to Gampopa's teaching on the creation stage practice.
Before he gets into the main topic, he lays the foundation by saying that
in order to bring our practice to fruition, we need to keep in mind some
basic truths, starting with impermanence and the uncertainty of the
time of death. We need to remember the karmic effects of our actions,
and we need to keep in mind the faults of samsara and the shortcomings
of the Hinayana. Gampopa is using the term "Hinayana" to signify
working for one's liberation alone. Our motivation needs to be strong
enough so that we practice and work for the benefit of others. This is
the motivation of bodhichitta, which grows from cultivating love and
compassion.

When we focus on the creation and completion stage practices of
the Vajrayana, we must never exclude the basic Buddhist truths, attitudes, and practices. Without these, our Vajrayana practice will not be

effective. Sometimes Westerners without much background see the Vajrayana as very ritualistic, and they wonder if Vajrayana practices are just Tibetan cultural trappings added on top of the real Buddhist teachings. The Vajrayana can seem very different from the Hinayana and the Mahayana. But this seeming discrepancy only exists when one doesn't go deeply enough into the Vajrayana to fully understand its meaning.

To practice the Vajrayana, we need a good general understanding of the dharma and the basic practices of the Hinayana, as well as the confident bodhichitta of the Mahayana. On top of that, it's very helpful and effective to practice the skillful means of the Vajrayana. The Vajrayana is part of the Mahayana; it is not outside of Mahayana practice. It is bodhisattva practice with special skillful means.

With that as a basis, the two methods of the creation stage and completion stage practice are the entranceway to the extraordinary great vehicle, the Vajrayana. It is said:

> *For those who are steadfast in the creation stage*
> *And want to undertake the completion stage,*
> *These skillful means, which proceed step-by-step,*
> *Were taught by the perfect buddha.*
> *The meditative equipoise of the two stages*
> *Is the dharma taught by Vajradhara.*

The skillful means of the Vajrayana contains two stages of practice: the creation stage and the completion stage. In brief, the completion stage is Mahamudra. The creation stage is quite different. It is a set of methods, primarily visualizations and mantras, which use our creative mind. We use our imagination, and in a way we are channeling our daydreams and wishes in order to change our habitual ways of seeing the world and ourselves.

Creation stage practice is more like shamatha meditation than *vipashyana* meditation. Shamatha is the type of meditation that stabilizes the mind by focusing on something and remaining there. But creation stage practice is more than shamatha; it works on our habitual tendencies. In deity yoga, which is another name for creation stage practice, we transform our habitual patterns into more positive ways of being. Usually, we pay more attention to the negative aspects of our life—our problems, our pain, and the various things that bother us. But in creation stage practice, we emphasize positive qualities and feelings by adopting a more enlightened way of being. We train in experiencing the enlightened body, speech, and mind in order to override our old habits of being hurt, getting upset, feeling bad, and on and on. We are changing this pattern into a feeling that everything is going very well.

Visualization and mantra recitation are merely methods, skillful ways of working on our habitual tendencies. The reason the Vajrayana is so effective is that it uses a variety of skillful means. These methods are not the ultimate truth, but they can change the way we feel about ourselves and our world, and thus free our mind. How effective they are depends on how well we understand them and how well we apply them. When we apply them as they should be applied, they are extremely useful.

In general, why do we meditate? We do it to train our mind. Meditation makes the mind calm and flexible, it helps us to see reality clearly, and it brings out the mind's innate qualities. For example, sometimes we use the breath as the focus of meditation. We sit down and become aware of breathing in and breathing out. Lightly focusing on the breath keeps us from being distracted. And when we do become distracted, we have the breath as a reference point to come back to. This is an excellent technique, an excellent skillful means for training the mind.

In the creation stage practice we take the same approach, but instead of focusing on the breath or another object, we think about an enlightened being, like Guru Rinpoche or Chenrezik, who is full of compassion and wisdom. What is the difference between these techniques? When we use the breath or another object, whether substantial or imaginary, it merely serves as a focus for our mind. In contrast, focusing on an awakened being activates other aspects of the mind as well.

What does it mean to be enlightened? What is a buddha? A buddha is someone who has developed wisdom and compassion to the fullest extent. We cannot focus on a buddha without focusing on compassion, wisdom, and other positive qualities. By doing creation stage practice, we are associating ourselves with these qualities; we are cultivating these qualities in our mind stream. Even though the visualization is our concept, to some extent we are experiencing and feeling enlightened qualities. We feel the presence of compassion and the presence of wisdom. We cannot feel anger or hatred while thinking of a buddha. With this type of practice, we are not only calming the mind, but we are indirectly transforming our mind's habitual tendencies.

There is a lot to be said about the creation stage practice. Gampopa explains it in this way:

> The creation stage practice can be explained in six points: (1) the types, (2) the essence, (3) the definition, (4) the purpose, (5) the measure of stability, and (6) the result.
>
> First, there are three types of creation stage practice: (a) the visualization is created in many steps, according to the particular sadhana, (b) the visualization is created in three steps, or (c) the visualization is created by instantly recollecting the entire form.

Gampopa sets out three styles of transforming ordinary thoughts and emotions into the clear appearance of the deity. The first style is to create the visualization in many steps, in accordance with the particular sadhana. There are many Vajrayana sadhanas; for example, there are sadhanas for Kalachakra, Hevajra, and Vajrayogini. Each of these sadhanas could be very elaborate, with complex mandalas, many deities and rituals, and lots of things to visualize, think about, and do. The same practice could be done less elaborately, it could be done simply, or it could be done extremely simply.

One reason for these variations is the differences between people. Some people have very creative or complex minds. This reminds me of the Indian style of mind, which is very complex and enjoys complicated ideas. It is very good with mathematics, and these days, with computers. This type of mind likes to have plenty to consider, such as deities with eleven heads and twenty-four hands, each holding something different. So the different styles of creation stage practice are suited for different styles of mind.

Also, there are different stages of the practice. Sometimes we visualize a deity step-by-step, and there can be many steps. The steps have particular purposes; they are working on different issues. We are not just thinking about some funny-looking figures; each part of the practice has a purpose.

The overall purpose of sadhana practice is to work on our traumas. Usually when we have a problem, we try to find the root of the problem so we can understand why we react the way we do. We locate the trauma and then try to work through it. Modern psychology usually focuses on things that happened to us in our early years. The Buddhist view goes even further back, since most of our traumas arose before childhood. Actually, our birth itself was traumatic. Birth and death are regarded as the biggest traumas that people experience.

The generation and dissolution practices, which are part of the creation stage practice, work on the way we experience birth and death. When we generate the deity, we are working with our birth experience. When we dissolve the deity, we are working with our experience of death. We have experienced birth and death many times over countless lifetimes. Birth and death have had a traumatic impact on us; they are the source of most of our fears and clinging. If we do not deal with birth and death, then no matter how much we work on other aspects of our personality, we will not completely outgrow our habitual tendencies. Therefore, we have to work on the traumas of birth and death, and in the Vajrayana, we do this through the generation and dissolution practices.

Creation stage practice takes us through the experiences of birth and death, but not in a traumatic way. We go through them in a very positive way. Stage by stage, we appear with many beautiful qualities, blessings, noble purposes, and wonderful experiences. We generate ourselves into something very positive; we have all the positive qualities of our nature. Similarly, the way we dissolve the visualization is easy and natural, without any pain or clinging. We learn how to arise and how to dissolve without any problems.

Right now, we have lots of problems with dissolving. Death is our biggest fear. Birth is also very painful. So, we work on these traumas within our mind by practicing the processes of generating and dissolving many times. Our accumulated experience and habitual tendencies of birth and death are replaced by positive experiences of generation and dissolution. In this kind of practice, the various stages of birth and death are created in our mind, and exercised again and again.

This is usually done in the form of a deity. "Deity" means a buddha, an enlightened being. The most essential point in the Vajrayana is the buddha nature, and all Vajrayana practices are based on understanding this. What is our buddha nature? It is not a thing that we have somewhere inside us, like a tumor. We won't be able to find our buddha nature in our heart or our brain. Buddha nature means there is no difference between the nature of our consciousness and a buddha's consciousness. A buddha's consciousness is not made of one material, and our consciousness made of another. They are exactly the same.

In that case, what is the difference between us and the buddhas? The difference is that they clearly see their nature; they understand what they actually are. And we do not clearly see and understand what we actually are. Therefore, we are confused, whereas they are not confused. However, both of us have the same enlightened nature.

There is no problem with our basic being; the problem is our confusion. Once we are no longer confused, we can become just as enlightened as a buddha. But right now, our confusion blocks our seeing. When we start seeing our nature clearly, then all the enlightened qualities naturally arise in us because they are all there. There is love and compassion and wisdom. Right now our love is very limited and mixed-up, whereas a buddha's love is not limited or mixed-up. Although we have some understanding, intuition, and clarity, generally speaking we have a lot more confusion. A buddha is totally free of confusion, and that is the real difference.

So, what we call a "meditation deity" is the same as a buddha. When you generate yourself as the deity, it means that you become your true self, without confusion. When you are free of confusion, you are an enlightened being.

To come back to the three styles of visualization, the first method entails an elaborate way of generating the deity in many steps. Some sadhanas have five, six, or even more stages before the full form of the deity appears.

The second method is to create the deity in three steps. This is called the three samadhis. In the first samadhi, everything becomes emptiness; in the second samadhi, the deity's seed syllable appears; and in the third samadhi, then the seed syllable transforms directly into the deity, or the seed syllable transforms first into the deity's symbol and then into the deity.

The third style of visualization is to instantly recollect the entire form of the deity. In one instant, the deity is complete. This is the simplest method.

If you look at various sadhanas, you will find these different ways of creating the visualization.

Second, the essence of creation stage practice is the transformation of your ordinary thoughts and emotions into the clear appearance of the deity.

The second category describes the essence of creation stage practice, which is to transform samsaric, painful experience into enlightened, peaceful experience. This is the main purpose, or the essence, of all aspects of creation stage practice.

The way we experience ourselves now is in human form. For instance, I think I am a human being named "Ringu Tulku," and I identify with this form. I also identify everything I have experienced in this life—especially in this life, but also in other lives—with this form. So, when I feel this "me," this "Ringu Tulku," then all my personal history comes up: "Ringu Tulku had this problem and that problem." I carry the burden of Ringu-Tulku-ness.

The idea here is that we could change our ordinary identification, let go of the past, and become something different. We need to go beyond our past, because otherwise it is all too much and we feel overwhelmed. We cannot resolve each and every thing that ever happened to us, even if we could remember them all. If we could see all the unconscious baggage we carry around with us, even a big garbage dump might not contain it all. We can't work on all these problems one by one. What we need is a total transformation.

The Vajrayana way of clearing away old baggage is to assume a new identity—a fresh, clear, and pure identity. This is the deity. So, instead of being an ordinary person, we could be Tara or Chenrezik or some other enlightened being. Then, no old baggage! Suddenly we have great compassion, great wisdom, and great ability. And as Tara or Chenrezik, we have been this way for centuries and centuries. Identifying with the deity is a skillful means; it is a very useful way to work on our confused clinging to a self.

Many students say they cannot visualize; they find it very difficult. This is because these students are trying to become something radically different from what they feel they are. In doing visualization, we are learning to connect with our true nature, which is already enlightened. In deity yoga, our undeluded nature appears in a perfect and pure form. It doesn't need to be beautiful; in fact, it can look very ugly. As you know, there are wrathful deities as well as peaceful deities. In whatever way the deity appears, we need to see it as pure and full of positive qualities.

Visualization practice involves more than seeing; it has many aspects. It resembles the way children learn. Educators say that learning happens through "SIFT." The letter S stands for "sensing," using our senses, and the I stands for "imagination." As we sense something, we naturally make an image in our mind. The F stands for "feeling." Along with the image, there is a feeling; we feel as well as see. The T is for "thinking." We also form concepts about what we experience.

Whenever we experience anything, we have all four aspects of SIFT. In visualization practice, we sense, imagine, feel, and think about our enlightened nature as the embodiment of compassion and wisdom. Whatever this enlightened nature looks like—Chenrezik, Tara, or whatever—doesn't matter. The meditation is exercising this new identity, this understanding of our inherent clarity and purity, over and over.

Don't be confused by thinking that now you have become someone else and you have two identities. Here you are assuming your unconfused identity, the buddha nature identity. Actually, the name and identity you have now is just as much an imputation as the deity's name and identity. In many ways, your regular identity is also your imagination. Each of us has many different identities. We change in relationship to others: In one situation we are a child, and in another we are a parent. We can be a teacher one day, and a student the next. We play many different roles.

What we are doing in this case is focusing on our original, unsullied, enlightened identity. With this technique, our problematic identity is abandoned, and our enlightened qualities are realized. We are bringing forth our true nature and identifying with it in a very clear way. This is the essence of the creation stage.

> Third, there are three parts to the definition of the creation
> stage: (a) the mind generates the body of the deity, (b) the
> body and mind clearly appear as the deity, and (c) the deity is
> known to be a mental imputation.

These three parts are practiced stage by stage. We first create, see, and feel the deity. Second, we see that the deity is a display of our mind, and it is not something to hold on to. Third, having understood that the deity is a manifestation of our mind, we realize that the mind is also a display. The mind is a magical thing—it is aware, and yet it is nothing in itself. It is awareness-emptiness.

> **a. In terms of the mind generating the body of the deity, instead of conceiving of your body as an ordinary, material body of flesh and blood, it clearly appears as the form of the deity.**

As its special skillful means, the Vajrayana uses the result as the path. This is in contrast to the general way, or the Mahayana way, where the cause of enlightenment is the path. In the Mahayana, we begin to practice compassion by thinking of someone who has given us a tremendous amount of love, and we wish that person well. We think about how much we want that person to be free of suffering. Not only do we think that, we also feel it very strongly. In Mahayana practice, we gradually expand this feeling to our friends and relatives. Then, we extend this love to people we don't know, people who are suffering intensely, and finally we extend love to all beings, even our enemies and people who have harmed us. This way uses the cause of enlightenment as the path.

The Vajrayana path uses the result, which in this case is the deity as an embodiment of enlightenment. This can be done in two ways, or in two steps. The first step is to visualize the deity in the space in front of you; you feel the presence of the deity outside yourself. You can feel the warmth of kindness and compassion radiating from the deity, and this love engulfs not only you but all sentient beings. In turn, you extend this feeling to all beings so that they will receive the light of blessings and the healing energy of this buddha. All beings, including yourself, become transformed.

The more you can feel this, the more you are exercising your loving-kindness, because you are the person feeling it. This is a way of developing compassion through the back door, so to speak. You are not contemplating suffering or generating a concept of compassion; you are simply feeling compassion, because you feel the energy radiating from the deity. This is the skillfulness of the Vajrayana.

The second step, which is more of an inner practice, is to visualize yourself as the deity. You see yourself as an enlightened being who is radiating warmth, wisdom, and the healing power of purification and transformation. When you feel yourself transformed, you feel that everything and everyone else are also transformed. You are a buddha, and your energy expands so that everyone else is equally pure, loving, and joyful. At this point, you feel completely good, beyond all negative emotions and problems.

You can take this even further and see yourself surrounded by all the buddhas and bodhisattvas. You can make your practice more inclusive by incorporating great masters of all traditions and religions. In this way, you multiply your intentions, and all of you together emanate light rays of blessings, goodness, and happiness to everyone. By practicing this repeatedly, you are using the result—being an embodiment of enlightenment—as the path.

We practice with visualized forms because our body and our mind are so strongly connected. The way we see our body is based on the habitual tendencies of our mind; we experience everything through our mind, even our body. For example, I have heard of people who stop eating because they think it is more beautiful to be very slim. Even when they become thin, they see themselves as too heavy when they look in the mirror. Our habitual tendencies are like that.

The way we see ourselves and the way we see others accord with our individual perceptions. People see differently. Some people seem to naturally see goodness, and everywhere they go, everything is fine. They are positive and optimistic, and everything seems to go well for them. Then, there are people for whom everything is a problem. Things constantly go wrong, everyone seems unpleasant, and they have many difficulties. We can see this happening all around us. Of course, there are lots of people in between these extremes as well.

In terms of changing the way we see ourselves and others, the change cannot be imposed from outside; it must come from within. In creation stage practice, we train in perceiving our body and mind without negativity. We train in seeing everything in a completely pure way. The more we see things in a positive way, the more positive we become. We are what we think. We have a certain way of looking at things, and we become that way.

Have you heard about the pessimists, the optimists, the realists, and the spiritualists? According to this way of looking at things, there are four kinds of people. The example for these types is four glasses of water. One glass is half-empty, one glass is half-full, one glass is completely empty, and the fourth glass is overflowing. Underneath the glasses there is written: pessimist—half-empty; optimist—half-full; realist—completely empty; and spiritualist—more than full. So, we Vajrayana practitioners are spiritual people. We work on seeing things as not only full but doubly full, or very positive.

This is how we train. At this very moment we can feel that we are enlightened beings, full of compassion and healing power. For example, if you want to become a doctor, first you have to think of yourself as a doctor. If you cannot see yourself as a doctor, you will not become one. You first imagine yourself wearing a white coat and walking authoritatively into the hospital. You might not know anything about medicine, but this is how you imagine yourself. Then, with training, you acquire the knowledge and skills to be a doctor.

All training is like this. To become a very compassionate and wise being, we start by feeling this now. The more we can feel this, the more we can exercise it. This is how we start to become a buddha.

When visualizing ourselves as the deity, we feel the deity's wisdom, we feel the deity's compassion, and then we relax. Compassion at this level is not dualistic; it is not the feeling that a subject has for an object. Often, when we contemplate compassion, we think of people who are suffering; we think that we don't want them to suffer, and then we feel bad. Here, we are talking about a different kind of compassion. As the deity, we are simply glowing with compassion, glowing with kindness, glowing with love. There is no need to think of particular people who are suffering, because this kind of compassion is not focused on suffering. It is just wishing people well, having benevolent feelings for everyone. In fact, this kind of compassion is sometimes called great bliss. Rather than being focused on suffering, this feeling is completely vibrant, joyful, and benevolent.

> **b. In terms of seeing your body and mind as the deity, you understand that the form of the deity is a display of the mind, like magic or a rainbow.**

The deity is not something we produce; it is a display. We don't need to get attached to the visualization, thinking we might lose it. As we have discussed, everything we experience is our mind, so it can display positive things, negative things, and all kinds of thoughts and emotions.

So we just relax in being the deity. It is a mistake to think, "Oh, I am about to lose this visualization, I need to focus more." Please don't do that; it won't work. The practice needs to be relaxed; it has to be natural. We need to let the visualization come and let it go. This is the second point, which is very important.

The third part of the definition is also very important. The text says:

> c. In terms of the deity being an imputation of the mind, the form of the deity is like a magical illusion. You understand that it has no basis. It is merely a name, merely a sign, merely an imputation, merely a designation.

Gradually, our practice matures so that we feel that all the displays of our mind are the deity. There is nothing that is not the deity; there is nothing negative. This is because everything is simply a display. By the end of the training, everything we see is the form of the deity; everything we hear is mantra; everything we think is wisdom.

At this stage, you do not need to think of yourself as the deity with a white face or a black face or certain ornaments, or that you are holding a lotus or a sword or whatever. You have passed that stage. You know the deity is a manifestation of your mind, and your mind is a magical thing. The mind is emptiness and awareness, and within empty awareness, anything can magically appear. The display is the nirmanakaya. The display is the deity.

With this view, there is nothing wrong at all; everything is okay. If there are negative feelings, it's okay; it is just a display. Things do not become negative unless we make them negative. If you hold on to something and grumble, then it becomes negative. If something simply happens, it is not negative. When we deeply understand this, there is nothing but the deity and nothing but purity. All that appears is the form of the deity; all that we hear is the sound of the mantra; all that we think is the display of wisdom. How could there be anything that is not the deity? Everything is a magical display of the mind.

Once we see this, we relax. We do not need to cling to things as good or bad, as wanted or unwanted. What previously frightened us is an illusory display of the mind, so it is also the form of the deity, or more simply, it is something positive. When we understand this, we are getting to the real meaning, or the root, of the creation stage practice. This is also called the "mandala principle" or the "view of pure perception." Since this understanding develops gradually, it is taught in the three stages we just discussed.

Sometimes, beginners wonder what would happen if they were to fully identify with the deity. They worry that they might go crazy or become schizophrenic. After all, people with multiple personalities get put in mental hospitals.

It is important to realize that every time we identify with something, it is merely a mental designation. It is similar to the way our identity changes as our roles change. For example, now I am assuming the role of the teacher, at another time I could assume the role of the student, and on another occasion I could be a brother or a son. This does not make me crazy, because I know these are roles that I am playing. It is important to recognize that all our designations and identifications— like being human, being Tibetan, being a monk—are imputations. They are images and names; they are not something solid and real.

Believing things to be solid and real is where all our problems come from. When you identify something as solid, and feel strong aversion or strong attachment to it, then problems arise. Most of our mental problems arise when we intensely dislike something or someone, and then feel aversion and fear. Or we may intensely like something or someone, and then become attached. These feelings arise from investing things with a substantial reality that they do not have.

It is much the same when you generate the deity. It should be clear that you are not assuming someone else's identity; you are assuming your own pure identity, but in a form that you can understand, a form that becomes familiar to you.

If a person's mind is stable, they will not think they have multiple personalities. However, if someone is already deluded in that way, then visualization practice might compound the problem. Although maybe it wouldn't be so bad for crazy people to think they are Chenrezik, since Chenrezik is full of love. Probably it would be much better for them!

I will tell you a sort of joke, although it is a true story. One time the first prime minister of India, Jawaharlal Nehru, visited a mental hospital. He went into a ward, and a patient who was getting better came up to him and said, "Who are you? What is your name?"

The prime minister replied, "I am Jawaharlal Nehru, the prime minister of India."

The patient patted him on the shoulder and said, "Don't worry, my friend! You are going to be okay. When I first came here, I thought I was Mahatma Gandhi."

Now we come to the fourth main aspect of the creation stage, which is its purpose.

> Fourth, as for the purpose of the creation stage practice, it has an overall purpose and specific purposes. The overall purpose is, at best, to attain the realization of nonduality. At a medium or lower level, the overall purpose of the creation stage is to become free of ordinary attachments.

Creation stage practice has two types of purpose: a general purpose and some special purposes. The general purpose also has two types: one is more ultimate and the other is more relative.

The ultimate purpose is the realization of the kaya of unity. This is another way of saying "enlightenment" or "nonduality." The more relative, short-term purpose is to become free of ordinary attachments. As we practice more, we become less caught up in the way we previously experienced things; we don't hold on to the world with our old habitual tendencies. More and more, we experience our positive nature in the form of the deity. So, the more relative aspect of the general purpose is to lessen our attachment.

> The creation stage practice has twelve special purposes. These are connected with the *samayasattva*, the *jnanasattva*, blessings, and empowerment.

The twelve specific purposes are connected with four main factors in creation stage practice: the samayasattva, the jnanasattva, blessings, and empowerments. The samayasattva refers to visualizing oneself as the deity, which we do after the preliminary section of the practice.

The jnanasattva refers to the truly enlightened beings, the buddhas and bodhisattvas, whom we invoke by radiating light from our heart. This light goes in all directions, inviting them to come and merge with our self-visualization. We do this because most of us feel that we are not really enlightened. It is more common to feel that we are imagining ourselves as the deity. So, to make the practice feel more real, we radiate light and feel that the truly enlightened beings arrive and enter us. They take their seat in our heart center, and we feel their presence. This is what we call the jnanasattva.

Then we receive blessings and empowerment as the deity. Receiving empowerments, such as the four empowerments, is a process of merging enlightened body, speech, and mind with our own body, speech, and mind, so that they become inseparable. This awakens our own enlightened body, speech, and mind, which is the key point of the creation stage.

All four aspects—the samayasattva, jnanasattva, blessings, and empowerment—have three special purposes of their own. These add up to twelve special purposes.

> First, there are three reasons for generating the samayasattva:
> (a) your ordinary delusions disappear, (b) you understand
> that you and your special deity are inseparable, and (c) gener-
> ating the samayasattva protects your *samaya* as a *vidyadhara*.

There are three reasons for generating the samayasattva. First, it is used to dismantle your ordinary delusions. Your ordinary way of seeing yourself and the world is transformed. Second, it is used for understanding that you and your special deity are inseparable. Third, it is used to keep the samaya of a vidyadhara. A vidyadhara is a Vajrayana practitioner with real, genuine experience. The samaya is like a precept, and the basic samaya of the Vajrayana is that your body, speech, and mind are understood to be the deity.

> Second, the jnanasattva fulfills three purposes: (a) you under-
> stand that you and your special deity are inseparable; (b) be-
> cause of recognizing that inseparability, you are blessed by the
> deity; and (c) it is used to quickly attain the supreme and ordi-
> nary *siddhis*.

The second group of three purposes is related to visualizing the jnanasattva. First, this makes you and your special deity inseparable. Merging with the jnanasattva is a way of recognizing that you are the same as the deity.

Second, by understanding your inseparability with the deity, you receive the blessings of the deity. Sometimes people wonder what the term "blessings" means. The blessings are the transformation. The more you see yourself as the deity, which is your pure buddha nature, the more you transform. Visualizing the jnanasattva helps you transform.

Third, the jnanasattva is used to quickly attain the supreme and ordinary siddhis. As your realization grows, you attain siddhis. *Siddhi* means "attainment." There are two main types of siddhis: the supreme siddhi and the ordinary siddhis. The supreme siddhi is enlightenment. It means realization, buddhahood, nonduality—whatever you want to call the highest attainment. Once you have the supreme siddhi, then nothing further is needed. It's all done; your work is finished. The ordinary siddhis are merely temporary, but they are useful. They are things like clairvoyance, being able to perform certain miracles, and being able to heal people. There are different ways of describing the powers and qualities you gain. Ordinary siddhis are not enlightenment, but they are very useful for benefiting beings.

> Third, blessing the body, speech, and mind fulfills three purposes: (a) blessings transform your ordinary body, speech, and mind into the pure body, speech, and mind of a *tathagata;* (b) blessings are an excellent protection against harm from human and nonhuman beings; and (c) through blessings, you completely accomplish the kaya of the deity.

The third aspect is obtaining the blessings of body, speech, and mind from the deity, which also has three purposes. First, blessings transform your ordinary body, speech, and mind into pure body, speech, and mind. By receiving the deity's blessings again and again, you are transformed again and again. The second purpose is that blessings provide a very strong protection against harm from human and nonhuman beings. Third, through blessings you completely accomplish the deity. Receiving blessings is part of the training, and they make the practice mature.

> Fourth, three purposes are fulfilled by receiving empowerment: (a) it distinguishes the Vajrayana from the Paramitayana; (b) through empowerment, all the emotional obscurations are purified; and (c) through empowerment, you completely accomplish the kaya of the deity.

The fourth aspect is receiving empowerment. Sometimes empowerment refers to receiving the blessings of the body, speech, and mind. Sometimes a vajra master gives the empowerment, and then you receive it. Blessings and empowerments are more or less the same.

The first purpose of empowerment is to distinguish the creation stage from the causal approach of the Mahayana, which is also known as the Bodhisattvayana and the Paramitayana. Empowerment is unique to the Vajrayana. As you probably know, there are three main yanas in Buddhism—the Shravakayana, the Bodhisattvayana, and the Vajrayana. In the Shravakayana we receive the precepts of the Vinaya, which are connected with conduct. There are five main precepts—to refrain from killing, stealing, lying, sexual misconduct, and intoxication—and we can take any number of those five. When people become monks or nuns, they take a very large number of Vinaya precepts. Taking refuge is part of this yana, and it can be considered a precept.

Then, the Mahayana has the bodhisattva vow. By taking this vow, we commit ourselves to work for the welfare of all sentient beings, particularly through the practice of the paramitas.

The entrance to the Vajrayana is empowerment. Empowerment is very important in the Vajrayana; it is an uncommon way of teaching or giving transmission that is not found in the Sutrayana. There are different kinds of empowerments, such as the seed empowerment and the result empowerment. The seed empowerment is given by the lama to the students. It could be in the form of a teaching, like a guided meditation, or a transmission of the lineage blessings or the blessings of the practice. Another type of empowerment is the "pointing-out," a pith instruction on the nature of the mind.

Empowerment can be a transmission of words, a transmission of symbols, or a mind transmission. In the most genuine type of empowerment, which is given by a very qualified teacher to a very qualified student, a mind-to-mind transmission happens. The student does not need to go through lots of teachings or lots of practice; there is just the mind transmission, and in one moment the student attains realization. Guru Rinpoche gave the mind transmission this way, and many other masters are able to do that.

The second purpose of empowerment is to clear away the *kleshas*, or emotional obscurations, such as attachment, aversion, ignorance, pride, and jealousy. The third purpose of empowerment is to accomplish the deity. This is the same as the third purpose of the blessings, which we discussed above. This concludes the twelve special purposes of the creation stage practice.

> Fifth, the measure of stability of the creation stage practice has three indications from the practitioner's perspective and three indications from others' perspectives.

Next, in terms of the creation stage practice, Gampopa explains how to tell what level of stability you have attained, or what levels of stability can be attained. There are three signs from your own point of view, and three signs from the point of view of others. In other words, it is a matter of the way you see yourself and the way others see you.

> From your own side: (a) the lowest level of stability is reached when you see yourself as the deity while you are walking, sitting, or sleeping; (b) the medium level is when you see the outer world as a palace, and all sentient beings as *yidam* deities; and (c) in addition to that, when you see all the deities as a dream, magic, or the moon in water, this is the highest level of stability.

From your own side, when the feeling that you are the deity continues even after your meditation session ends, you have reached the first level of stability. In the midst of your regular activities, like sitting, standing, sleeping, dreaming, and so on, you continue to know you are the deity. This is a very great stability, but it is not the highest stability; it is only the first level of attaining stability.

Second from your own side, when you see the outer world as a pure realm and all beings in it as *yidam* deities, this is the medium level of stability. At the medium level, not only do you see yourself as the deity but you see the whole universe as a pure realm. This means that you are pure and free of problems, and the whole world is pure and free of problems. Seeing the outer world as being essentially the mandala of the deity is a much greater level of stability. This is the medium level.

In addition to this pure perception, if you see the deities as like a dream, an illusion, or the moon reflected in water, this is the highest level of stability. At the third level, you realize there is no purity or impurity. Seeing everything in this way is the highest level of stability from your own point of view.

So it goes like this: seeing yourself as pure is the first level, seeing everyone and everything else as pure is the second level, and seeing the illusory nature of purity is the third level.

When Gampopa says that you see yourself as the deity, it doesn't mean that you literally see yourself with many heads and hands, or things like that. Seeing yourself as the deity means that you see there is nothing wrong with you. More specifically, your body, speech, and mind are experienced as not different from the enlightened body, speech, and mind of the deity. As your practice matures, you see your form, and all forms, as appearance-emptiness. All sounds resonate in emptiness. All thoughts are awareness-emptiness. This experience is what is meant by seeing yourself as the deity.

Of course, it is also possible to see yourself in the form of the visualized deity. There are many stories about this, like the one about the young boy who went to a lama and said, "I want to learn to meditate. Please give me instruction."

Perhaps the lama thought the boy was too small or too stupid, so he said, "Okay, go into that hut and visualize a big horn on your head."

So the boy did that. People kept sending in food and the boy did not come out, and this went on for a long time. Finally, the teacher went to the hut and said, "What are you doing in there? Come on out."

The boy said, "I cannot come out because of my horn."

The lama said, "What do you mean? Just come out."

The boy said, "But I really have a horn on my head." And when people looked, they actually saw some kind of horn on his head.

When you are clear about something and your mind projects that, it can be seen and felt by others as well as yourself. If we keep on focusing on something or looking for something, we will find it. For example, if we look for faults in someone, we will find them. And if we look for good qualities in someone, we will find those, too. This is why at times we find certain people attractive, and other times the same people look bad. These appearances are our mind's creation.

The whole world is created by our mind, by the way we see and project things. I have heard that there were experiments in Russia where people lifted very heavy objects by applying the strength of their mind. I've also heard that DNA can be changed by the mind. Not that the

structure of DNA changes, but its effect changes. For example, if someone assimilates a lot of stress, it makes an impression on the DNA that
can be transmitted to the next generation. The mind is so strong that it
can create things.

> For the measure of stability from the point of view of others:
> (a) when you are liberated and others see you as the deity, this
> is the highest level of stability; (b) the medium level is when
> you appear as the deity all the time; and (c) the lowest level is
> when the hungry ghosts see you as the deity.

Next, from the point of view of others, the highest level of stability in
creation stage practice is when you are a liberated being and others can
see you as liberated or as the deity. For example, there are stories of empowerment ceremonies in which the students could see the lama as the
deity while the lama was giving the empowerment. When you reach the
highest level of stability, you feel completely liberated, and some people
can see you that way.

At the medium level, even though you are not fully liberated, you
see yourself as the deity, and sometimes others can see you as the deity
as well.

At the lowest level of stability, the spirits see you as the deity. Other
humans may not see you in that way, but the spirits do.

As our visualization becomes more stable, our mind becomes clearer
and calmer, and our habitual reactions change. If we change our way of
seeing, then we change our way of reacting. This is the Buddhist approach to breaking old habits, and it is very effective. You purify the way
you feel and experience yourself so that your experience becomes very
positive. We cannot change everything outside ourselves; we have to
change the way we experience. Since everything is a manifestation of
our mind, once we have changed the way we experience, we have
changed our whole world. This is what creation stage practice is leading
toward.

Having a stable visualization is important, but for enlightenment,
more is needed. Along with stability, the creation stage practice needs
wisdom and compassion. Wisdom and compassion are the most important elements of dharma practice. Any kind of practice we do has to
contribute to the increase of our wisdom or our compassion. If the

practice doesn't do either of these things, then it is not real practice. Every practice has to move directly or indirectly toward this goal.

A stable creation stage practice can make your mind very strong, particularly through the practice of mantras. But a stable mind alone cannot liberate you. There is a Tibetan story about a man who had done a lot of creation stage practice and developed great stability. However, since he lacked compassion, after he died he was reborn as an evil spirit. One time this evil spirit appeared as a very negative vision to a sincere lama who was in retreat in a cave. The lama recognized the spirit as merely a negative vision, and he decided to exorcise it. The lama was also a very stable practitioner, and he visualized himself as a wrathful deity and said wrathful mantras. But the evil spirit was able to visualize himself as an even more wrathful deity, and he said even more powerful mantras back to the lama.

It became clear to the lama that this spirit knew how to do creation stage practice, and that the spirit must have once been a strong practitioner who went wrong in some way. Seeing this made the lama very sad, and he felt genuine compassion for the spirit. He thought, "What a pity! This person must have done so much practice and spent so much time in retreat, and this is what he has come to be. How unfortunate!"

While the lama was thinking this, he forgot about visualizing and saying mantras, and just felt strong compassion. He looked up and saw that the vision was becoming smaller and smaller and dissolving away. As the vision was disappearing, he heard it say in a very quiet voice, "This is exactly what I did not have." In other words, the spirit recognized that what he was missing was compassion.

It's hard to tell about the quality of visions. Sometimes practitioners have visions of the deities, or visions of lamas or buddhas; there are many different kinds of visions. Some visions are just imaginary, like a dream. They are neither good nor bad. Some visions show a negative influence, while others are very positive. These are the real visions.

How can you tell which vision is which? They say you can tell by its smell. It's like the saying, "Something smells fishy." A good vision smells good—you feel very positive and warmhearted. If it makes you more compassionate, it is a real vision. If it smells bad, then you know it isn't good. Negative visions make us uncomfortable, dissatisfied, or depressed.

Sometimes people have visions while in retreat. I heard about a man in a three-year retreat in Canada who heard a voice saying to him, "You should go out and do something to benefit beings. You are wasting your time here, just doing retreat." This happened over and over.

The man thought this was a good idea, so he left retreat. He went to see a lama—I think it was Kalu Rinpoche—and told the lama about this sign that he needed to go out and work for the welfare of others. The lama told him, "No, that was an obstacle for your retreat. You should immediately go back in."

But the student did not go back. He left, and as he tried to work for others, everything went wrong. He couldn't accomplish anything, and then he started drinking and became an alcoholic. He was kicked out of the place where he was living and had to live on the streets. After several years, he realized that he had been mistaken. So he went back into retreat, and after completing a three-year retreat, he eventually went into lifelong retreat.

In any case, visions can be obstacles that arise in our practice.

> The sixth point about the creation stage practice is the result, which has two aspects, temporary and ultimate. The ultimate result is the arising of the two form kayas. The temporary result has three levels: (a) at best, in this very life, you see the truth; (b) at the medium level, in your next life you become a *chakravartin* king; and (c) at the lowest level, you obtain a good rebirth as a human or a god.

Now we come to the sixth point, the result. This has two aspects: the temporary result and the ultimate result. The ultimate result of creation stage practice is the accomplishment of the two form kayas: the nirmanakaya and the sambhogakaya. This complements the ultimate result of the completion stage practice, which accomplishes the dharmakaya.

The temporary result has three levels. At best, in this very life, you see the truth. At the medium level, in your next life you will become a chakravartin king, or someone with enormous positive influence in the world. Chakravartins have the ability to bring peace to the world without the use of force. The lowest level of the temporary result is attaining a good rebirth as a human or a god.

This concludes Gampopa's six points on the creation stage practice. All these points can be summarized into three stages of understanding. First, when you do the self-visualization, you find yourself being transformed into the deity, into an enlightened being. As you practice again and again, you feel the enlightened qualities increase.

At the second stage, you know that the self-visualization is merely an exercise. You understand that this process is a creation of your mind, just like everything else you experience. You are simply becoming habituated to the compassion, wisdom, and power of your own mind.

Third, since the deity is created by your mind, you recognize it as the radiance of the mind's nature. The deity has the same ultimate nature as the mind: clarity-emptiness, which cannot be pinpointed. So, even while feeling that you are an enlightened being, you know that this is not something concrete or real. Enlightenment is as empty, or as unreal, as everything else.

These three stages show how the creation stage practice is united with the completion stage practice of Mahamudra. The further one takes the creation stage, the more ultimate wisdom manifests. When your understanding reaches a very deep level through this kind of practice, you realize the true nature of your mind, and therefore, you realize the true nature of everything. This is what makes the creation stage practice so profound.

NINE

Stabilizing Recognition of the Nature of the Mind

NEXT, GAMPOPA TALKS about the completion stage practice, which focuses on awareness of the nature of the mind, or the nature of reality. Before beginning the main topic, Gampopa urges students to be diligent. The text says:

> *Take advantage of this human boat;*
> *Free yourself from sorrow's mighty stream!*
> *This vessel will be later hard to find.*
> *The time that you have now, you fool, is not for sleep!*[1]

In this quotation from the *Way of the Bodhisattva*, Shantideva is pointing out that it's foolish to waste our time and waste the freedom we have to practice. This quote also reminds us of our good fortune in having a human form endowed with so many qualities and abilities. Gampopa adds his own commentary to this verse by saying:

> At this time we have attained the precious human body. We have entered the door of the precious teachings. We have heard the precious dharma. We have met the precious, genuine teacher. This is the time to practice the instructions, which

takes diligence. It is said: "After stabilizing the root, which is devotion, you should stabilize bodhichitta."

First, for the general path to arise in your being, it is very important to stabilize devotion as the foundation. Then, to firmly maintain bodhichitta, you need to recognize the nature of your mind, because this is the heart essence of the entire dharma.

In order to refresh our dharma practice, it's good to look back and recall our purpose. What are we doing? Why we are here? What do we really want? What is most important?

In taking up dharma practice, devotion must be the foundation. We discussed this topic thoroughly in chapter 2. To recap, we are not talking about devotion as some kind of blind faith but devotion as inspiration, aspiration, and certainty. These three qualities come from understanding what is genuine and true. This inspires us to practice and study further. The more inspired we are about something, the more we want to explore it and experience it. This is the aspect of aspiration. And the more deeply we penetrate something, the more we understand it. This brings certainty; we get the message. We can say, "Yes, this is true. From whatever angle I look at it, I know that the dharma is true."

Certainty is the heart of devotion. Once we are certain about the dharma, we cannot help but be devoted to it. This becomes a fourth quality of devotion, called irreversible devotion. This is the strongest foundation for practice. Until we have this, our practice is somewhat unstable. We could safely say that the stronger the devotion, the stronger the practice. As our inspiration and certainty grow, our practice becomes clearer and stronger. We need to gradually develop this kind of devotion as the foundation of our practice.

With devotion as the basis, you are ready to do the main practice, which is working directly with your mind. All the various methods, such as the creation stage and the completion stage with form, are skillful means for making the mind more positive, clear, and focused. Then you are able to practice the essential point, which is to clearly see and experience what you are. From one point of view, you are your mind. What you are is your awareness. Why? Because without your awareness, there wouldn't be any "you."

Once you know the nature of your mind, you understand the phrase:

"By knowing one, you know everything." If you clearly know this one thing, then there's no problem in understanding everything else. This "one thing" is the nonconceptual nature of the mind. If you don't know the nature of your mind, then even if you know all sorts of other things, you will still be confused. This is because all the other things are concepts. Until you know your own nonconceptual nature, you won't know the true nature of anything else.

> In terms of understanding this, outwardly there are perceived objects, and inwardly there is the perceiving mind. The internal mind arises as the mind and mental objects. These are said to be the mind's essence and characteristics. "Outer objects" refer to everything outside the mind, including one's own body.

There are two factors involved in understanding the nature of the mind: an outer factor, which means the perceived outer objects; and an inner factor, which means the perceiving mind. The perceiving mind also has two parts: the mind that experiences, and the mental objects that are experienced. In other words, the perceiving mind arises as the main mind and its mental events.

Let's discuss what these statements mean. For example, when I say that everything I experience is my mind, I'm not necessarily saying that other people are my mind, or the wall in front of me is my mind, or the chair I'm sitting on is my mind. I'm not saying that the whole world is my projection. If that were the case, then when I'm not here, there would be nobody here; there would be nothing. This is obviously incorrect. The outer world is here for as long as it is here. It arises interdependently.

The perceiving mind is a very important part of this, and it is also interdependent. Even if I am not here, other people will be here for as long as they have the karmic conditions to be here. In other words, as long as there are people with similar human bodies, brains, and faculties, they will see a similar kind of world. I see basically the same world that they see, because we are alike. Different types of beings, like humans and animals, see the world in different ways. Although various perceptions do occur, true existence or non-existence is another matter.

We cannot say that the outer world does not exist, nor can we say that the outer world does exist. The world arises interdependently, and the perceiver is a key element in its arising.

Whatever you experience in the world is completely your own experience. The way you experience the world is with your eyes, your ears, your body, and your mind. You cannot experience in any other way. My experience may be similar to yours, but it's not the same. There are outer objects that we both experience, and then there are our individual experiences of those objects. "Outer objects" refer to everything outside your mind, including your own body.

Objects are always experienced in the mind, and this is what Gampopa is referring to when he says that the inner, perceiving mind has two parts: the mind that does the experiencing, and the mental objects that it experiences. The essence of the mind is what experiences, and the characteristics of the mind are the objects being experienced.

The Vajrayana approach of Mahamudra starts with recognizing the nature of the perceiving mind. This is different from the way one proceeds according to the Mahayana approach of Madhyamaka. We looked at this in chapter 6, but let's go over it again.

In Madhyamaka, one starts by looking at the outer world, or what is considered to be the outer world, and analyzes it. For example, you look at an object like a cup or a watch, and ask, "What is the nature of this cup? What is the nature of this watch? What is the nature of substantial things?" You examine by asking questions like, "Does this object have different parts? Is it one thing or is it many things?" Madhyamaka has various ways of reasoning, such as the reasoning of "neither one nor many," that you can apply in your investigation.

When you look for the nature of things, what you find is interdependence. The nature of everything is relative, transient, and based on causes and conditions. In other words, the nature of everything is emptiness. Once you are clear about the nature of outer objects, then you begin to look at the mind, you look at the perceiver who is investigating, and you apply the same kind of reasoning. This is the usual method in Madhyamaka and the Mahayana.

In contrast, in the Vajrayana, particularly in Mahamudra, one first looks directly at the mind itself. If you can directly see the mind's nature, then the nature of the perceived objects is not so important. This is because you are always working with your own experience. The key factor is how you experience yourself, and how you transform your experience.

> To begin with, the nature of the mind needs to be recognized. In the middle, it needs to become familiar. At the end, there needs to be oneness.

There are three stages in practicing the nature of the mind: recognizing the nature, being familiar with the nature, and becoming one with the nature. These three stages are also called ground Mahamudra, path Mahamudra, and result Mahamudra. These three aspects of Mahamudra are basically the same as the three stages. The ground Mahamudra is the nature of the mind, the path Mahamudra is the process of becoming familiar with the nature of the mind, and the result Mahamudra is being completely one with the nature of the mind. That's it! There is nothing more we need to do. We become enlightened by knowing and experiencing the nature of the mind, directly and completely.

Your initial, direct experience of the true nature of your mind is called recognition, which is the first stage. Recognition is like a glimpse, and from that recognition you get a deeper understanding. So, you need to work on it, meditate on it, and familiarize yourself with it. This is because the recognition can go away. Sometimes you have a glimpse of the nature, a moment of recognition, and then it's gone. You see the nature, but then you forget it.

The second stage of becoming familiar is the hardest part. There is no alternative to meditating again and again and again. At this stage you can have many different experiences—some are very nice, which makes you feel enthusiastic and inspired, and at other times nothing happens, which makes you feel dull and hopeless. There are many ups and downs in practice. But if you keep going, eventually your experience becomes realization, which is the third stage. The recognition is stable, and you know it cannot be lost. It can no longer be forgotten because it is a deep, ongoing experience of being one with the nature.

Gampopa was a great master of Mahamudra, and he goes through these three stages in detail. Even the first step, recognition, has three aspects.

> To explain these, first, recognition has three aspects: (1) the
> essence of the mind is recognized, directly and experientially,
> as coemergent wisdom; it is clarity-emptiness, which cannot
> be pinpointed.

First, we need to directly recognize that the mind's essence is coemergent wisdom. What do we mean by "coemergent wisdom"? It is the
mind's simultaneous clarity and emptiness, which cannot be pinned
down. Sometimes in meditation, we look at the mind and ask, "What is
the mind?" What we find are the thoughts, emotions, perceptions, and
feelings that we experience as mental arisings. In Tibetan, these mental
factors are called *sem*. They arise and dissolve over and over. For instance, every time we go to sleep, they dissolve. If they did not dissolve,
we could not sleep. This dissolving is the process of falling asleep.

Is there more to the mind than the mental arisings? Yes, there is the
awareness, the consciousness in which all the arisings take place. This is
called *rigpa*. This subtle awareness never dissolves or ends. At the time
of death, the consciousness—the gross mind and its mental factors—
dissolves into this subtle awareness. Even after death, this subtle awareness does not dissolve or stop.

In looking at the mental factors and the consciousness itself, the next
question is: Where is this mind? Where are these thoughts and emotions arising? Where is my consciousness? When you look for the mind,
can you find it? Can you pick it up and hold it?

What you find is that you cannot pinpoint anything. The mind cannot be seen; it has no shape, it has no color. There is no object called "the
mind." Even if you had tiny, tiny tweezers, you could never pick something up and say, "This is my mind." The inability to find the mind is
the mind's emptiness. Emptiness does not mean being empty of something. It means that there is no object to be grasped, there is nothing you
can hold on to.

Yet at the same time, there is always the mind's clarity. Because it is
clear but cannot be pinpointed, the mind can be described as clarity-
emptiness. This is the mind's nature. Here, clarity means awareness.
What is awareness? Where is awareness? Finding and experiencing this
directly—that your mind is clarity-emptiness and nothing other than
that—is the first step of recognition.

(2) There is recognition that the radiation of various thoughts and emotions is inseparable from the essence.

Whatever arises in our mind—whether it's a thought, an emotion, a sensation, or a perception—is the arising of coemergent wisdom. It is the radiation of the mind's emptiness and clarity. Every arising is a temporary arising—one thought comes and goes, then another thought comes and goes. All our thoughts and emotions just appear and disappear.

This is very important, because we usually grasp at whatever occurs. For instance, when sadness arises, we hold on to this feeling and think, "I am so sad, I am so depressed." But from the Mahamudra point of view, what has happened? A feeling has arisen in the mind, like a cloud. Like a cloud, it appears and then it disappears, and that's all there is to it. This time it is sadness arising, the next time it may be happiness, the next time it may be anger, and later it may be kindness. All sorts of things arise, like wildflowers in a spring meadow. All sorts of flowers grow; all sorts of thoughts and emotions arise. They are all okay; they're nothing special. When we understand what our thoughts and feelings are, and we experience them in this way, we are able to let them come and let them go.

The important point is seeing that there is not some "me" that is sad. Whatever arises, like sadness, is simply an arising; it is not that "I" am sad. If we identify with what arises and think we are that, then it becomes solid. It takes on an identity, and then we're in trouble.

This new way of understanding our mind and its arisings is very deep. Since this completely changes the way we relate to our mind, it is quite profound.

(3) Then, there is knowing that the various colorful, outer objects are inseparable from the mind. All three of these factors are inseparable.

There is one more step in recognizing the nature of the mind. Besides seeing that emotions and thoughts arise from our mind, we need to see that the external objects we experience also arise from the mind. Outer objects are not completely separate from the mind. We usually think that what we see is really out there. However, when we truly understand interdependence or the relative nature of things, then these objects are not necessarily there.

Take colors, for example. We usually think that yellow is always yellow, and blue is always blue. However, I have been told that nothing is actually a color like blue or yellow or red. Rather, the color we see indicates the degree to which light is absorbed or reflected. And yet we think that the colors are really there.

In reality, there is nothing absolute; everything can be many different ways. The more deeply you understand this, the more lightly you take things. When you directly know this, you have recognized the nature of your mind. This can be completely liberating. It changes the way you look at things and the way you look at yourself. Ordinarily, we think that we are over here, and some object is over there. One thing is good, and another thing is bad. We want what is good, and we don't want what is bad. This is how our mind manages to stay very, very busy.

But in truth, things are not like this. What is good is your reflection, and what is bad is your reflection. It is not the case that there is some "you" here and some separate thing there. Everything you experience is "you." It is always your experience. For instance, ordinarily when you look in the mirror, one day you like yourself because you're smiling, and another day you don't like yourself because you're frowning. But once you understand that all your perceptions are merely the arisings of your own mind, then you can laugh at yourself. You take things lightly. Because this kind of recognition brings freedom, it is an essential part of Mahamudra.

> **At the intermediate stage, there is familiarity. This happens by practicing properly and diligently in a solitary place or a charnel ground.**

After we have recognized the nature of the mind, we need to practice and become familiar with it. Gampopa says we need to practice appropriately with great diligence, alone in the wilderness or a charnel ground. Many great masters like Milarepa and Gampopa practiced in solitude in the mountains, and also in charnel grounds. The charnel grounds were places outside of towns where dead bodies were taken.

Charnel grounds were inhabited by wild animals that would tear apart the corpses and eat them. People would usually avoid these places because they were frightening and dangerous.

There used to be many charnel grounds in India, but I doubt there are any left since India has become so populated. So, it's not really possible to practice in a charnel ground anymore. But there are still places we can practice without much distraction, and this is where Gampopa recommends we go to familiarize ourselves with the nature of mind.

This does not mean that people cannot practice unless they are in solitude or a long-term retreat. There are many lineage holders who never lived in solitude, and yet they accomplished their practice. For example, Tilopa lived in cities, and for thirteen years he had a job extracting oil from sesame seeds. There were no machines at that time, and he spent his days pounding sesame seeds by hand. Marpa is another example. He was a farmer and householder with a wife and many children. However, all the lineage masters practiced; they practiced a lot. Without practice, stabilizing recognition of the nature of the mind is impossible.

> Familiarity arises in three stages: (1) meditation and post-meditation are different, (2) meditation and postmeditation are comparable, and (3) meditation and postmeditation are inseparable.

There are three stages of stabilization. First, your experience is different within meditation and outside of meditation. Second, the meditative mind is present both while meditating and after meditating. Third, meditation and postmeditation are inseparable. These are three levels of practice, and each goes further than the previous one.

> 1. Meditation and postmeditation are different when the recognition of the nature is there during meditation, and it is not there outside of meditation. At this stage, the inner thoughts and emotions do not harm you, yet you cannot eliminate them. Therefore, stay in solitude and continuously pray to your lama. Along with having unfailing devotion, it is very important to rest the mind one-pointedly in evenness.

Now, this is very advanced. Even though it is called the first level, it is a long way from the usual first level of meditation. Gampopa is describing the situation where one recognizes the nature of the mind during meditation, and everything is completely okay. But when one is not meditating, everything is not completely okay. It's important for us to remember that this already shows a level of attainment. Simply recognizing the mind's nature is very difficult at first.

In any case, when people experience this level of attainment, they might think that since everything is okay while they are meditating, it means they don't need to meditate much anymore. They think that instead of meditating, they will do other things. However, this is a grave mistake. This is precisely the time when people need to meditate more. They need to remain dedicated to their practice, because at this stage they are on the verge of becoming enlightened.

So, Gampopa recommends staying in solitude and continuously praying to the lama. Of course, at this level a practitioner understands that the lama is not external; the lama is not outside the practitioner's mind. Still, one needs to cultivate devotion. One must continually ground oneself in devotion and practice. At this level, you know there is nothing to meditate on, but you must continue to meditate until there is no difference between meditation and postmeditation. Until you reach the second level of familiarization, there is still a distinction between abiding during meditation and not abiding outside of meditation.

> **2. Meditation and postmeditation are comparable when the nature is present while meditating, and after meditating, it is unharmed by the four daily activities of sitting, standing, moving, and lying down. You become decisive that all the radiant thoughts and emotions are inseparable from the nature of the mind. However, sometimes you perceive outer colorful appearances as illusory and empty, and at other times you perceive them as real and definite things. At this stage, some meditators get a strong urge and think, "It would be better for me to travel than to stay here." However, it is very important to remain alone in a solitary place.**

Gampopa says very clearly that even though at this stage the true nature is experienced outside of meditation, it is still too soon to leave retreat. It's important to continue with the training until every experience arises as illusory and empty.

3. In the final stage, meditation and postmeditation are inseparable. Coemergent appearances are the radiance of the dharmakaya. The coemergent nature of the mind is the dharmakaya. Outer objects and all phenomena of samsara and nirvana are realized as the great bliss of nonconceptual equality. There is no difference between meditating and not meditating. No matter which of the four daily activities you engage in, you never waver from resting in evenness. All the time, your practice is like the continuous flow of a river. There is no need to be mindful and concentrate, or to think and investigate. The nature is simply there all the time. At this point, it makes no difference whether you travel or remain in one place. Since practice is what meditators do, it is more appropriate to stay than to go. It is said that in general, there are two types of meditators—one type wears out their shoes, and the other type wears out their seats. Among these two, the one who stays put is more joyful.

For example, Lama Milarepa stayed in the mountains for forty-two years. He lived until the age of eighty-four, going from mountain to mountain. He simply transferred his meditation place from one mountain to another. Our precious teacher Gampopa once asked Milarepa, "Lama, why do you stay in the mountains all the time?" Lama Milarepa replied, "For me, there is no difference between staying in solitude and staying in a marketplace. However, at this time, in this body, I have taken all beings into my heart, and I am trying to liberate them from samsara. Living in town is not the real way of a meditator."

Our precious teacher Gampopa acted in the very same way. We need to practice and train as he did. Let us all be very clear about this.

At this point, one is enlightened, and it makes no difference whether or not one meditates. Milarepa continued to meditate and stay in caves, but it was probably to provide an example to his followers and to their followers in the future.

As you may know, the Kagyu lineage, which came down from Milarepa and Gampopa, is known as the practice lineage. Kagyupas are renowned for doing lots of practice, and they are not known for studying very much. Some other lineages accuse the Kagyupas of not knowing anything except how to meditate. But if you look back, many of the great writings of Tibetan Buddhism were composed by Kagyu masters. I can't say how this happened, but it did.

In any case, I think I need not comment on this section of the text, because probably none of us is at this stage. So, I will leave the root text to stand on its own, and you can contemplate it as a guide to show you how the path will unfold once you are familiar with the nature of the mind.

TEN

The Qualities of a Genuine Teacher

Next, Gampopa talks about the qualities of a genuine teacher.

> Lama Rinpoche said: After people have begun to experience the general path, if they want to enter the uncommon path of the Vajrayana, it is very important to attend a genuine Mahayana teacher. A genuine teacher has the following characteristics: (1) a lineage that is connected to the lineage, (2) a lineage that is connected to living words, (3) words that are connected to an authentic transmission, and (4) an authentic transmission that is connected to blessings.

Sometimes students ask me if they really need a teacher or a guru. My answer is that if they have a good guru, then it is much better to have a guru. If they have a bad guru, then it is much better not to have a guru. The issue isn't whether or not to have a guru; the issue is whether or not the guru is genuine. You don't benefit from a relationship with someone who is not a genuine teacher or practitioner. Therefore it is very important to understand what makes someone a genuine guru.

I suggest that students do not start out by trying to find a spiritual teacher. It is better to start out by trying to understand the dharma. It is by studying the dharma that you will know whether a teacher is good or not. Once you understand the dharma, you will find a suitable teacher.

Until then, you need not be too particular about whom you study with. It is better to focus on studying the genuine, classical teachings of the Buddha and getting a deeper understanding of them. As you pursue that, you will find a spiritual teacher as well.

We read in the traditional teachings that we are supposed to use pure vision and see the guru as perfect, or see the teacher as a buddha. But it seems to me that trying to see with pure vision too soon does not work. You need to be realistic and objective before you accept someone as your guru. It can happen that you see a fault, but you think you're not supposed to think that way, so you pretend and deceive yourself. This is not helpful. It is very important to be honest and objective in observing a teacher. Once you find a teacher you can trust, someone who has the right qualities, then a pure view will naturally evolve.

If you feel some hesitation about a teacher, the way to work with your hesitation is to ask questions and get clarification. Why would you want to become the student of someone you have doubts about? Nobody is holding a sword over your head and telling you to become someone's student.

Another point we need to understand is that there are many levels of gurus. This topic is discussed in Gampopa's book, the *Jewel Ornament of Liberation*. There are gurus who are enlightened incarnations, gurus who are great bodhisattvas, and gurus who are ordinary, samsaric beings. Even in this era, some gurus may be great bodhisattvas or nirmanakaya buddhas. But most of the gurus—most of the people like me who are teachers—are just ordinary people. I am not saying that all lamas are ordinary people, but I myself am an ordinary lama.

Students need to realize that the teacher is a samsaric being not very different from themselves. Usually a teacher has received more teachings, or studied and practiced more, or at least comes from a good lineage of teachers. That kind of teacher would probably not say anything totally contrary to the dharma. If that person is genuinely sharing his or her understanding and knowledge without a hidden agenda, then that person could be a genuine teacher.

Be careful that you don't superimpose the idea of enlightenment on someone just because that person is a teacher. Sometimes students think, "This person is a teacher, so this person must know everything and be highly realized. This teacher must be enlightened!" This attitude can cause problems when the teacher actually doesn't have much real-ization. If you keep your eyes open, you can usually see without much difficulty that the teacher is not enlightened. Gampopa mentions in the *Jewel Ornament* that it is not wrong to have an ordinary person as a teacher, because this is the level where we usually start. An ordinary being can be very important for our progress on the path.

Gampopa begins describing the characteristics of a genuine teacher by discussing the kind of lineage the teacher holds:

> 1. A lineage that is connected to the lineage means that the lin-eage of realized beings has remained unbroken since the time of the perfect Buddha. It must not be a lineage of beings who have transgressed samaya or violated the precepts.

The first thing to find out is whether the teacher possesses an authen-tic lineage. A good guru will possess a lineage of genuine teachings, which means teachings experienced by a fully realized being. Since the time of that fully awakened being, or buddha, the teachings have been passed down pure and intact by a succession of other teachers. This suc-cession should be unbroken, not only in the words and meaning but in terms of the practice. The teachers of the lineage need to have practiced those teachings, and it is best if all the lineage holders have fully experi-enced them.

A lineage holder is someone who has actualized the teachings that came from a fully realized being. All the students who have reached a certain level of experience are considered holders of the lineage. There can be many lineage holders; there is not only one at a time. The lineage primarily refers to the practice and experience people have. The lineage is not just information; information is something you can get from books. Lineage holders must not have transgressed the samayas or bro-ken the precepts. If they have done something totally mistaken, realiza-tion will not be there. Genuine practice and experience are correlated with not violating vows and precepts.

> 2. A lineage that is connected to living words means that the oral lineage is transmitted from mouth to mouth, from ear to ear, and from mind to mind. It should not be a lineage of black ink on paper, or moldy old books.

The lineage needs to be connected through speech, which means the teachings come through oral transmission—mouth to ear, and mind to mind. You can't just read a book and become a lineage holder. It must be personally taught. For example, saying, "I have a lineage; my lineage comes from the Karmapa," is not enough. You need to receive teachings from him; the teachings must be transmitted to you.

There have been a few exceptional cases where not much teaching passed between a master and student, and yet the lineage was received. There is a story of the Second Karmapa, Karma Pakshi, and the siddha Ugyenpa. They met only once, at a river crossing. They were traveling in different directions and stopped in the same place for a tea break. They had tea together and talked for a while, and then the Karmapa said to Ugyenpa, "You now hold my lineage. You know everything I know, and you will be my lineage holder."

This is very unusual. I think this is probably because Ugyenpa was already realized. There are a few cases like this, but in general, one must receive teachings and practice them before becoming a lineage holder.

3. A lineage that is connected to an authentic transmission means that the lamas have definitely realized the meaning of the teachings and mastered them.

Third, the lineage must be connected to an authentic transmission. This means that a genuine teacher should truly understand the meaning of the teachings. This person needs real mastery of the teachings.

How does a lama, or any student, get the transmission? In the Vajrayana, there are three aspects to transmission: the empowerment, the reading transmission, and the practice instructions. Students receive the blessings and the permission to do the practice through receiving the empowerment and the reading transmission. The practice instructions are also very important because this is where students get a detailed explanation. If people don't understand, they can ask questions and get clarification. When all three aspects have been received, then the transmission has been received.

All these qualities are closely related with being able to pass on the lineage. The teacher needs to have received teachings from an authentic lineage holder who is endowed with the blessings to transform others. If the teacher hasn't really received the teachings, then it isn't possible for the teacher to pass them on.

I don't think I can say too many times that simply receiving the transmission is not enough. The teachings must be practiced and assimilated. A genuine lineage lama should be someone who has not only received the empowerment, instructions, and reading transmission but has also learned, practiced, and truly understood them.

> 4. An authentic transmission connected to blessings means that since the lineage is unbroken, it contains the blessings that generate virtue in the minds of others.
> For these reasons, search for a lama with these qualities.

The fourth quality is having an authentic transmission that is connected to blessings. This means there is continuity in the lineage. Not only should the lineage not be broken, the lineage should be endowed with blessings. To be a lineage holder, a lama must have the ability to bring the blessings to others. This can happen only in a practice lineage. An "unbroken lineage" refers to two things: there have been no substantial transgressions, and the people who have received the lineage have actually received the blessings.

Blessings are very important, especially in the Vajrayana. Even at the level of Mahamudra and Dzogchen, blessings and devotion are important. In Mahamudra, simply being clever or intelligent doesn't matter; what matters is having an open heart. An open heart is another way of saying "having devotion and blessings."

All the Vajrayana lineages are based on blessings, especially the Kagyu lineage. I heard a story about a Nyingma lama asking Dilgo Khyentse Rinpoche about this. In case you don't recognize his name, Dilgo Khyentse was one of the greatest Nyingma teachers of the twentieth century. He was also a Ri-me master and one of His Holiness the Dalai Lama's teachers.

In any case, in this conversation between a Nyingma lama and Dilgo Khyentse Rinpoche, the Nyingma lama said, "Most Kagyu monks haven't studied much, and they don't know a lot. But many of them go into samadhi when they die. How does that happen?"

Dilgo Khyentse replied, "Oh, it's from the blessings. Any practitioner who does the Eighth Karmapa's *Guru Yoga in Four Sessions* throughout their lifetime will certainly enter samadhi when they die, even without much understanding. This is because that practice carries great blessings."

A genuine, unbroken lineage has great blessings, because it includes the blessings of the whole lineage, as well as the blessings of the personal teacher who transmits the lineage to you. Even if there are one or two lineage holders who do not have very high realization, as long as they have not broken their samaya, the blessings will continue.

> **In other words, a Mahayana spiritual friend possesses either the eye of dharma or the eye of wisdom.**

As his next point, Gampopa says that a Mahayana spiritual friend should have one of two qualities: they should either be a person with the eye of dharma or a person with the eye of wisdom. The eye of dharma means clearly understanding the teachings, and the eye of wisdom means having both the understanding and the real experience of wisdom. Of course, it is much better to have the eye of wisdom, but a teacher should at least have the eye of dharma.

> **Or the qualified teacher is described in three ways: (1) through great wisdom, the teacher has the ability to lead others on the path; (2) through great compassion, no sentient beings are left behind; and (3) the teacher has not even a hundredth of a hair tip of attachment to the concerns of this life.**

There are three more qualities a teacher should have: great wisdom, great compassion, and non-attachment. Through great wisdom the lama can lead others on the path, through great compassion the lama does not neglect even one sentient being, and through non-attachment there is no interest in power, popularity, or pleasure. Gampopa uses much stronger language—that a genuine teacher should not have even a hundredth of a hair tip of attachment to the concerns of this world. These qualities of great wisdom, great compassion, and great non-attachment are ideal, but they may not be so easy to find.

Recently, when the Seventeenth Karmapa was teaching at the Kagyu Monlam in Bodhgaya, India, he told the lamas and monks present that the most important precept for them to keep is to never cheat their students and patrons. He said that these days there are lamas going around who are deceiving people in order to gain money and power, and this is happening especially in the Chinese communities, both outside and inside Tibet. The Karmapa said that someone who does that should not bother to come see him. For a teacher, the worst violation of the precepts is to use people for personal gain. Teachers must go beyond ordinary, worldly concerns. Having no worldly concerns at all is quite an advanced state, but at the very least, a teacher should never take advantage of students or of people in general.

> Or the lama can be said to have four characteristics: (1) genuine devotion to the three jewels, (2) genuine compassion for sentient beings, (3) genuine realization of the profound meaning, and (4) motivation to teach the dharma with no consideration of personal gain.

Gampopa sums up the discussion by stating four qualities a genuine teacher should have. These four points come from different sutras and tantras taught by the Buddha, and Gampopa has listed them together. These are devotion to the three jewels, compassion for all beings, realization of the true meaning, and the motivation to teach without concern for personal gain.

> We need to attend a lama who has these qualities. A lama who acts like a fox or a monkey is useless as an escort from samsara to nirvana.

Gampopa concludes by saying that this is the sort of spiritual teacher we can rely on to take us from samsara to nirvana. Lamas who act like foxes and monkeys cannot help us. Personally, I'm not sure why he mentions foxes and monkeys. Maybe they are animals who are sneaky and steal things. Foxes are known to be sly; they are clever, but not in a good way. Monkeys are known for jumping around and being agitated. Maybe Gampopa mentions monkeys because he is thinking of having a mind that is grasping and unstable.

In any case, Gampopa gives us a clear idea of what qualities to look for in finding a teacher. This is because the teacher is always selected by the student. A lama will not come to you and say, "I am your lama; you must become my student." If somebody comes and says that to you, run away as fast as you can! In the Tibetan tradition, the student examines the lama to see if that person has good qualities, and if so, the student can choose that person as their lama.

I heard that some students in the West went to a high-ranking Tibetan lama and asked if they could call their teacher "Rinpoche." In case you don't know, "Rinpoche" means "precious one." And the high lama said that they could call their teacher "Rinpoche" if they wanted to. That's how the Tibetan system works. There are no official pronouncements of what someone will be called. For example, I can take someone as my lama and use whatever title I prefer, like "His Holiness" or "Rinpoche" or "Yizhin Norbu," which is a name given to the Dalai Lama that means "wish-fulfilling jewel." The lamas wouldn't call themselves that; it is only the students who use those names to honor their teachers.

So, how do you go about selecting your guru? You look around for someone from whom you could learn. When there is no problem with the teachings that are given and the teacher seems like someone you could trust, then you can take that person as your guru. It's good to take time to examine the teacher, but it isn't necessary to be totally certain—sometimes we can't be completely convinced. But we can still receive teachings from a trustworthy person; the teachings are the most important thing. The teachings are more important and the teacher is less important, especially at the beginning. Perhaps later on, the teacher becomes more important, but that comes later. At first you need to learn how to practice; that's how you will progress on the path.

Sometimes people ask, "How can I tell who is my root guru?" I would say that your root guru is whoever has given you the teachings and guidance that have helped you the most. There is a story about Atisha Dipankara, who had fifty different teachers. When anyone would mention his teachers, he would immediately fold his hands and bow his head in respect. But when anyone mentioned the name of Serlingpa, his teacher from Indonesia, Atisha would bow down and shed tears. People asked him why he did that, and he said, "It is because Serlingpa was the one who helped me to generate bodhichitta. It is due to his teachings and guidance that compassion has arisen in me. I have the greatest respect for him. This is what makes him my root guru."

Another question I often hear in the West is whether you should have only one root guru, because if you were to have many gurus, you might get confused. From my point of view, you are not limited to only one lama. It's not like dating several women but being allowed to marry only one. It's fine to receive teachings from only one lama, but if you receive teachings from two lamas, it might be even better.

The main reason I don't believe in having only one guru is that I personally have many root gurus. I have received many teachings, not only from Kagyu lineage lamas but from Nyingma, Sakya, and Geluk lamas. In all that time, I have not heard contradictory teachings from any of them. The genuine dharma is without contradiction.

It is also okay to have only one root teacher. If you find a very good teacher, and you remain with that teacher, there is nothing wrong with that. If you like to study with many teachers, and you find more than one root teacher, that is also fine.

One other point: there are aspects of your personal life that you don't need to ask your teacher about. Otherwise, you make your life impossible. There are things connected with your culture and your lifestyle that you understand much better than a Tibetan lama would. I have heard of misunderstandings arising when students asked their lamas about things the lamas were unfamiliar with. Then, the students say, "My lama said I should do such and such, but it's not working out and I don't know what to do." When you ask the lama for advice but then don't do what the lama says, you feel bad for not obeying your teacher. However, if you do what the lama says but you don't really like it, then you still suffer. You have to decide many things for yourself in accordance with the situation. If you know how to do this, then there is no problem in having many teachers.

It can be confusing if you ask for their opinions. Perhaps you ask your lamas what color to paint your room. One teacher might like yellow best, and another might like red, and a third might like blue. But this has nothing to do with the dharma; it has to do with their opinions. In other words, you need to learn which questions are appropriate to ask a lama and which are not. I think you will not be breaking samaya if you don't paint your room in the lama's favorite color.

So, the lama is probably not the one to ask about where to live or what college to attend or which person to marry. What you are looking for in a lama is someone who is qualified to guide your dharma practice, and Gampopa has given us very clear guidelines for this.

ELEVEN

How to Actualize the View, Meditation, Action, and Result

> Jetsun Rinpoche said: For a good practitioner who has cut attachment to worldly concerns: (1) the view is connected with realization, (2) the meditation is connected with experience, (3) the action is connected with the time, and (4) the result is connected with benefiting others.

GAMPOPA STARTS BY saying that good practitioners are not caught up in worldly concerns. To see if this applies to us, let's review the meaning of the term "worldly concerns." There are eight main things that people think will make them completely happy or completely miserable. There are several ways of describing them. One way starts with the pair of wealth and poverty. Some people think if they were rich, they would have everything they want. Or if they were poor, their life would be ruined. The second pair is being powerful or powerless. Some people think that without being in a position of power, they would be nothing. Another pair is being famous or popular compared with being unknown or insignificant. People often think it would be wonderful if everyone admired them and knew who they were. Others think that by having lots of luxuries and sensory pleasures they would always feel wonderful, and without these things they would be miserable.

It is fine to have positive things, but they will never bring lasting happiness. When we know this for a fact, we will look for happiness somewhere else. Where we need to look is inward: we have to work on our own way of experiencing. When we work on our own way of being, our own way of reacting, then we become genuine practitioners. Real satisfaction, or true peace, has to come from our own heart and mind.

So, first of all, for a good practitioner who is no longer attached to worldly things, the view needs to be connected with realization. What is the view? It is an experiential realization of the nature of mind, with its two aspects of the coemergent mind and coemergent appearances.

> 1. The view has two main aspects: the coemergent nature of the mind is the dharmakaya, and the coemergent appearances are the radiance of the dharmakaya. The coemergent nature of the mind, which is the dharmakaya, is present in the mind stream of every sentient being. The coemergent appearances manifest as various thoughts and emotions, and appear as colorful objects. These two aspects—the coemergent appearances that are the radiance of the dharmakaya, and the coemergent mind itself, which is the dharmakaya—are inseparable and completely pure in nature.

Gampopa says that when you look inward, the coemergent mind is the dharmakaya, and the coemergent appearances are the radiance of the dharmakaya. This is how the nature of mind is usually described in the Mahamudra teachings: it is the dharmakaya and the radiance of the dharmakaya, or the buddha nature and the radiance of the buddha nature. This nature is present in every sentient being. The nature of the mind itself—the consciousness, the aware and empty aspect of the mind—is the dharmakaya. This is the coemergent mind, which is sometimes called the ordinary mind, or tamel gyi shepa.

All sorts of arisings come out of the ordinary mind. By "arisings," I mean all our perceptions, emotions, thoughts, and sensations. The coemergent appearances manifest as various thoughts and emotions and outer objects. These are the radiance of the dharmakaya.

An analogy for this is the sun. If there is a sun, then there will be the sun's radiance as well. They are inseparable, and in essence, they are pure. In other words, there is nothing at all wrong with the way things are. If we just let everything be, in a completely natural way, then the mind and all its manifestations are perfect just as they are.

> They are perfect, beyond words or expressions. They are primordially and naturally spontaneous. They are uncompounded—not created by causes or conditions. The basic space of phenomena and primordial wisdom are inseparable. This is the fundamental way of abiding. It is not something that ancient buddhas created, or that clever sentient beings fabricated. This way of being is called the view.

The nature of mind is clarity-emptiness and its radiance. It is the union of space and wisdom, beyond concepts and beyond words. It is unfabricated, spontaneously present, and unconditioned. It is our fundamental way of being. When we truly understand this, we feel confident because we realize that nothing needs to be removed, and nothing needs to be added. We can let everything be as it is.

This is very deep. Understanding this in a deep and experiential way is the view. We need to understand what our mind is, what our nature is. To experience this, not as a concept but as a genuine experience, is the realization of the view.

> This is something that must be realized. If it is not realized, then it does not help. Lama Rinpoche said: The view that has not been realized is called free of extremes, but this is still a mental construct.

This is a very important point. The view is not a set of concepts. Having a conceptual understanding is good, of course; there is certainly nothing wrong with it. But a conceptual understanding and the actual experience are very, very different. A conceptual understanding, however close it may be to the fact, is still a chain of thoughts. Realization is direct experience. Conceptual understanding and direct experience are as different as reading the description of a place and actually being there. Realization does not come from study and reflection. Of course, study and contemplation are helpful and important, but realization has to be a personal experience.

And exactly what is to be realized? Gampopa says:

> What is to be realized is that the coemergent nature of the mind is the dharmakaya, and the coemergent appearances are the radiance of the dharmakaya. All appearances of samsara and nirvana, without exception, arise as the great bliss of equanimity.

Both nirvana and samsara arise as the great bliss of equanimity. This is like the line we chant in the Short Mahamudra Prayer: "May I realize the inseparability of samsara and nirvana." Students sometimes wonder about this: How could samsaric appearances and nonsamsaric appearances be inseparable? It is because both of them are simply the radiance of the dharmakaya. In truth, they are nothing more than that.

Gampopa calls this "the great bliss of equanimity." Equanimity does not mean being numb or indifferent. Equanimity is knowing very clearly that whatever experience we have is coming from within. Our experience is merely the radiance of our own mind, the radiance of the dharmakaya nature of the mind.

The implication of this is that you can experience anything and enjoy everything. Whatever experience comes, whether it is positive or negative, enjoyable or not enjoyable, it is okay. Once you have this realization, then everything arises as great bliss. Great bliss means that there is nothing unsatisfactory, nothing traumatic. Nothing is actually wrong.

When the true nature is experienced deeply, and you become very familiar with it, then you can say, "This is it." There won't be any question of whether you have the experience or not. You will know that you have realized the view.

Actually, having the view is the most important part of Buddhist practice. The key point is to thoroughly know the nature of your mind. Once you have this view, then meditation is nothing more than becoming fully familiar with it. And the result is nothing more than completely actualizing it.

Everything we are doing in our practice, beginning with understanding impermanence, interdependence, and emptiness, is geared toward realizing the view. All the various practices and meditation are also directed toward this. Once the nature of the mind is completely experienced, this is what we call wisdom. Having wisdom is more than having a good understanding; it is having the complete, direct experience—we see the nature and we are the nature. This is the goal of all the study we undertake, all the teachings we receive, and all the practices we do. Gradually we come closer and closer to this end.

In the Mahayana, we work on perfecting the six paramitas of generosity, discipline, patience, diligence, meditation, and wisdom. It is said that these virtues become paramitas only when wisdom is present. Without the wisdom of knowing the true nature, these qualities are not real paramitas. When wisdom is there, then everything becomes perfected and accomplished.

It is similar in the Vajrayana, in which the emotions are seen as wisdom. In the Vajrayana we talk about transforming or transmuting the emotions. It is not that you have a lot of negative emotions and suddenly they turn into wisdom. Rather, by understanding the nature of mind, we recognize all the emotions as the radiance of the dharmakaya. We understand that we do not need to fight our emotions, nor do we need to be their slave. Our emotions are neither our enemy nor our boss. We can let them come and go. They arise, and then they dissolve. Since they are our own mental arisings, we have no problem with them. This is how the emotions turn into wisdom.

Anything and everything we experience is like this. Realizing the nature of the mind is the single medicine that cures all disease. Deeply knowing the nature of the mind is regarded as the most important point; it is the heart of Mahamudra.

> **This realization is not the wisdom of understanding that comes through study and reflection, but it comes from deep within, through a great deal of meditation. If you have this realization, then the view is connected with realization.**

Mahamudra is a lifelong practice. Directly realizing the nature of the mind is not as easy as it sounds, and it can take a long time. Different methods are usually needed as stepping-stones. For example, as part of our Mahayana practice, we contemplate impermanence and interdependence, work on our attitudes and habitual tendencies, cultivate compassion, and so on. Vajrayana practice usually starts with the

Ngöndro. Sometimes people do the Ngöndro practices one hundred thousand times, four hundred thousand times, or a million times. Some people do Ngöndro their whole life without doing any other practice, and some people never do it at all. It doesn't matter how many times you do it. To do the main practices of the Vajrayana, we need to receive the pointing-out instructions, and then do the creation and completion stage practices. What matters most is gradually training the mind to understand the true nature.

All the practices are geared toward the realization of Mahamudra. We study and practice the dharma in order to open up fully and awaken our buddha nature. In this lineage, we take Mahamudra as the main practice, the highest and deepest practice, but if we cannot experience it straightaway, then we progress through other methods.

Mahamudra practice is very individual; it is best taught one to one. In order to realize Mahamudra, some people need more shamatha, some people need more investigation, some people need only the key instructions. For example, the amount of investigation varies from person to person. It also varies depending on when in your training you do the investigations—at the beginning, in the middle, or near the end. Some people are very intellectual and need more understanding before they can let the mind rest. It all depends on the person. There are many Mahamudra instructions, and students don't need to follow them all. Some will fit one person, and some will fit another.

Therefore, it's essential to have an experienced teacher to guide you. Although there are books of written instructions you can work with, if you want to experience Mahamudra fully, you need a personal teacher.

It is the experience of Mahamudra that really liberates us. The path is all about overcoming ignorance, and the way ignorance is dispelled is by understanding and experiencing the nature of the mind. This is why Mahamudra is said to be the quintessence of all the sutras and tantras.

> 2. In terms of the meditation being connected with experience, what do you experience? You experience realization. Realization is the meaning of experience.

Next, Gampopa says that the meditation has to be connected with experience, and what we experience is the realization. What we realize is the view that we have been discussing, and we work on it through meditation. Meditation is not something other than the view. Meditation is the way we train to have a full and direct experience of the view.

> However, there are incidental experiences that are not connected to real meditation. These include coincidences between the inner channels and the wind energy; different appearances seen by the eyes; different sounds heard by the ears; experiences of bliss, clarity, and nonthought while doing shamatha; there being no object to perceive or not experiencing perception; and the feeling of being completely immersed in emptiness, like a completely clear sky. Although these incidental experiences are there for a while, later they are gone. It is taught in the *Lamdre,* or *Path with Its Result,* that these are circumstantial experiences.

We can have many different temporary experiences during meditation, which include heightened sense perceptions and changes in the channels and wind energy inside the body. During shamatha, or calm abiding, we can feel deep peace, bliss, clarity, or nonthought. Here, nonthought refers to having no thoughts for a long time. This is not a sleepy feeling but a kind of samadhi, where we might not even know how many days have passed. Other incidental experiences mentioned in the text are having no perception, or there being nothing to perceive, or a feeling of being immersed in emptiness. All these are considered incidental experiences, because they appear for a while, but then disappear.

Gampopa mentions that the Lamdre tradition, which is the main practice of the Sakya lineage of Tibetan Buddhism, describes all these as circumstantial experiences. We might have a very nice experience, but then it goes away, and we wonder what happened. Experiences, like the ones mentioned here, simply come and go. They are not particularly useful, because they are not liberating.

Liberation means that you know what is happening; you know "what's what." You have the view, and once you reach liberation, you never lose it. At that point, you know how to self-liberate your thoughts and emotions, so they are no longer problematic. In other words, you know how to liberate yourself. This constitutes real wisdom. Realization is not about having positive experiences. You might have some great experiences, but when they are over, they are over. You might be left with no idea of how to go further.

This is why Gampopa is pointing out the difference between incidental and real experiences. Real experience means that you deeply understand what to do, how to do it, and why it works. You know how to liberate your thoughts and emotions. It is not something that you can do today but can't do tomorrow. With real experience, no matter what happens, you know how to work with your mind. You know that you are not bound by samsara, and that fundamentally you are not deluded. This experience is liberating. It is real wisdom, and it is what cuts the root of samsara.

> Well then, what experiences are connected with real meditation? These are having a personal experience of the essence, a personal experience of coemergence, a personal experience of the natural state, and a personal experience of Mahamudra. All these refer to knowing the nature of your mind. What is this nature like? The nature of the mind is not something existent, because not even a hundredth of a hair tip can be found. Yet it is not non-existent, because it is experienced and realized. The nature of the mind is clarity-emptiness, which cannot be pinpointed. Clarity-emptiness cannot help but arise and is never interrupted. When this has become apparent, then the meditation is connected with experience. This is also called experience and realization occurring simultaneously.

When this happens, meditation has been actualized. At this point, meditative experience is called realization. With the correct view, we cannot go too far wrong because we know what we are doing. Earlier, we talked about needing a teacher so we can learn how to practice. Once we truly know how to practice, there is no more need for a teacher.

> 3. Next, the activity connected with the time has four levels: (a) a beginner acts like a young monarch, (b) a yogic practitioner acts according to the secret Mantrayana, (c) an accomplished master, or siddha, acts according to crazy wisdom, and (d) a wisdom holder acts according to great equanimity.

In the Vajrayana, the entire path is included in the view, meditation, action, and result. In contrast, the Mahayana describes the path in terms of the six paramitas, and the Hinayana focuses on the four noble truths and the eightfold path. Here, Gampopa uses the Vajrayana approach. We have briefly discussed the view and meditation, and now we will discuss the action.

Gampopa's main statement is, "The action is connected with the time." Here, "time" refers to the level of your practice or realization. You must behave in accordance with the stage of the path you are on. He mentions four different levels or times. At the beginning, the practitioner acts like a young monarch. At the level of a yogi, the practitioner acts in accordance with the tantras, or the secret Mantrayana. Once one has the realization of a siddha, one acts according to crazy wisdom. And finally, a wisdom holder acts according to great equanimity. A "wisdom holder" means a vidyadhara, a completely accomplished master.

Among these four levels, the most important one for us is what to do as a beginner. Gampopa says you need to act like a young king or queen. When you first become the king, you have to be careful and you have to be mindful. You have to be vigilant in dealing with your advisers and ministers, as well as your subjects. It is the same for us as we begin training in the Vajrayana.

> **a. The activity of a young monarch entails observing and not transgressing whatever precepts one has taken, such as the *pratimoksha* or *upasaka* vows. One also maintains one's commitment to the bodhisattva training in aspiration and application bodhichitta, and to the samayas of a vidyadhara. The hundred thousand samayas can be condensed into fourteen root downfalls and their branches. One begins by studying and understanding the various vows, and continues to guard them from degenerating. Finally, if a vow is violated, one makes the effort to repair it, purify it, and uphold it.**

Gampopa says that first of all, we need to keep whatever precepts we have taken without transgressing them. He mentions the pratimoksha and upasaka vows. The pratimoksha is the code of the Vinaya, and the upasaka vows are those taken by householders, like the five precepts: to refrain from killing, stealing, lying, sexual misconduct, and intoxication. The Vinaya vows could be one or more of the five precepts, or if you are not keeping any of them, you must at least uphold the refuge vow. It is important to be aware of what you are doing with your body, with your speech, and with your mind.

On top of that, there is the bodhisattva training. This includes compassion, aspiration and application bodhichitta, and trying to practice the six paramitas.

So, a Vajrayana practitioner has to keep three levels of precepts: the Vinaya precepts, the bodhisattva precepts, and the Vajrayana precepts. There are many Vajrayana, or vidyadhara, samayas. Sometimes it is said that there are a hundred thousand samayas. We might prefer not to know about all those! But all the Vajrayana vows can be condensed into the fourteen root and eight branch samayas.

As Vajrayana practitioners, we work on all three levels of vows at once. The correct conduct is to maintain our vows and guard them from degenerating. It is important to study the precepts, understand them, and try to live by them. They all boil down to refraining from negative actions and becoming more accustomed to positive actions. If there are any violations of the vows, we try to repair them, purify them, and resume them. In essence, we are training to live mindfully, so that we become progressively more positive and less negative.

Incorporating the vows into our life is very important. To some extent, we may understand the view that everything arises equally from the dharmakaya. But we have not yet accomplished this view. If we let our actions follow the view, we might think, "Since everything is the radiance of the dharmakaya, then everything is equal, beyond accepting or rejecting. This means I can do whatever I like." Such thoughts mean that recognition of the dharmakaya is lost. This is not crazy wisdom. With this attitude, the wisdom is gone, and one just goes crazy. We mustn't try to be a crazy yogi too soon.

This is why Guru Rinpoche said that even though our view may be very high, our actions need to be precise and down-to-earth. We must continue being mindful, and we must continue working on how we act and react. This takes training, and it takes time. Even though we might have some sense of the view and meditation, our habitual tendencies are still samsaric, so we need to keep working on them. This is the first level of action, which is appropriate for us as beginners.

In terms of our actions being in accord with the time, we have to discern what we can and cannot do in particular circumstances. The best approach is to do something good for oneself and good for others, both now and in the long run. But we have to be realistic. It is not a matter of following rules that were written down long ago, or following a map that says there is no cliff when you can see for yourself that there is one. You have to use your own eyes; don't walk off a cliff. This is why Gampopa says that you have to act in accordance with the time and the situation.

In the remainder of this chapter of the root text, Gampopa discusses levels of realization far beyond most of us, and I don't see a need to comment on them at this point. The rest of this chapter of the root text is included below, and just as I did earlier, I will leave the text to stand on its own.

> b. A yogic practitioner of the secret Vajrayana acts according to the path of transformation. This entails practicing in retreat in an isolated place, like a charnel ground. In this kind of practice, the body is transformed into the meditation deity, the speech is transformed into mantra, and the mind is transformed into the true nature. The *Mahamaya Tantra* states:
>
> > *Mantras, forms, and the absolute nature*
> > *Are the three yogas.*
> > *By means of these three yogas,*
> > *One does not become stained by the faults of samsara.*
>
> Transforming one's body into the deity refers to meditating on the stages of generating the illusory body, the form of the deity. Transforming speech into mantra means, at the highest level, to meditate on the wisdom wind of *chandali*, or Inner Heat. The medium level is to count the ordinary breathing pattern of exhalation, inhalation, and retention. The lowest level is to recite the mantra of the deity. Transforming your mind into the absolute nature means that you engage instantaneously in formless meditation, such as Mahamudra, and practice the various special skillful means of the Vajrayana.
>
> In terms of the secret mantra, what does "secret" mean? It is said that you keep the deity secret, you keep the lama secret,

you keep the teachings secret, and you practice by keeping your body, speech, and mind in secrecy.

c. An accomplished master acts in accordance with crazy wisdom. In relation to the yogic activity described above, the siddha's body has been transformed into the deity, the speech has become mantra, and the mind is the true nature. Therefore, it is said that one is able to bring the dead back to life and to make things appear and disappear. These are the activities of a crazy wisdom master.

d. The actions of a wisdom holder reflect the realization of great equality. In all four daily activities, this person acts spontaneously in a state of uninterrupted bliss-emptiness. This is the state of unity of no more learning, beyond meditation and postmeditation. There are no activities to be done or not done. In essence, all action is spontaneous; a wisdom holder has no agenda.

For these four types of people, the higher should not act like the lower, and the lower should not act like the higher. When one's activity is related with one's capacity, then the activity is connected with the time.

4. In terms of the result being connected with benefiting others, for a real yogi, there is no duality of perceiver and perceived. There is no need to be deliberately mindful or think about anything. Without effort, the yogi is naturally immersed in the realization of great equality. At the level of the result, when the nets of the body come apart at death, then the body, speech, and mind become inseparable from the enlightened kaya of great bliss. The result is attained when actualization becomes spontaneous. Then, in terms of how the result is connected with benefiting others, from the dharmakaya the form kayas naturally and effortlessly arise to act for the welfare of others.

Each of us needs to apply the view and actions described here. Please carefully consider all of this.

The Importance of Recognizing the Ordinary Mind

AS BEFORE, this chapter begins with "Jetsun Rinpoche said." Of course, "Jetsun Rinpoche" refers to Gampopa, who leads into the main topic in this way:

> As practitioners, please remind yourselves of death and impermanence. Do not forget karmic cause and result. Recognize the shortcomings of samsara as well as the shortcomings of the Hinayana. Recollect loving-kindness, compassion, and bodhichitta. From now on, if you want to be liberated from samsara, you need to recognize tamel gyi shepa, the ordinary mind, since it is the heart of all the dharma.

As our foundation, we need to remind ourselves of impermanence again and again, and try to see things clearly. Impermanence is obvious, but most of the time we don't want to see it. We often prefer to be caught up in our current situation, but this kind of attachment leads to trouble. Our problems multiply because we don't know how to let go of things; we don't see that what is happening now is going to change. Sometimes even little problems overwhelm us. There is no reason to be so strongly affected by small things. We might die tonight, or next week, or soon after. If we thought more about impermanence and death, then our small problems might seem like no problem at all.

We need to free ourselves from samsaric states of mind. As long as we have a mind that gets caught in fear and clinging, we won't be free from suffering, nor will we find lasting happiness. So, whenever we begin our study or practice sessions, we need to remind ourselves of these fundamental things.

All beings are just like us in not wanting to suffer and in wanting to be happy. Along with freeing ourselves, we need to help free everyone else. It's important to cultivate love, compassion, and bodhichitta, and to make aspirations. When the wish to free all beings becomes our greatest concern, then what is the best thing to do? What will enable us to solve their problems as well as our own? From the Mahamudra point of view, the solution is to recognize tamel gyi shepa.

Tamel gyi shepa is a Tibetan phrase that is usually translated as "ordinary mind" or "ordinary consciousness." However, it is important not to confuse ordinary mind with our regular, habitual way of experiencing things. That kind of ordinariness is not tamel gyi shepa. This term refers to the basic awareness that is the nature of the mind. Our mind in its natural state is peaceful, joyful, compassionate, and clear. In fact, the mind is so clear that in its own state, it is omniscient. It has tremendous natural power and ability. This is the actual nature of our mind.

This understanding of the mind is regarded as the most profound teaching of Buddhism; Gampopa calls it "the heart essence of the entire dharma." When we talk about the realization of Mahamudra or Dzogchen, this is what we are talking about. From this perspective, the ordinary mind is not theoretical. It is not something produced over time. With the right understanding and the right way of being, we can experience the natural state right now. The teachings of Dzogchen and Mahamudra always include the introduction to the nature of mind. If the right circumstances are created, if you have the right conditions, then you can experience this right away, at this very moment. And if you do, you experience the enlightened mind.

Enlightenment is not something far away; it is in our experience right now. The problem is that since we haven't consciously experienced it, we don't know how to access it. Although this basic awareness is always present in us, we are so accustomed to reacting in limited ways that we don't open up to the vastness of what we are. If we could let go of our small, self-centered thinking and instead completely open our heart, we could experience this now.

The natural state is very simple, but experiencing it is not easy because most of us do not dare to do this. In general, we don't like surprises and we don't like to be shocked. For instance, why are we afraid of the dark? Because we don't know what is there. We don't want to encounter what we haven't experienced before. In the same way, our fear keeps us from looking at ourselves completely and thoroughly.

We need more daring! To realize the nature of the mind, we must be more courageous. Also, we need to be prepared. What will prepare us are the attitudes Gampopa mentioned at the beginning of this chapter: we need compassion—the feeling that our heart is open to everyone. We need renunciation—the feeling of being fed up with our aversion and attachment and all the problems they cause. And we need to let go of our ignorance—our age-old patterns of pretending and hiding ourselves.

Sometimes people find samsara so difficult that they want to get away from everyone; they want to go to the forest and live in solitude. It would disturb them if anyone came along. This is a misunderstanding of renunciation. As your understanding of samsara grows, your understanding of people grows, and your ability to relate to their problems grows. You become more capable of dealing with the difficult aspects of the world. The more renunciation you have, the more compassionate you become. You want to help people solve their problems because you see how all of you are in the same situation. It naturally follows that you become more easygoing and find it simpler to be with people. This is how renunciation and insight lead to compassion.

We need to explore our mind, to open up and become truly familiar with what we are. This is how we will uncover our true nature. If we are willing to go through whatever it takes to know ourselves fully, then it becomes possible to experience our true nature. From one point of view, every aspect of dharma practice—like prostrations, mantra recitation, and meditation—could be seen as methods that prepare us to experience the nature of our mind.

> **What is the ordinary mind? It is your own consciousness, unadulterated by anything, unspoiled by any kind of worldly consciousness. No matter what sort of dullness or thoughts hide it, it remains in its natural state. If you realize it, it is the**

wisdom of pristine awareness. If you do not recognize it, it
is coemergent ignorance. When you realize this, it is called
rigpa. It is called the essence. It is called coemergent wisdom.
It is called the ordinary mind. It is called the primordial state.
It is called free from extremes. It is called luminosity.

So, the ordinary mind is our own undisturbed consciousness. It is
the mind remaining in its natural state.

This brings up the question of thoughts. When we look at our mind,
we see all sorts of arisings—different thoughts, emotional reactions,
sensations, and perceptions. From the Mahamudra point of view, these
are regarded as the radiance of the mind. If the natural state of mind is
like the sun, then the mental arisings are like the rays of the sun.

The true nature of our consciousness, the subtlest form of our consciousness, is just awareness. This is the ordinary mind, tamel gyi shepa,
or rigpa. If you look at this awareness, there is nothing to find. You cannot say your awareness is here or there, or that it resides in this cell or
that cell of the brain. You cannot find anything, and yet awareness continues. Because of awareness, it is called luminosity. Luminosity does
not refer to something glowing, like a light, but it means that the mind
is self-aware, that awareness is always present. Since awareness does not
have any form or shape, it is sometimes called awareness-emptiness. It
is nothing in itself, but at the same time, we experience being aware.

Awareness itself is not affected by any of our thoughts, perceptions,
or feelings. They are simply the radiance of awareness, like the waves of
the ocean. The waves are not different from the ocean; they are part of
it. They simply appear on the surface without disturbing the ocean. In
the same way, the various thoughts and emotions appear without disturbing the fundamental consciousness.

When we recognize the ordinary mind and see our experience as its
radiance, we realize there is no reason to be disturbed by whatever happens. We don't need to be attached to our experiences, and in fact, we
can laugh at them. We don't need to run away from them or run after
them. They are simply displays of indestructible awareness. Seeing our
experience in this way is the hallmark of being enlightened. Whatever
experience arises is okay, because in its nature and its depth, awareness
is not disturbed by anything. Anything that appears is simply the mind's
own radiance.

It is similar to your shadow. You don't have to be afraid of it, you don't need to be attached to it—it is just there. When it's there, it's okay, and when it's not there, it's okay. Your shadow doesn't bother you. If you know this about your thoughts, emotions, and sensations, then you know how to liberate yourself.

Connecting this with meditation, it is important to remember that having a focused or stable mind is not enough to free us from samsara. It just calms us down, that's all. It doesn't do much long-term good. The real training is in knowing how to liberate ourselves from fear and attachment to our own experiences. Once we know that all our experiences are just the radiance of our ordinary mind, then they can come and go without our being attached to them or wanting to get rid of them. This is how liberation happens.

Gampopa says that if you realize this, it is the wisdom of pristine awareness, but if you don't realize this, it is coemergent ignorance. When we talk about realizing or recognizing, we are talking about experiencing our basic awareness without it being an object of awareness. Usually when we are aware, we are aware of something. We have an object of awareness—something we see or hear. But the experience of coemergent wisdom is just being aware. It is not a vague, dim awareness but a very clear awareness. When you realize this, it is called rigpa. It is called the essence. It is called coemergent wisdom. It is called the ordinary mind. It is called the primordial state. It is called free from extremes. It is called luminosity.

> If you realize this, you become more qualified than a scholar who knows the five traditional sciences. This is because scholars understand through concepts and words. They may know everything, yet they are stumped on this one point. However, if you understand the ordinary mind, then by knowing one thing, you know everything. Since you have gotten to the real point, your qualities are greater.

This is the crucial point, and the reason why it is has been said: "By knowing one thing, you know everything." Rather than being a great scholar who knows everything and yet knows nothing, by knowing this one thing—how to liberate yourself—you know everything you need to know.

> It is better to understand tamel gyi shepa, the ordinary mind,
> than to have shamatha that is so stable that you do not know if
> it is day or night. That kind of shamatha meditation is com-
> mon; even the long-life gods, and the prairie dogs, bears, and
> other animals that sleep in holes have that. The ordinary mind
> is uncommon; this is why it has greater qualities.

It is better to understand tamel gyi shepa than to have shamatha
meditation that is so stable that you lose track of the days and nights.
People can have that kind of experience, but its effect is very limited.
When you come out of that state, since you have not cut the root of the
mind poisons, all your attachment and aversion can come back. But
deeply understanding tamel gyi shepa cuts the root of the mind poisons
because you know your real essence. When you directly know that all
your emotions and thoughts are inseparable from wisdom-awareness,
then they are cut through.

> It is better to understand tamel gyi shepa, the ordinary mind,
> than to receive the four empowerments in sequence, practice
> generating the deity, and experience the signs of contacting,
> hearing, and seeing the yidam. Seeing the face of the deity is
> the pure relative truth, and it is a sign of exhausting one's ob-
> scurations. However, knowing the ordinary mind is the ulti-
> mate truth, so its qualities are greater.

Please don't misunderstand—to accomplish the creation stage practice and experience pure perception is a great achievement. However,
Gampopa says that directly experiencing the ordinary mind is even
greater. Seeing the face of the deity is the pure relative truth, but knowing the ordinary mind is the ultimate truth.

> It is better to understand the ordinary mind than to have the
> five higher perceptions of the eyes and ears and so on. These
> higher perceptions come with defilements. Even ghosts and
> animals can have them. When you understand the ordinary
> mind, your higher perception is undefiled, so it is more won-
> drous. A scripture says:

> *Wisdom, wisdom is the great distinction.*
> *One with wisdom understands existence and non-existence.*[1]

The higher perceptions of the eyes and ears are things like clairvoy-ance and clairaudience.[2] It is possible to develop miraculous powers from meditation. But these powers are not as special as tamel gyi shepa. The various intuitive powers and healing powers are the ordinary sid-dhis, the common spiritual accomplishments. But the experience of the true nature of the mind is the supreme siddhi, the ultimate accomplish-ment. By gaining the supreme siddhi, you reach liberation and cut through all samsaric states of mind. This is why tamel gyi shepa is so valuable.

> It is better to understand the ordinary mind than not to expe-rience perception, or for there to be no perceptible objects, or to have flashes of experience, or to be immersed in emptiness like a completely clear sky. This is because these are general-izations formed through inference. However, the ordinary mind reaches the real point; it is based on direct perception, which makes its qualities greater.
>
> Realizing the ordinary mind is the king of supreme know-ing. Since this is not an object of discriminating knowledge, it is said:

> *With great knowledge, in one instant*
> *All phenomena are completely understood,*
> *All phenomena are completely realized.*

This is why it is the king of primordial wisdom. All five types of primordial wisdom are contained in tamel gyi shepa, so it is the wisdom of the basic space of phenomena. Through realizing that the grasper and the grasped are not separate, it is discriminating-awareness wisdom. It is said:

> *In one instant, specifics are discriminated,*
> *In one instant, perfect buddhahood.*
> *In one instant of mind, everything is known.*

There is no need to progress through the five paths, and so on. In one instant, all purposes are accomplished, so it is all-accomplishing wisdom. Since all things in the relative world are realized to be like reflections in a mirror, it is the mirror-like wisdom. All of samsara and nirvana are equally one's own awareness, so it is the wisdom of equanimity. Therefore, it is said:

> Buddhahood has no beginning or end.
> The primordial buddha has no cause.
> The stainless, single eye of wisdom,
> The embodiment of wisdom is the Tathagata.

This is how the ordinary mind is the king of wisdom. The ordinary mind is the king of all qualities. There are no greater higher perceptions than those mentioned above, yet tamel gyi shepa is greater than that. The ordinary mind is the king of all samadhis. Once it is realized, no matter what kinds of samadhi are experienced, they are like outer shells and husks. The ordinary mind is the essence of the entire dharma and the root of all samsara and nirvana, so it all comes down to whether you recognize tamel gyi shepa or not. Therefore, it is very important to recognize the ordinary mind.

In a way, the whole practice of Buddhism is about realizing the ordinary mind, especially in Vajrayana, Mahamudra, and Dzogchen. We do Ngöndro practice, three-year retreats, and all sorts of meditation, reflection, and study in order to experience the nature of the mind. When you comprehend this, you know where the Buddhist path is taking you.

To fully recognize the ordinary mind is not easy. Maybe I shouldn't say this, since it is also said to be very easy if you know how to recognize it, or if you have the right conditions. Then you just get it!

There are three ways of getting tamel gyi shepa. Some people get it through a mind-to-mind transmission. If there is a meeting of minds between a great teacher and a great student, then click! It's done.

The second way is through a sign transmission from a vidyadhara. A great teacher makes some sign, gives an empowerment, or throws a shoe at your head and hits you, and you get it!

The third is the mouth-to-ear transmission, where the teacher explains what to do. But the key here is still your own experience. In Mahamudra practice, you meditate and work on understanding and experiencing what you were told. Then you tell your teacher what you have understood and experienced. The teacher usually says, "No, that's not it," and sends you back to your cushion. You practice more and have more experience, and revise your understanding again. In this way, little by little, full recognition comes.

Sometimes people think that realizing the ordinary mind means that one goes beyond ordinary perceptions. But realization isn't a matter of not seeing things or not feeling them. Ordinary perceptions are there, but when you have realized the ordinary mind, what changes is the way you react to your perceptions. You know there is no reason to be afraid or cling to whatever happens.

Of course, there are different levels of realization. These depend on habitual tendencies and the degree to which you've experienced the nature of the mind. Generally, what happens first is that you realize there is no need to habitually react to what you perceive. Great masters do not hold on to their feelings. Although some never get angry and always seem easygoing, there are others who are very emotional.

A good example of this is His Holiness the Dalai Lama. His emotions are very vibrant. Scientists who have observed the Dalai Lama say that his emotional reactions are just like those of other people. He sheds tears like other people, and he laughs fully from his heart. He is far from being numb and indifferent. What is unusual is the way his emotions change very quickly; he doesn't get caught in one emotion. He feels and expresses his emotions very clearly, but he doesn't hold on to them. When he is sad, he can be very sad, but in the next moment, he can be very happy.

One time, some neuroscientists were meeting with the Dalai Lama in Dharamsala when news came that a child in the Tibetan Children's Village had passed away. The Dalai Lama's face got very sad; it crumpled up and he shed tears, like a father who has lost his child. Everyone could see his emotion; there was no doubt he was brokenhearted. But then, in the next moment, he was talking about other things, laughing heartily, and back to normal. What was so striking to the scientists was the speed at which he could change from one emotion to another.

So, our problems don't come from having feelings and emotions;

they come from holding on to them. As Buddhists we are training in non-attachment, not indifference. Indifference means you don't care, whereas non-attachment means you don't cling. So, as our realization of the nature of mind grows, we will be able to experience our emotions fully, and immediately let them go. No longer caught in emotional experiences, we will know how to liberate ourselves.

THIRTEEN

The Ways in Which a Realized Yogi Is Free

NEXT, GAMPOPA describes how yogis can tell if they are realized, or truly free. Freedom is the most important point, and there are many ways in which we need to be free.

It sometimes happens that people have meditation experiences and think they are realized. But if you think that you are realized when you are not, it can create problems for both you and others. If you have understood and experienced the ordinary mind, then just how much realization do you have? It is important to be able to judge this, to have some criteria to determine how free you really are.

> Jetsun Rinpoche said: For a yogi who realizes Mahamudra: (1) the view is free from two desires, (2) the meditation is free from three stages, (3) the action is free from earlier and later activities, and (4) the result is free from hope and fear.

Gampopa says that the view, meditation, action, and result must all be free. Let's go through these one by one.

> 1. In terms of the view being free from two desires, first, having realized the fundamental way of abiding, we might like others'

views to resemble our own, without any disagreement. Second, we might want our practice of the true nature to give rise to one result after another. We need to be free from these two desires.

Let's begin by reviewing the meaning of the term "the view." The view is not philosophy; the view is direct understanding. It is how we see everything. In Mahamudra, directly experiencing tamel gyi shepa is the view. Of course, our way of understanding is also the view, but that is more of a conceptual view. In truth, the view is experiential.

The first desire is connected with the tenets that we hold about the ultimate nature. Having developed an understanding of the true nature, we usually want others to hold the same view that we do, and we're afraid that their view will contradict ours. Usually, we take the way we see things and think, "This is obviously right. If you see things differently, you must be wrong. I don't like that. In fact, if your view is different, I don't like you!"

Sometimes when I give a talk, people come up to me afterward and say, "Oh, you are a great teacher. You said exactly what I think." On the other hand, if I had said the opposite of what they think, they might have hated me! So, wanting others to have the same view as we do is the first desire that Gampopa warns us against. As you progress toward realization, this attitude lessens until it is no longer there.

The second desire is connected with wanting your practice of the true nature to bring one result after another. The problem here is that you still desire results. If you actually have the right view, that *is* the result. It is not the case that after this experience there will be some other result. If you think that you have the right view and still wonder when the result will come, then you do not have the right view. The right view *is* freedom. There is no more desire, no more feeling of wanting "this" and not wanting "that." Once you have the real experience of the view, you are liberated.

2. The meditation is free from the three stages. Rather than meditating in some way as the preparation, meditating in some way in the main part, and meditating in some way as the conclusion, at all times one's practice is free from these three stages. It needs to be yogic meditation, like the uninterrupted flow of a river, never moving away from the true nature.

The second point is related to meditation. The three stages being referred to here are the preparation, the main part, and the conclusion. For someone who has realized the view of the ordinary mind, there is no first "this," there is no second "that," and there is no third "something else." The practice of a realized yogi never wavers from the true nature. There are no different stages. The experience of the true nature is the preparation, it is the main part, and it is the conclusion. There is no need to do anything else. One's whole being has become meditation.

At the level of realization, one's meditation resembles the uninterrupted flow of a river. This was said of Milarepa; he had a flowing, river-like samadhi. A river flows all the time, day and night. A river doesn't need to take a break from flowing. In the same way, a realized yogi's meditation is always there, without any special activity. A yogi is simply in that state. Realized beings understand what they really are. They know completely, so they are always in meditation.

> 3. **The action is free from earlier and later activities. This means being free from thoughts like, "First I will do this, and then I will do that." In brief, one has no agenda. Another way of saying this is that one's actions are free of rejecting and accepting. One is free from wanting to get rid of emotional afflictions and wanting to accomplish wisdom as their antidote. We need to be free of all negating and affirming.**

"The action is free from earlier and later activities" means that you no longer think in terms of the past and the future. In other words, you have no agenda. Having no agenda for yourself is the whole point. With realization, you know that you already have everything you need. You're not running after one thing and running away from another. You have no need to get rid of or accomplish anything.

This does not mean that realized yogis do not intend to fulfill the purposes of others. Once you are realized, you still have one item on your agenda: to help other beings. In terms of having no agenda, Gampopa is not implying that yogis are crazy, although sometimes they can seem a little crazy.

There is a Tibetan saying that yogis do not get along well in society. Ordinary people want certain things and not others, and yogis may think and act very differently. Yogis have their own ways of thinking and doing things, which may be completely unconventional. Their activities are done for the sake of others; they are no longer concerned about themselves.

This reminds me of one of the stories about Drukpa Kunley, the crazy yogi of Bhutan. There are many stories about the outrageous things he did. During his time, there were three famous crazy yogis: one in central Tibet, one in western Tibet, and one in Bhutan. They were all realized beings. People knew these men were siddhas, but they were called "crazy" because they did such strange things.

The story goes that one time there was a drought near Lhasa. It had not rained for months and everything was drying up. Various lamas did *pujas* and rituals, but nothing seemed to help. Finally, people asked Drukpa Kunley, "Can't you do something? You are supposed to be a realized yogi."

He told them, "I can help you, but you must do exactly what I say."

They agreed to do whatever he asked. He said he wanted all the monks of the three big monasteries—Ganden, Drepung, and Sera—to assemble at a certain place and to bring with them a great deal of tsampa, or roasted barley flour. When the monks came, Drukpa Kunley took off his clothes until he was completely naked. He stood on his head and told the monks to put the tsampa on his buttocks. As they were piling on the tsampa, he started farting, and the tsampa billowed up in the air, making a big cloud with a very bad smell. The cloud went higher and higher, and grew larger and larger, and then it began to rain.

This story is supposed to illustrate the realization of a yogi who no longer cares about himself but cares only about others.

> **4. The result is freedom from hope and fear. There needs to be freedom from the hope of attaining nirvana and the fear of wandering in samsara. In short, by realizing that samsara and nirvana are inseparable great bliss, there is no wish to rise up to buddhahood and no fear of falling down into samsara.**

Fourth, a realized yogi has gone beyond both hope and fear. Having no hope does not refer to feeling hopeless and discouraged; it means not having any expectation or longing for something better. The reason there is no expectation is that everything is already accomplished. Your understanding is complete, and you are satisfied. At the same time, there is nothing left to fear. You have gone beyond wanting to get out of samsara and get into nirvana. You know that samsara is just a state of mind filled with clinging and fear. When realization happens, samsaric states of mind no longer arise, so there is no more samsara. And once there is no more samsara, then there is no more nirvana, since these two exist only in relation to each other. Everything is enlightened; it's all good. It is sometimes said that actual liberation is being free from the concepts of samsara and nirvana. This is the result of realization.

This is very important. Even if you feel like you have a very high view, or you have good signs or meditative experiences, as long as there is any hope or fear, you are not completely free. Good understanding and good experiences do not make you highly realized. When people have wonderful experiences of clarity, peace, or bliss, they sometimes think that they have reached realization—they feel so good, and everything is so nice. In order to clear away this misunderstanding, Gampopa tells us what to look for in our experience. The main measure of realization is being totally free of desire, hope, and fear.

FOURTEEN

The Ideal Way to Listen to the Dharma

HAVING THE EXPERIENCE of Mahamudra does not mean you are fully enlightened. Simply saying that you understand the nature of the mind is not enough. Although it's possible for realization to happen instantly, most people need to develop wisdom first. There are three main ways to cultivate wisdom: study, reflection, and meditation. In this chapter, Gampopa briefly explains how to study or listen to the dharma.

> Jetsun Rinpoche said: In general, listening to the dharma has two aspects: the ideal intention and the ideal application.

So, Gampopa is going to tell us the best motivation for study and the best method for study.

> The ideal intention involves four attitudes: (1) "I wish to listen, not because I want to be famous, but in order to take all beings across the great ocean of samsaric suffering."

The way to tell if your study or practice is moving toward enlightenment is by looking at why you are doing it. It's good to check your motivation to see the direction in which you are going.

Intention is extremely important, whether in connection with study, practice, or anything else. We shouldn't have the intention to study and become a great scholar in order to impress everyone. The best attitude is to think: "I want to study the dharma because I wish to help sentient beings. All beings are suffering due to samsaric states of mind, and I want to help them cross the ocean of samsara. To be able to do this, I need to study."

>   (2) "I wish to listen, not to obtain honor and gain, but to ob-
>   tain the wisdom of omniscience."

Second, with the right motivation, you are not studying to be honored or increase your income. You sincerely want to understand and develop your wisdom, to the point of becoming omniscient.

>   (3) "I wish to listen, not to be victorious in arguments, but to
>   be victorious over the enemy army of my mental afflictions."

Third, you are not motivated by wanting to be able to argue well and win debates. Competitiveness often surfaces among students. I'm sure you know that monks in the Tibetan monastic colleges spend a lot of time in debates. Debates can come close to violence. Sometimes debaters get very excited and jump around. I even saw one man stomp so hard that he broke the flooring. In some traditions, when the best debaters defeat everyone else, then all the other students have to take off their debate hats, and the winner gets to walk on everyone's hats. If one of the defeated debaters does not take off the debate hat, the winner is allowed to take it off and throw it far away. However, I can assure you, that is not recommended! What Gampopa is recommending is that we use our study to work on our negative emotions and delusions. This is what we need to defeat.

You might be interested to know that I heard that monks adopted an aggressive style of debate in order to drive away the nuns. The more violent style developed when the nuns were participating in the debates, and many of them were brighter than the monks. Some monks were unhappy with that, so they started debating with loud voices and rough gestures, and the nuns went away. I don't know if this is true. But I do know that these days the nuns are coming back. I heard that recently there was a debate in Dharamsala between some monks and nuns, and the nuns won.

> (4) "I wish to listen not because I want to expose my teacher's mistakes but to show respect for my teacher and the teachings."

The fourth motivation discusses the relationship with the teacher. Sometimes students listen with the intention of spotting the teacher's mistakes so they can correct the teacher. Their real motivation is to show off how much more they know. Gampopa warns against this, and says that we need to show respect for the teacher and the teachings.

> The ideal application has three parts: the preparation, the main part, and the conclusion. (1) The preparation is motivated by bodhichitta, while knowing that everything is like a dream or an illusion.

Once again, Gampopa is directing our attention to bodhichitta, because as bodhisattvas-in-training, bodhichitta precedes all our activities. Bodhichitta is usually thought of as compassion, but it is more than compassion; it is compassion inseparable from wisdom. Bodhichitta focuses on two things: sentient beings and liberation. Ordinarily, when we feel compassion, we focus only on sentient beings. We see that people have problems, we feel very sad about that, and we strongly wish for them to be free from suffering. Usually, it doesn't go further than this.

The problem with focusing on the suffering of others is that this kind of compassion can be painful for us as well. We see the suffering of others, but we don't see the illusory nature of their suffering. When we see this illusory nature, we see that their suffering can end. But if we don't see this, we don't see what can be done to end their suffering, and this leaves us feeling hopeless and sad.

Bodhichitta also focuses on liberation. When you have compassion with wisdom, not only do you see the suffering of others and want it to end, you also know there is a way out. This makes bodhichitta a hopeful, optimistic kind of compassion. Your enthusiasm comes from knowing that there is a path out of suffering. You may not know exactly how to become free, but you know that it's possible, and you intend to explore this and work on it.

With bodhichitta as the basis, whatever you do is for the benefit of all beings. Inspired by compassion and wisdom, you act with enthusiasm and purpose. Bodhichitta gives you a clear vision; your compassion becomes focused, directed, and optimistic.

(2) The main part is to practice all six paramitas while listening to any sort of teaching.

The six paramitas are generosity, discipline, patience, diligence, meditation, and wisdom. Let's look at how each of these could be applied to listening to teachings.

To begin with the first paramita, generosity, you give your time and attention to listening. Generosity includes making preparations for the teachings, like obtaining flowers for the teacher or setting up the environment for the event. At the teaching itself, making a mandala offering is another aspect of generosity that is part of receiving teachings.

The second paramita, right conduct or discipline, is practiced by sitting up with good posture and keeping your body, speech, and mind positive and disciplined. For instance, you would avoid having negative thoughts during the teaching.

The third paramita, patience, is applied when the teachings seem too long, or when tolerance is needed for the other students who are there. If some parts of the teaching are difficult to understand, then you apply patience by listening carefully and asking questions, and by not getting agitated if you don't understand right away.

The fourth paramita, diligence, is applied when you listen with joyful interest, and you don't get irritated or lose interest. Diligence brings a sense of joy to hearing the teachings.

The fifth paramita, meditation, is present when your mind is focused on the teachings. You don't get distracted outwardly or let your mind turn inward and fall asleep. It's best to focus your mind during teachings in the same way you do while meditating—not too much and not too little—so that you are awake and hear everything being said. If you concentrate too much, your mind gets dull and can't grasp or retain the material. When your mind is balanced without either concentration or distraction, you comprehend better and retain more of what was said.

The sixth paramita, wisdom, is applied to clarify your understanding. With wisdom, your faculties are clear, so you can ask questions and investigate the topic from different angles. Wisdom is also involved in retaining what you heard, so that you don't forget either the words or the meaning.

These are some of the ways that you could apply the six paramitas while listening to dharma teachings. Of course, there are other ways as well, but this is an overview of how all six could be applied.

> (3) The conclusion is to dedicate the positive results of listening toward the perfect enlightenment of all beings.

Dedicating the merit is always important. After listening or studying, we conclude by dedicating the merit for the enlightenment of all beings, just as we do in all our dharma activities.

> To practice all these points together, think: "I will establish in enlightenment all the limitless sentient beings, who are like a magical illusion or a dream. For that purpose, I will attain perfect enlightenment. And to accomplish that, I will listen to the precious instructions. I will understand them, I will realize them, and I will practice them." We need to generate this kind of special intention. In general, it is important to have a completely pure intention in listening to the dharma.

Pitfalls in Experience and Deviations from the View

Jetsun Rinpoche said: Of all the pitfalls, which is the greatest? It is the attachment to worldly things. Unless we turn our mind away from worldly things, there is no way to become a great meditator.

IT'S LIKE THIS: if we think that some worldly thing—like having money, power, or a special relationship—is going to bring us lasting happiness, then we will not practice the dharma. Because if one of those things could bring us lasting happiness, why do anything else? This is not to say that all practitioners should become monks or nuns, or live in monasteries or caves. Obviously, we live in the world, and we need to do what is necessary in the world. Practically speaking, it is good to have worldly things; the more we have, the easier our life can be. But if we think that worldly things are going to bring real happiness and satisfaction, then our practice won't get very far.

For instance, many wealthy people are unhappy. This does not mean that wealth causes unhappiness; of course, one could be wealthy and happy. But there are many people who are powerful and unhappy, many people who are famous and unhappy, and many people who are comfortable and unhappy. External conditions are not the cause of happiness.

I hope it is clear that there is nothing wrong with having wealth or success or comfort. But lasting happiness comes from within. This is what our practice is all about. Dharma practice is not about having one thing or another, or believing one thing or another. Dharma practice is about learning to live in such a way that we have lasting peace and happiness. This is why it is so important to understand our own mind and know what we actually are.

Even if you gave up everything and went to sit in a cave, you could still have plenty of attachment to the world. Not having something is not the same as not having attachment; in fact, not having something can lead to even more attachment. For example, if someone has no shoes, that person might become very attached to shoes. Or if you have no food, then your attachment to food gets very strong.

I've had a little experience of this while doing Nyungne, the compassion practice that involves fasting for almost forty-eight hours. I remember one time while doing Nyungne I could smell the tsampa from a hundred feet away. Roasted barley flour usually has very little smell or taste, but when I smelled it during Nyungne, it was heavenly! I even started dreaming about it. On the final morning, when the bland, watery soup was served, it seemed like the most delicious food in the world! So, the key point is not whether we do or don't have something but whether we are attached to it. What is there on the outside is not very important. What is there inside us is much more important.

In practicing, there are three pitfalls connected with experience and four deviations from the correct view. Of the three pitfalls connected with experience, the first pitfall is to be concerned about having a comfortable body, a happy mind, and experiences of bliss pervading the body.

Sometimes we can experience bliss in meditation. The body becomes very comfortable, the mind becomes very happy, and various blissful experiences arise. However, these can cause problems as well. The main purpose of practice is to free ourselves from suffering. But if we get attached to happiness, it doesn't make us happier. Instead, we get caught in thinking, "I want to be happy, I want to feel good." But then we don't want to lose it. We become afraid it will go away and not come back. Right there, the happiness is lost.

Even though there can be a lot of bliss in meditation, it is very important not to be attached to it. Meditative experiences are usually temporary. They are nice; there is nothing wrong with having them. But attachment to them causes suffering when they are no longer there. It is important to learn to let go of blissful experiences, and even to deliberately disrupt them. Training in cutting through bliss is a good way to practice. Otherwise, we get caught by our wanting, and find ourselves back in a samsaric way of reacting.

If bliss is not a real sign of good meditation, then what is? The most important experience is equanimity. With equanimity, when the mind and body feel good, we can enjoy that, but it doesn't matter if good feelings go away. We're not afraid of losing them. If we can let our mind relax when we experience bliss without wanting more, then our practice is very good.

However, it is more often the case that our experience is not so blissful. Our mind can be disturbed or depressed, and our body can be uncomfortable or sick. Our practice is very good when we can say in the midst of pain, "I can handle this; it's not a problem. The pain can come and go. It's okay with me." If we can accept both positive and negative experiences in this way, we have real stability of mind.

When we have become truly stable, then all experiences are good. Bad experiences are workable, and of course, good experiences are good experiences. So, in a way, there are no more bad experiences. When we are confident that we can deal with whatever kind of experience comes along, we are making real progress on the path.

Please don't confuse this kind of equanimity with being numb or not feeling anything. Good meditators feel things fully and clearly, but they are not overwhelmed by their experiences, whether positive or negative. We are training to let everything come and go, without fear or clinging. This is the main reason we meditate.

> Through attachment and overt clinging to these things, they become extremely important, and this is the cause for perpetuating the desire realm. If people die in that frame of mind, they deviate by going to the desire realm. After experiencing the bliss and rapture of the desire realm, there is no difficulty in traveling endlessly in the lower realms.

Gampopa is warning us that if we get attached to pleasurable or blissful experiences, we will go no further toward liberation than the desire realm of the gods. The desire realm is still within samsara, and being born there is not a great achievement.

The Buddha taught that there are three main realms: the desire realm, the form realm, and the formless realm. The six realms of sentient beings, which we are more familiar with, are within the desire realm, except for the god realm, which also extends into the form and formless realms. One way that beings are reborn in the three levels of the god realm is through attachment to meditative experiences. The first pitfall Gampopa mentions is attachment to meditative bliss. This state is similar to the desire realm of the gods, and if we die while attached to an experience of meditative bliss, we could be reborn there.

> **The second pitfall is connected to the experience of clarity that arises in the absence of drowsiness and dullness. By clinging to clarity and giving it the highest importance, one deviates by going to the form realm. After experiencing the bliss and rapture of that realm, there is no difficulty in falling into lower states of existence.**

We usually have both coarse and subtle dullness in our mind. Here, Gampopa is referring to the meditative experience in which coarse dullness has been clarified. The mind can become extremely clear; the meditator can see through things and become clairvoyant to some extent. People can become attached to clarity and think they are having an important experience. Sometimes people think, "I am so clear now, I must be enlightened." This meditative state is similar to the form realm of the gods. If you die while attached to the experience of meditative clarity, you could be reborn in the form realm of the gods. You can enjoy that realm for a very long time. But eventually the experience is exhausted, because it is still within samsara. When it ends, you fall into lower states. It is a pitfall because it is not a state of freedom or enlightenment.

> **The third pitfall is connected with the experience of being unmoved by the winds of thoughts and emotions. Attachment to that state of mind, and holding it as supreme, is the cause of perpetuating the formless realm. If people die in that frame of**

mind, they deviate by going to the formless realm. After experiencing the bliss and rapture of that realm, one travels endlessly in the three lower realms.

In this experience, your mind has become extremely stable. It is not moved by thoughts and emotions, so it is very peaceful. This is a state of complete stability and peace. But if you become attached to this state of mind and perpetuate it, you will deviate into the formless god realm, and when that ends, you will suffer.

It is helpful to differentiate between pitfalls and obstacles. Pitfalls are connected with good experiences, whereas obstacles seem to be negative. Obstacles seem to get in your way. When you have a good experience, if you are not skillful in the way you handle it, it can become a pitfall where you get stuck. The meditative experiences we are talking about—bliss, clarity, and peace—are very good. However, you have to be careful not to become attached to them. It is great to feel blissful, clear, and peaceful. The only problem is longing for these experiences and clinging to them.

Actually, in terms of meditation, Gampopa is referring to advanced levels of practice. But these experiences happen in our daily life as well. We need to learn to handle our good experiences without getting so attached. And we need to be able to undergo our negative experiences without getting overwhelmed or depressed. We are training in the dharma so we can skillfully deal with problems as they arise. Unless our practice is connected with our life, it is not real practice. If we are skillful, then obstacles can be transformed into something positive.

The main point is not to be afraid and not to be attached. We have talked a lot about attachment, but fear is another area where we often get caught. We need a deep understanding that fear is useless and unnecessary. When something happens to us, we simply have to go through it. Whether it is good or bad, our only choice is to keep going. Fear doesn't make it any better, although it can make it much worse.

We need to understand through our own wisdom that there is no need for fear. This doesn't mean that we should give up being careful, and not bother to avoid danger. This is not what I am saying. If you find that something is causing you problems, that it is harmful for you and others, then leave it alone. Not out of panic or fear, but because you understand that it's not good. Once you see this, you avoid whatever it is, or reduce how much you do it. If we look carefully, we have the wisdom to understand what is wholesome and what is not wholesome, what is right and what is not right. Try to understand, try to investigate, and then do your best.

We need some courage. We need a little daring in dealing with our everyday life, as well as some daring in our practice. Without some courage, you can become frozen and think, "I can't do this and I could never do that." I am not suggesting you become a daredevil, but you have to be courageous. Especially when you feel you can't handle something, this is when you need to be daring. You will not get stuck in a situation if you face it with courage.

There is a very moving story in the *Jataka Tales* about fearlessness.[1] Once there was a parrot who lived in the forest, and one day the forest caught fire. Since the parrot was able to fly, she started to fly away. Then she heard the crying of the animals and insects trapped in the forest. They could not fly away like she could. When the parrot heard their anguish, she thought to herself, "I cannot just go away; I must help my friends."

So, the parrot went to the river, where she soaked all her feathers, and then flew back to the forest. She shook her feathers over the forest, but it was very little water, not nearly enough to stop a forest fire. So, she went back to the river, wet her feathers, and did this over and over again. The fire was so strong and hot that her feathers were scorched and burned, and she was choking on the smoke. But even though she was about to die, she kept going back and forth.

Up in the god realms, some of the gods were looking down and laughing, saying, "Look at that silly little parrot. She is trying to put out a forest fire with her tiny wings."

Indra, the king of the gods, overheard them. He wanted to see for himself, so he transformed himself into a big eagle and flew down just above the parrot. The eagle called out, "Hey, foolish parrot! What are you doing? You're not doing any good, and you're about to be burned alive. Get away while you can!"

The parrot replied, "You are such a big bird, why don't you help me to put out the fire? I don't need your advice; I need your help."

When the little parrot said this with so much courage and conviction, the eagle, who was actually the king of the gods, shed tears because he was so moved. His tears were so powerful that they put out the fire.

Some of Indra's tears also fell on the parrot's burned feathers. Wherever the tears fell, the feathers grew back in different colors. This is said to be the origin of parrots' colorful feathers. So, it turned out that the little parrot's courage made the fire go out, and at the same time, she became more beautiful than ever.

> **Even if one does not deviate in these three ways, there are four ways of deviating from emptiness.**

Following the three pitfalls, Gampopa goes on to discuss four ways of deviating from the view of emptiness. Emptiness must be understood in the context of interdependence. When we say that the nature of things is emptiness, this doesn't mean there is nothingness. It means that everything arises interdependently, whether it is the largest universe, the smallest subatomic particles, or the minds, emotions, and karma of sentient beings. All these things appear due to causes and conditions. If the causes and conditions do not come together in a certain way, these things will not happen. If even one condition is missing, something totally different will occur.

Sometimes Buddhists say that everything is the mind. This doesn't mean that there is nothing other than your mind's projection; it doesn't mean that if you leave a room, everything in the room will disappear. All these things are not simply your projection; they won't disappear when you walk out. Saying "Everything is the mind" means that everything is interdependent and experienced within your mind. You cannot experience anything outside the range of your mind.

We usually think that what we see and experience is the way things are. We come into this room, see and experience the walls, the colors, the furniture, and so on, and think our experience of these things is the way they are. The Buddha said it a little differently: the way we see is very much connected with the way we are. For example, if our eyes were not in the condition they are now, if instead we were looking through a microscope, then we would see something very different. Similarly, our mind has developed in certain ways because of how we've been educated and conditioned. This definitely influences what we perceive.

Sentient beings that are similar to us see more or less the same things we do. You and I are enough alike that we see similar things and can communicate with each other. But a being with a different structure and way of experiencing would not see what we do; it would see something else. The way things appear is dependent on the way we are.

Emptiness means that everything changes according to conditions. The Buddha said that we can never find anything with an independent, unchanging basis. This is because an independent thing couldn't function. And if something was unchanging, if something couldn't change, it couldn't be affected by anything nor could it affect anything else, and this would make it totally useless and irrelevant. So, everything that is growing, living, or functioning must be interdependent and changing.

Emptiness is another way of saying that there is nothing independent. Emptiness does not mean that nothing is there. Everything we know is there, but its way of being is fluid and ever changing. Everything is conditioned, so everything can be affected and changed.

Things are actually more like a dream or a mirage. A mirage is a very good example: It is very strange how you can see water where there is no water. When you are driving through a hot, dry area, you can sometimes see a mirage ahead on the road. The person you are riding with can see the mirage, too. The mirage can even reflect a car coming from the other direction. How can something be reflected on water that is not there? How can this happen? It is due to causes and conditions coming together in a particular way. You can see it from a distance, but when you get close, it is gone.

Similarly, everything appears as it does due to particular causes and conditions. This includes yourself. Like everything else, you have no independent existence, but you are still here. Even your mind, or awareness, is this way. Awareness is here, it is functioning, but if you try to find it, there is nothing you can pinpoint. Awareness is nothing in itself.

From a different point of view, this means that your awareness cannot be destroyed. It is indestructible because it's not a solid thing. It is always present, but it is unfindable at the same time. Understanding this deeply is what allows you to become free from fear and attachment. When you know that your awareness can never be destroyed, you see that there is no reason to feel insecure.

Of course, your body has no security. It is changing all the time, so it is impossible to secure the body. Really, there is no so-called security. Everything is changing in every second, so security is impossible. But in relation to your mind, there is nothing to be afraid of. Your mind can never be destroyed because it is not a thing. When we know this fully, we transcend our samsaric reactions and liberate ourselves.

Concerning the first way that people deviate from correctly understanding emptiness, Gampopa says:

> 1. It is a deviation to treat the ground of being as an object of knowledge. Someone might say, "All phenomena of the grasping mind and the grasped objects are primordially pure and primordially liberated. Right from the beginning, there is enlightenment. Right from the beginning, there is spontaneous presence. Through meditating, things do not get better, and by not meditating, things do not get worse. There is nothing positive or negative. Doing positive deeds does not help; doing negative deeds does not harm. Putting your hand into a black bag and putting your hand into a goat's intestines are equal." Speaking in this way is just mouthing empty words. This is how one strays from emptiness by turning it into an object of knowledge.

This first deviation is to make emptiness into something intellectual, something known through the conceptual mind. This leads to mistaking emptiness for nothingness, which is nihilism. A nihilist would say that there is no good or bad; ultimately there is nothing positive and nothing negative. Holding the view that there is nothing but emptiness can be dangerous, because it implies that negative actions do not cause harm. If someone thinks that it doesn't matter what they do, they are deviating into a wrong view.

The correct understanding of emptiness is interdependence. The more you understand the nature of emptiness, the more your confidence in karmic cause and effect grows. You become very clear about what to do and what not to do. This is because you understand interdependence; you see the effects of your body, speech, and mind on yourself and on others.

A correct understanding of emptiness does not make you irresponsible, but just the opposite—you become much more responsible. If your view of emptiness makes you feel that you can do whatever you want, and that your negative actions will not cause pain and problems for yourself or others, then your view has clearly deviated from the right understanding of emptiness. Therefore, holding on to an intellectual understanding of emptiness can have very negative consequences.

> 2. One deviates from emptiness by regarding it as an antidote. In general, our study, contemplation, and meditation are geared toward being antidotes to the kleshas. This applies to study and reflection, ranging from the *Karika*, which is the Vinaya text of a novice monk, up to the *Guhyasamaja Tantra*. This also applies to topics of meditation, ranging from death and impermanence up to the unborn nature, and to practices like keeping the precepts, accumulation, and purification.
>
> It is very important to cut the root of the kleshas. If you can cut the kleshas at their base, it is like cutting a tree at its root. If you are unable to do that, then when the five poisons or three poisons arise, you might make assertions, based on analysis, that since their nature is emptiness, they are not truly existent.[2] Although it might seem helpful to meditate on them as unestablished, this would neither lessen nor suppress them, much less cut them at the root. This is the deviation of using emptiness as an antidote to the kleshas.

Of course, every dharma practice is designed to be an antidote to the kleshas, or mind poisons. If our practice doesn't affect our emotions and habitual reactions, then it isn't working. Gampopa is emphasizing the need to get to the root of confusion. The more we understand the nature of the mind and the nature of all phenomena, the less we react with negative emotions. When we truly know the emptiness nature, we can allow our emotions to come and go. This transforms negativity at the root. The emotions are self-liberated by thoroughly understanding their nature.

Someone might think, "Focusing on emptiness will make everything all right. I am going to meditate on the emptiness of my problems so that they will go away." This approach simply won't work. Applying the concept of emptiness doesn't make anything disappear. In order for thoughts to self-liberate, we must directly know their nature. We train by first developing a correct overall understanding, and then we practice cutting the root of thoughts by directly experiencing their nature. Simply thinking, "This doesn't truly exist," won't help very much.

> 3. Another deviation is to superimpose emptiness onto phenomena. As an antidote to clinging to things or actions as having substance and characteristics, you might logically analyze them through reasoning such as "neither one nor many," to prove they are empty of existence. Or you might try purifying them with the *shunyata* or *svabhava* mantras.[3] Or you might try to establish them as non-existent by maintaining the nonconceptual supreme knowing of threefold purity. Initially focusing on something as substantial, and later imposing emptiness on top of it to make it non-existent in nature, is the deviation of superimposing emptiness on phenomena.

Another mistaken approach is to perceive something as real, and then superimpose the notion of emptiness on top of it. For instance, you might say, "This watch is emptiness," while still holding the idea that the watch is there. This is a misunderstanding of emptiness.

Sometimes we use analysis to understand that things are not truly existent. This lessens our clinging to some extent, but it is not the real experience of emptiness. Real experience happens when you are not grasping at all. You understand and relax without grasping. This applies to concepts, emotions, perceptions, or whatever. Direct experience without holding on to anything shows a real understanding of emptiness.

The word "emptiness" does not really count. Emptiness is not something in itself. Nor is it a matter of imputing "All this is emptiness." Rather, emptiness is a way of experiencing in which there is no grasping and no urge to grasp.

The points Gampopa is making about emptiness are subtle but very important. Buddhists talk a lot about emptiness, but this doesn't help much because it is just the conceptual aspect of ultimate reality. It seems to me that a lot of talk about emptiness is not useful, and at times it can even be misleading. There is nothing called "emptiness" that you could put on things to make them go away or make them okay. Rather than focusing on emptiness, it's more helpful to focus on interdependence.

There is no ultimate nature apart from the relative. It is very important to clearly understand how everything exists only in relationship. Seeing how the relative world works is seeing the emptiness nature.

When we talk about karma, it is the same thing—it is interdependence. If you understand how everything arises in dependence upon other things, then you understand karma. Since the way that you see people affects the way you feel about them, you realize that by changing the way you see, your feelings will also change, and liberation can take place.

> 4. Finally, there is the deviation of regarding emptiness as the path. In general, when the true nature, or Mahamudra, is realized, then all three—the cause, path, and result—are complete in this single nature. The true nature is not produced by the mind; it arises from within. In relation to this, *Chanting the Names of Manjushri* states:
>
> > *Buddhahood has no beginning or end.*
> > *The primordial buddha has no cause.*
> > *The stainless, single eye of wisdom,*
> > *The embodiment of wisdom is the Tathagata.*
>
> Without this understanding, you might think, "By using the meditation on emptiness as the path, I will gain the result—the signs and marks of an omniscient buddha, endowed with three kayas and five wisdoms." This is the deviation of regarding emptiness as the path.
>
> In general, it is very important not to make these mistakes.

The Mahamudra teachings discuss ground Mahamudra, path Mahamudra, and result Mahamudra. These are not three different things; they are the same. The experience of emptiness or the nature of the mind is the ground, it is the path, and it is also the result. Ground Mahamudra is the way things are. Realizing the nature of the ground is in itself the result.

You might misunderstand, thinking that the process of doing one practice after another is what will make you a buddha. However, it is not a matter of meditating on emptiness for a long time, and then the result appears. Nor do the enlightened qualities gradually manifest from meditating on emptiness. Instead, once you fully experience the nature of your mind, you *are* a buddha. Awareness of your true nature is the stainless, single eye of wisdom.

The distinction between being enlightened and not being enlightened is whether you experience your nature fully or not. In seeing your nature, there is nothing to see, because there is nothing there. This experience could be called emptiness, but it is not like designating or imputing something as being emptiness. Instead, it is being aware of your nature in the way we discussed in chapter 12 in the section on tamel gyi shepa, the ordinary mind of Mahamudra.

The experience of emptiness, the nature of the mind, and Mahamudra are all the same. If you try to find this experience, there is nothing to find. This means there is nothing that comes into being and nothing that could be destroyed. The subtle nature of the mind, the ordinary mind that we discussed earlier, is the Buddha. And the nature of buddhahood has no beginning and no end. It has no cause.

These four deviations connected with emptiness are subtle and not easy to grasp. I should add that these four are not the only ways that emptiness can be misunderstood. The Buddha taught eighteen types of emptiness, because there are at least eighteen ways of misunderstanding it.

I don't want to sound overly critical of gaining a conceptual understanding of emptiness. Using analysis and reasoning can lead to the understanding of emptiness. Applying reasoning through debate can be particularly useful, because in debate you develop the ability to think from different angles, and you are presented with another person's understanding, which the two of you analyze together. Buddhism offers many useful approaches. Having an intellectual understanding can give you a broader view and a more holistic sense of how the teachings fit together.

However, the bottom line is that emptiness is an experience and not a concept. A concept is like a map. You could have a map of Barcelona, and say, "This is Barcelona." But is it really Barcelona? No, it's only a map of Barcelona. The concept and the reality are quite different. Often we mix these up. Concepts are in the head, and experience is in the heart. That is why it is sometimes said that the longest journey we take is the journey from the head to the heart.

SIXTEEN

Illusory, Dreamlike Bodhichitta

> Jetsun Rinpoche said: In the system of the Mahayana, what-
> ever the level of practice—whether observing the precepts, ac-
> cumulating and purifying, or giving generously—the things
> themselves are not of primary importance. The most impor-
> tant factor is one's intention. In any sort of dharma activity, it
> is very important to start with a pure motivation. To give rise
> to a special motivation, one generates bodhichitta in an elabo-
> rate, medium, or brief way.

FROM THE MAHAYANA point of view, motivation is extremely important, since what is positive and what is negative is not always apparent on the surface. We could do seemingly positive deeds that are
actually negative; seemingly negative deeds that are actually positive;
seemingly positive deeds that are truly positive; and seemingly negative
deeds that are truly negative. These are the four possibilities.

We might look like we are doing something positive, and everybody
thinks that is what we are doing, but actually our action is not positive
because of our selfish motivation. Conversely, it can seem that someone
is doing something wrong, but if the reason behind the action is compassionate, then it is not a negative action. For instance, a particular
action may have been done to prevent much greater harm coming to a
large number of beings. In terms of the karmic consequences, the decisive factor in our actions is our intention.

Gampopa mentions observing the precepts. Generally speaking, the Vinaya precepts are vows to refrain from negative actions. There are five main precepts: to refrain from killing, stealing, lying, sexual misconduct, and intoxication. The Vinaya is action oriented. If you do not break the rules, then your conduct is faultless.

The Bodhisattvayana is much more concerned with the motivation behind the action. For example, a person might take monastic vows in order to have an easy life. Many of you don't realize how easy a monk's life can be. Most people's problems occur in personal relationships, right? This is what students tell me. But in Asia, if you are a monk, relationships are not an issue, and people give you food and a place to sleep, and you needn't work hard all day. It's a picnic! However, wanting everything to be made easy for you is not a positive motivation. Some people might even become monastics for negative reasons, which is worse. So, being positive or negative is not determined by what we seem to be doing but by the intention underlying it.

On the spiritual path, creating a higher motivation and correcting a lesser motivation are very important. In terms of doing formal Buddhist practice, the key factor is not which practices you do or how much practice you do: the key factor is having a positive intention. With a vast intention, even a small action can have a very positive effect. Basing our motivation on bodhichitta is especially important.

All of us have bodhichitta to some extent, since everyone wishes to be happy and free of suffering. In the West I have been told that there are people who hate themselves and have a death wish. I cannot agree with this. People don't wish for death; they wish for freedom. When someone is really suffering, they naturally want the situation to end. Things might seem so bad that they can't see any way out of their problems except to end their life. In this case, what people are calling a "death wish" is more a wish to be free of problems. I don't think people actually hate themselves; they just hate their problems.

Sometimes people get angry or upset with themselves, and think, "I'm not good enough. I should be different. I should be better than this!" If you get annoyed with yourself in this way, it is because of expecting too much from yourself. Although you might chide yourself in this way, it is not the same thing as hating yourself. It is simply expecting too much.

Everybody wants happiness, and everybody wants freedom from suffering. That is the primary motive for everything we do. On top of that, all of us have someone for whom we feel goodwill. For instance, if I were to say to you, "You can be free, but everybody else will have to suffer," would that make you happy? I doubt it. There are others, like your family and friends, whom you want to be happy. Happiness for oneself alone is not enough. Maybe we don't care whether everyone in the world is doing well, but surely there are some people we care about. This applies even to strangers: when we hear about people we don't know who are experiencing great difficulties, we wish their suffering would end. And this applies not only to humans but to animals; their suffering also touches our heart. Most people are like us in wishing other beings well, not only our near and dear ones.

There are many, many people in the world who are naturally caring and altruistic. Recently I heard about two men in Ireland who jumped into the sea to save a couple of young girls from drowning. These men had no previous connection with the girls, and in the act of saving the girls' lives, the men died. Lots of times people act instinctively, without thinking, in order to help others in distress. This willingness to jump in and help others, without thinking of one's own safety, is a trait of animals as well as human beings. We naturally have compassion; it is our nature to wish others well and want ourselves and others to be free from pain.

This brings up the question of what would be the best way to accomplish this. What should our priorities be? There are so many things that seem good and helpful, and we have to choose. We cannot do everything. If we try to do everything that looks interesting, we will not accomplish anything. We have to understand what activities contribute most substantially toward this goal.

Here, what Gampopa suggests is that we first transform ourselves through practicing the dharma, and especially by practicing meditation. After transforming our confusion and suffering, we will have the knowledge and ability to help others transform as well. This is not to say that practicing the dharma is the only thing we can do. There may be other things that would be important and useful, and we could do those things as well. Whatever it is we decide to do after we have established our priorities, we need to work on that.

> **The elaborate way of generating bodhichitta is to think: "I must take across the ocean of samsara all the limitless beings, who are like dreams or illusions. I am not going to take them to**

the shravaka enlightenment or the *pratyekabuddha* enlightenment of the Hinayana, but I will establish them in unsurpassable enlightenment. Therefore, I myself must attain complete,
perfect enlightenment. And to do that, I will perform various
types of meditation, practice, and dharma activity."

Here, we are thinking that we would like to benefit sentient beings,
not only a little, but so they will have the greatest possible joy and benefit. Once they are completely free of suffering, they will also be able to
benefit others greatly. The wish for the highest enlightenment is not just
for a few people but for all beings. No one should be left behind in samsara. In order to do this, we need to study, practice, and thoroughly train
our mind. With this elaborate style of motivation, we generate the intention to do whatever is necessary to establish all beings in enlightenment.

Then, there are shorter and shorter versions of the same aspiration:

The medium-length way of generating bodhichitta is to think:
"In order to bring to complete enlightenment all sentient beings, who are like illusions or dreams, I will do this and that."
The short way of generating bodhichitta is to think: "I will
perform this dharma activity to benefit all the illusory, dreamlike beings."

This way of generating bodhichitta emphasizes the illusory, dreamlike nature of beings. Whether we are talking about sentient beings,
ourselves, or dharma activities, none of them is beyond the nature of
emptiness. The more you understand emptiness, the easier it becomes
to help others, because you are less caught up in attachment and aversion. Also, you don't become overwhelmed and burdened by the inten-
sity of others' suffering. In this way of arousing bodhichitta, Gampopa
is emphasizing the dreamlike nature of beings.

Generally, in relation to whatever accumulations and purifications are done, in the beginning they are motivated by illusory
and dreamlike bodhichitta in its expanded, medium, or condensed form. In the main part, the dharma is practiced like an illusion or a dream. At the conclusion, the illusory and dreamlike
merit is dedicated for sentient beings. The dedicator (oneself), the

> object of dedication (sentient beings), and the positive effects
> of what is dedicated are all illusory and dreamlike, so they are
> inseparable from one's own mind. All of them are a magical
> display of the nature of the mind, nondual in essence.

When we talk about everything being illusory, when we say that nothing exists on its own, there is a danger of people becoming nihilistic and thinking that it doesn't matter how they act. This is a wrong view, because it does matter. What we do with our body, speech, and mind affects our experience, it affects our future, and it affects others. This is our karma: our actions have effects. Of course, the effects are also illusory, but still we experience them. We don't like suffering, even if it is illusory. As long as we don't like illusory suffering, we should not act in the ways that produce it. Instead we need to act in positive ways that bring happiness and well-being, even though these too are illusory.

People who truly understand emptiness become more careful; they become more mindful of their body, speech, and mind and how their actions affect others. Actions have subtle, far-reaching effects. It is because things are not fixed but illusion-like that karmic cause and effect operate. And yet, because of understanding the dreamlike nature of phenomena, you needn't take things too seriously. You become much more relaxed, especially about yourself.

Sentient beings are emptiness, but they don't understand that. Beings are actually enlightened, but they don't see that. Ultimately, they are beyond suffering, but until they realize it, they will suffer. With bodhichitta, we want them to get out of suffering, but this intention is also a dream. When we understand this, all our experience becomes a magical display.

Even though the world is a dream, it's important for us to work with relative reality. Experiencing the ultimate nature does not stop us from doing positive bodhisattva activities. Actually, knowing the ultimate nature makes us much more effective because we see the effects of our actions and reactions more clearly. Although we know that our actions are not ultimately real, our actions still have effects.

So, the ultimate and the relative—the nature of things and the way they manifest—do not go separate ways but always come together. They work together, and the more we understand the ultimate nature, the easier it is to apply our bodhichitta motivation in the relative world.

SEVENTEEN

Gampopa's Heart Advice
to Retreatants

> Jetsun Rinpoche said: All you great practitioners assembled
> here, if you want to do genuine practice, you must cut the ties
> to the concerns of this life, to the extent of giving up every-
> thing, even your body and life.

IN THIS SECTION of the text, Gampopa is giving advice specifically to
practitioners in retreat. Retreat is all about practice. If you truly want to
become enlightened in this life, you have to practice with your full attention. You need to be willing to give everything—all your time, all
your energy, and all your focus.

This applies not only to dharma practice but to other pursuits like
sports. People who are training for the Olympics don't do anything else;
they work on their sport all the time. It is the same here. If you really
want to be enlightened in this life, you can't be halfhearted, merely
doing a little here and a little there. You need to give everything you
have to it. Of course, the less worldly concerns you have, the better.
Once you are in retreat, you should not be concerned with food, clothing, and things like that. You need to be satisfied with very little.

> Reduce your food and clothing to the bare necessities, and
> then do the practice. In order to truly practice, you need to

remain in solitary retreat. The best practitioner goes to the glacier mountains like a lion. The medium practitioner goes to the forest like a tiger. The lesser practitioner goes to the rocky hills like a vulture. Do not skirt the edge of town like a fox ready to sneak into a charnel ground.

I heard a story about a lama who went to see the Sixteenth Karmapa, and told him, "I am trying to go crazy, but I am not able to do so." I think he meant that he didn't want to be worldly; he didn't want to be an ordinary person anymore. The Karmapa replied, "If you really want to be crazy, then go to Mount Kailash and stay there for eighteen years." The lama agreed and went straight to Mount Kailash, where he stayed in retreat for eighteen years.

When the lama returned to Tsurphu Monastery, he found a new Karmapa; the previous one had passed away. So, he reported on his retreat to the Seventeenth Karmapa. Years later, when the lama died, there were wonderful signs of realization.

This is what Gampopa is recommending: be free of hesitation, and be completely one-pointed in your practice.

At the same time, however, it is important not to overdo it. Do only what you are capable of doing. First, work on your motivation, and become very clear about what you want to do and what you are capable of doing. Then go ahead and do it. But be careful not to push yourself beyond your capacity. Train step-by-step. It is not a matter of merely having some understanding, and immediately going into retreat on Mount Kailash. That could be disastrous.

Generally, if you are too attached to food and clothes, you cannot stay in the mountains. It is important to be able to wear only one cotton cloth. Rely on just a small amount of food. No matter what purpose you wish to accomplish, whether it is great or small, when life goes well, that is okay, and when things go badly, that is okay. No matter what happens, this is the way to think.

In general, if you are going to practice the dharma, do not expect much from other people. Do not be hard to please or easily annoyed. It is better not to count the number of kind deeds you have done for others. I have not kept track of the kindness I have shown to people, although I do think I have been a great help to all of you.

This advice is not only for dharma practitioners or retreatants but for everyone. The more we expect, the harder we are to please. We get easily annoyed and depressed when things don't work out right. It's good to train in being satisfied with very little.

Gampopa's second point is also very important. It is better not to count the good deeds we have done for others, because the more we think about what we have done, the more we expect in return. People won't necessarily repay your kindness. Generally, the way you behave with others is the way they behave with you. But if you do some kind act with the expectation of getting something in return, it rarely comes back to the degree you wish it would, and this leaves you dissatisfied and unhappy. So, if you do something good, simply do it for the sake of helping someone. Don't expect anything in return. This is very important no matter where we are.

Generally, whether the students' behavior discredits the teacher, or the teacher's behavior discredits the students, it is all the same. I do not want to disgrace you. The best result would be for all my students to reach supreme enlightenment in this life. Next best would be for my students to become enlightened in the bardo, and at the least, they would be enlightened in a future life.

The way a teacher would discredit their students is by not practicing dharma properly or not teaching the dharma correctly. The way a student would discredit their teacher is by misbehaving. Both teacher and student have a responsibility to practice properly. Gampopa says that he is trying his best to help his students, but the students must also help themselves. Their degree of attainment will depend on their own practice.

The best result is to attain enlightenment in one lifetime. Attaining realization in this life can include attaining realization in the bardo. It is said to be easier to recognize the true nature when the clear light dawns right after death than it is to recognize the true nature while we are alive.

> I ask of you: please do not beat up on yourselves. If you show
> real kindness to yourself, then things will certainly turn out as
> I wish.

Here, the Tibetan literally says, "Don't hit yourself on the head." It
means to be kind to yourself; don't do things that will harm you. Think
of it this way: if you are not kind to yourself, will others be kind to you?
Try to do things that are good for yourself and good for others as well. If
this is really your intention, the best thing you can do is to transform
yourself, and the best way to do this is by practicing the dharma.

> In general, when you practice the dharma, do not be someone
> who just talks about practicing, or who practices only a little
> on the side. Do not look for easy dharma practices, or practice
> only once a year.

Next, Gampopa counsels us about merely pretending to be a practitioner. Literally, he says, "Don't practice dharma with your mouth." In
other words, don't be someone who talks about practice but doesn't actually do it. Don't say you are a practitioner when your interest is only
intellectual. Nor should you practice dharma as a sideline or a hobby,
like someone who practices a little when they have plenty of time. We
should not practice in the easiest way, or do only easy practices. And
even more extreme, we shouldn't practice only once a year.

> Even if you are known to others as a practitioner, and you
> think of yourself as a practitioner, there is the danger that you
> could die as an ordinary person. It is very important to medi-
> tate on the stages of the path of the three types of individuals,
> on death and impermanence, and on karmic cause and result.
> These meditations become the whip of diligence.[1]

This is implying that we could even practice the dharma secretly.
We don't need to make an announcement that we are Buddhist practitioners. Patrul Rinpoche said, "Dharma practice is not like a goldsmith
making ornaments." In other words, we don't need a lot of tools and
techniques to work with, and we don't need to make a display of our
practice. Dharma practice is simply our mind working on our mind.

What we need is clear awareness, along with some mindfulness, bodhichitta, renunciation, and understanding of how to work with the mind. A great deal of learning or scholarship is not necessary. It's more a matter of having a clear understanding of the direction we want to go, and being more mindful and aware. There is nothing about our practice that we need to display. We don't need to broadcast that we are working on ourselves. And yet the work definitely needs to be done. It's not a matter of talking about it, or getting interested in it, or knowing about it. Even if we know everything about the teachings, if we don't apply them to our mind, the teachings will not transform us.

For example, there was a student of the Buddha who listened to the Buddha for about twenty years. He knew all the Buddha's teachings and was so proud of his learning that he didn't practice. As a result, he didn't receive real benefit from being near the Buddha all that time.

Practicing the dharma means using whatever methods you know and integrating them with your mind. The technique you use need not be complicated or a particularly high teaching. Fully understanding one small point and using it on yourself could transform your life. Without a doubt, there is definitely a need for more practice.

> Generally, the way it works for those who have entered the dharma is that the best practitioners die smiling, full of joy and deep confidence. They are going from happiness to happiness.

One test of whether someone has practiced well is the way they handle their death. One of my favorite songs by Milarepa talks about his realization of the true nature of death. Milarepa sang: "I was afraid of death, and so I ran away to the mountains. I meditated on the uncertainty of death to the extent that I realized deathlessness. So now, even when the Lord of Death comes, I will have no fear."

There is so much uncertainty in our relationship to death. But the very notion of death is a misunderstanding. It's a mistake to think that we aren't changing now, but at the end of our life we will undergo a huge change. It is more that everything is constantly changing. Constant change is the nature of reality. This means, in a way, that there is nothing changing at all. There is nothing to die, there is nothing that could die, because death is happening all the time. This is what Milarepa called deathlessness. By realizing the significance of constant change, Milarepa was able to be completely at peace and completely fearless.

Gampopa says that the best practitioners die smiling, full of joy and confidence. I would add that even better than dying with joy and confidence is living with joy and confidence. Living with a smiling face is even better than dying with a smiling face.

> At death, medium-level practitioners are free of dread. Lower-level practitioners are free of regrets, without thinking, "I did this and I did that with my body, speech, and mind."

Medium-level practitioners have no fear at the time of death. Lower-level practitioners have no regrets because they know they did as much as they could with their body, speech, and mind.

These teachings are not only for dying well; they apply to living well. If you have one of these attitudes, then you are a good practitioner.

> Great meditators stay in solitary retreat because they have given up all their activities, they have given up all their distractions, and they want to do spiritual practice one-pointedly in seclusion. If you are involved in distracting activities, then it seems appropriate to stay in town and live in society. However, if you do go into retreat, do not create more distractions than in the city. Be diligent about your spiritual practice. Because dharma practice is a great, inexhaustible treasure, it is like a wish-fulfilling jewel. Since it is the accumulation of all your lifetimes, it is very important.

If you are living in retreat, then you need to practice one-pointedly. Don't create distractions for yourself. If you want to be distracted, it would be much better to live in the city.

> Once dharma practice is begun, it needs to be perfected through familiarization. The view needs to be applied in meditation. This will assure the welfare of others. Without doing it this way, acting for others' benefit can harm oneself and make it difficult to be of any help. Therefore, the preliminary step is

to accomplish your own purpose. After that, you can nurture
students. In order to accomplish your own purpose, it is very
important to remain in solitude.

The main purpose of dharma practice is to help yourself and then to
help others, not in a small way but in a big way. First you need to transform
yourself, and once you know how to do that, you are ready to help others.
You cannot save someone who is drowning if you don't know how to swim.
Once you are a strong swimmer, then you can save others. So, we need to
change ourselves first, because that is something we can do.

I heard a story about this in Scotland. A Christian priest in Edin-
burgh had some words like these written on his tombstone: "When I
was young, I wanted to change the world. I prayed to the Lord God,
'Please give me the wisdom and power to change the world.' I tried my
best, but as I got older, I realized that nothing changed. Then, I thought
that in order to change the world, I needed to change my near and dear
ones. If I could change them and make them an example, then maybe
the world would change. So, I prayed to the Lord God, 'Please give me
the wisdom and power to change my near and dear ones,' and I tried my
best. But as the years passed, I found that nothing had changed. When I
was very old, I realized that I needed to change myself first. If I changed,
if I was an example, then perhaps my near and dear ones would change.
And if they became an example, then the whole world might change. So
I prayed to the Lord God, 'Please give me the wisdom and the power to
change myself.' I started to do my best, but then it was too late."

Working on ourselves first doesn't mean we have forsaken others. We
are working on ourselves in order to help others. The more we know
how to help ourselves and free ourselves, the more we will be able to
help others.

If you are a good practitioner, one who knows how to practice and
really works at it, the best way to help others is to do your own practice,
do retreats, and work on yourself first. The better you practice in solitude, the more beneficial it is for others in the long run. But if you don't
know how to meditate and you don't practice well, then you won't transform in retreat. In that case, it would be better to do other projects outside of retreat to help others. But to reiterate, if you do practice well, the
best thing you can do to help others is to stay in retreat and practice.

In terms of being able to live in retreat, the Kadampas teach five points:
1. Have conduct that is free of hypocrisy.
2. Ensure that the antidotes hold up under various circumstances.
3. Gain mastery of the instructions.
4. Invigorate yourself through devotion.
5. Have the strength to overcome small problems.

The first point is being free of hypocrisy. Especially when you are on your own, like in solitary retreat, your conduct needs to be genuine and free from pretense. When you are with people, you might want to appear to be well, but when you are alone, you should be completely genuine.

Second, in terms of antidotes, whatever instructions or antidotes you apply need to be strong enough to withstand difficult conditions. You need confidence that the teachings and practices you are applying will hold up under various circumstances.

As for the third point, mastering the instructions, you must understand and know them very well.

In terms of the fourth point, your devotion needs to be stronger than your emotions. This is very important because emotions go up and down. If your devotion is not strong enough, your emotions can overpower you to such an extent that you feel unable to practice. Devotion, which includes aspiration, inspiration, and certainty, needs to be very strong.

The last point in this set of instructions is to have the strength to ward off small problems. You need enough determination and courage to deal with the problems that arise in retreat. Sometimes the problems are physical, sometimes they are environmental, and sometimes they are mental. Whatever comes up, you need to maintain your strength and keep going.

These five guidelines provide an important foundation for doing well in solitary retreat, and they are also good guidelines for practitioners not in retreat. Retreats are all about training, whether the retreat is short or long, in a group or alone. We train in retreat so we can practice these principles throughout our life. If you can learn these five things, then wherever you go later on—whether you are in a city working with people, or whatever the situation might be—you will be able to maintain your stability and clarity of mind.

> Similarly, our own enlightened teacher, Lord Gampopa, said
> there are four points involved with staying in retreat:
> 1. Have confidence in the instructions.
> 2. Have confidence in your own ability.
> 3. Have confidence in your experience.
> 4. Have confidence in the view.

Here, Gampopa mentions four things you need to have confidence in while you are in retreat: the instructions, your ability, your experience, and the view. These are things you would develop with the guidance of your teacher or spiritual friend. If you don't have confidence in these four aspects of practice, you shouldn't go practice alone in the wilderness, particularly in a place as challenging as Mount Kailash.

> To act according to these points, regard your teacher as a buddha. Supplicate the lama continuously and spend a long time
> in your teacher's presence. It is not right to snatch the teachings and then take off, like a chicken snatching a bite. On the
> other hand, do not get too familiar with the teacher. Do not get
> jaded with the instructions, and do not let your devotion get
> stale. These points are very important.

The more confidence you have in your teacher, the more confidence you will have in the teachings and your practice. The way that you see your teacher could be a way of gauging how much you have benefited from the teacher. It is not a matter of pretending or trying to see your teacher as a buddha, thinking, "My teacher is not a buddha, but I know that I am supposed to see my teacher as one." That just won't work!

Gampopa goes on to say that you need to spend time studying with your teacher, because this is how you learn. If you do not study and apply the teachings, there is no point in having a teacher. It is also important to know the right way to receive teachings. It is inappropriate to think, "I need that teaching, so I will go get it, and once I have it, I will leave." You can't just receive a teaching and think it's all finished. It is also a matter of learning from the teacher's inspiration and example. Hearing the words is only one part of learning from a teacher.

It can also happen that when you become very familiar with your teacher, you start to see the teacher's faults, and personal problems develop. This happens even more often in relation to the people surrounding a teacher. There is a Tibetan proverb that it is better to live at least three valleys away from your teacher. Becoming overly familiar becomes a problem, not necessarily with the teacher but mainly in dealing with the people very close to the teacher.

Another pitfall Gampopa points out is becoming jaded because we have already heard the teachings many times. This can lead to devotion getting stale. Sometimes people think, "I have heard those teachings before; in fact, I've heard them so many times that I don't need to hear them again." Even when students have the opportunity to be near the teacher, they sometimes become complacent and think, "I could go to those teachings, but right now I'm so busy. I'll get those teachings another time." It's good to maintain a certain degree of urgency about receiving teachings and to cultivate a strong interest in them.

For example, Patrul Rinpoche taught the *Bodhicharyavatara,* or the *Way of the Bodhisattva,* over one hundred times. One of his students, Khenpo Kunpal, said he received this teaching from Patrul Rinpoche fifty times. He listened to the same teaching from the same teacher fifty times! Later Khenpo Kunpal wrote a great commentary on the *Bodhicharyavatara* according to Patrul Rinpoche's way of teaching it. The Khenpo said that each time he heard Patrul Rinpoche teaching on this text, he learned more. He didn't have the attitude of "I already know that, and I'm finished with it."

> We need to think this way: "I have obtained a precious human body, entered the gateway of the precious teachings, received the precious dharma, met with a precious, genuine teacher, and been given precious instructions. I now have the freedom to practice. All these auspicious conditions have come together, so I must meditate." If you meditate at a time like this, it is impossible for the meditative state not to occur. If it does not occur, it is because you are not meditating.

Here is another important point. Most of the time, when our practice is not bearing fruit, it is because we don't know how to meditate. Learning how to meditate is a practical thing, and sometimes it can take a very long time to learn exactly how to do it.

> In order to please the teacher, the best type of service is to do the practice. The medium level is to give service through body and speech. The lowest service is to give material things. If the dharma is practiced genuinely, it will fulfill all aims—both your own and others. You will be happy in this life and in all your future lives. Other people will appreciate you. However, if you do not practice like this, then you will suffer. People will scorn you and put you down. It will result in your going to the lower realms.
>
> To practice the dharma in a heartfelt way, generate the power of devotion, respect, joyful effort, and the antidotes. Do not disgrace your lama and your dharma brothers and sisters. Do not be a cause for others to commit negative actions. At the very least, I ask each of you to refrain from a negative lifestyle.

If you wish to serve or make offerings to your lama, the best offering you can make is to practice the dharma. The most satisfying reward for genuine lamas is for their teachings to be practiced and yield results. When students are truly benefited by the lama's teachings, then the lama's work has been accomplished. So, the highest offering is to follow through and do your practice as instructed. The second best offering is to serve the teacher with your body and speech, and the third best is to make material offerings.

When you work on your dharma practice and get some results, you become happier and can deal with problems better. Your life becomes easier, and you are easier for others to live with. These results are directly correlated with the amount of practice you do. The more you do, the more you can benefit yourself and others. Your teacher will be happy as well. All your effort and the teacher's effort will not have been wasted. In this way, everyone's aims will be fulfilled.

EIGHTEEN

Ten Ways in Which Students Attend Their Lama

WE'VE REACHED the last chapter of this book, which is Gampopa's advice on ten ideal ways to attend your teacher. This is how Gampopa himself did it, and this is how Milarepa and Marpa did it. Their behavior was ideal; certainly, not all of us will be able to attend a teacher like they did.

The first condition necessary is to have a great and genuine teacher, and to know how extraordinary your lama is. Without this kind of teacher, this kind of devotion may not be possible. So, the first and most important thing is to have a genuinely realized teacher, and to have confidence in the lama's realization.

In accordance with the Kadampa tradition, Jetsun Rinpoche taught ten ways in which students should attend their lama.

In terms of the wording here, "attending" a lama has a similar sense as attending a conference or attending school. Saying "serve the lama" sounds a bit subservient, and "follow the lama" or "rely on the lama" each have certain associations that don't convey the right meaning. As we go through these ten points, you will see what Gampopa means by attending the lama.

1. Attend the spiritual master with devotion, without becoming tired and bored. In doing this, you should follow the example of the mahasiddhas.

This is similar to what I was saying about following the example of the lineage fathers like Marpa, Milarepa, and Gampopa.

2. Attend the teacher by offering material wealth without stinginess. This is similar to what is said in the scripture, the *Fifty Lamas:* "Give even the things which are not given, like your child, your wife, and your own life."

If your teacher is a genuine teacher, I doubt your teacher will ask for your spouse or children. The implication here is that you would be willing to give up even your greatest attachments. This level of non-attachment comes from a mind that is very devoted and a heart that is very open.

3. Have a flawless and noble intention when attending the teacher. The flaw would be the motivation of a shravaka or pratyekabuddha or any lesser motivation. Instead, the motivation should be completely pure and noble.

You should not have the motivation of an ordinary person, or that of a shravaka or pratyekabuddha. The best motivation is completely pure and full of goodwill toward everyone. In other words, you are motivated by bodhichitta, which is the desire to help all beings to enlightenment. Ideally, you would attend a teacher with a greater intention than just benefiting yourself alone.

4. Have undeluded wisdom when attending the spiritual friend. This means you should not be confused about the lama's instructions, including the logic involved.

Having wisdom refers to being able to receive the instructions, reflect on them, and understand the meaning as well as the words. We need the ability to use reasoning and ask for clarification.

Gampopa himself was a good example of this. Gampopa became Milarepa's best student, even though he stayed with Milarepa a relatively short time. Many of Milarepa's students spent much more time with him; some stayed all their lives. Later, people asked Milarepa why Gampopa was the best when others had been there much longer. Milarepa said that Gampopa knew how to ask questions and get clarification. He would apply logic and practice until he fully understood.

We should take the same approach. Instead of thinking, "The lama said such and such, and I should accept it without doubt," we need to ask questions and gain certainty through reasoning.

> 5. Attend the teacher by having respect and not being arrogant. This means seeing the lama as a doctor, yourself as a patient, and the dharma as medicine. Honor your lama just as patients honor their doctor.

Students need to have respect and not be arrogant when attending their teacher. The traditional analogy is to see the lama as a doctor, oneself as a patient, and the dharma as the medicine.

> 6. Attend the teacher with unhesitating service. This means trusting, without a doubt, in whatever the lama says.

We need to attend our teacher with respectful service and have confidence in whatever our lama says. However, this doesn't mean we should not ask questions, especially when we do not understand.

> 7. Attend the master truthfully, without deceit. Give up lies and deception and have heartfelt respect.
> 8. Attend the teacher by being flexible, rather than rigid and proud. Rather than being hard-edged, or conceited about your background, you need to be humble and peaceful. For example, if you were writing and the vajra master were to ask you to cut off the bottom of the letter *P*, then you would just do it.[1] You need to do whatever the lama says.

Students need to be flexible. It is a fault to be rigid or stubborn, or to be proud about your family background or social class. Be humble and easygoing, and do whatever the lama says. The example here—cutting off the bottom of a letter such that it becomes unrecognizable—is just an illustration of how far one would go to follow the lama's instructions. But again, I want to stress that this doesn't mean you don't ask questions.

> 9. Attend the spiritual friend with patience and without anger. This means you need to be like Lama Naropa undergoing his twelve trials.
> 10. Attend the teacher as an extraordinary form of the deity. At all times, see the lama as a buddha rather than as an ordinary person.

Students need to treat their teacher as a buddha instead of a regular person like themselves. A renowned example of this is the way Gampopa related to Milarepa. In the first chapter of this book, I told the story of Milarepa telling Gampopa that when Gampopa truly saw his guru as a buddha, then Gampopa would be ready to teach.

But actually, right from the beginning of their relationship, Gampopa more or less saw Milarepa as a buddha. Gampopa had complete trust in Milarepa; he was very inspired by his guru. The more teachings he received from Milarepa, the more certain he became that the teachings were true. Not only that, but because of the way Milarepa guided him through different experiences in meditation, Gampopa became convinced that Milarepa was as good a teacher as Buddha Shakyamuni himself. This is the kind of attitude that Gampopa is advising us to take.

> In order to attend a lama, it is important to have these qualities. It is inappropriate to simply do whatever you like.

The main point here is for us to trust our teacher. Trust is important. We can have a lot of problems if we don't have trust, although we can also have problems if we place our trust in an inappropriate person or situation. But I think more problems arise from our unwillingness to trust each other.

Often we are too scared to trust; we fear getting hurt if our trust is misplaced. We know from experience that when we trust someone and they let us down, we feel shocked and hurt. As a consequence, we might decide to never trust anyone again. But if we can't trust anyone, we are going to be very lonely. There is no way around it.

If there is even one person you can fully trust, then you feel much more stable and much more connected. You know that you have someone you can rely on. For instance, people can usually trust their family members. Or at least in previous times they could! But in general, people have become so fearful that everyone seems suspect and dangerous. It almost reaches the level of seeing others as potential enemies. It's important to have some trust, because we cannot live very well without it.

At the beginning of your relationship with a teacher, it is important to examine this person. This is probably the most important step for establishing trust. Observe the lama over time, and find out if the lama is trustworthy. If you determine that the teacher is reliable, then allow yourself to trust. As time goes on, the trust will develop further, and you will have someone you can depend on.

If you have more people you can trust, this is even better. Rather than carrying fearful scenarios in your imagination, your mind becomes more trusting. This brings confidence. The more confidence we have, the more clearly we know what's going on, and we can dare to be ourselves. When we dare to be what we really are, we are getting closer and closer to reality.

These were some teachings of the precious Lord Gampopa, which were put in writing by the monk Sherap Shönu. May this be virtuous!

We have reached the end of the text, with a very brief colophon written by Sherap Shönu, the monk who compiled this collection of Gampopa's teachings. He was probably a direct student of Gampopa, although that isn't certain. It's also possible that some of these teachings were added later by others.

Sherap Shönu ends with a short dedication and aspiration: "May this be virtuous!" This is a traditional way of ending a text, with the wish that it may be beneficial and auspicious. I will conclude my teachings here with the same intention. May this be virtuous!

Gampopa's Great Teachings to the Assembly

NAMO RATNA GURU[1]

[1. THE LINEAGE OF THESE TEACHINGS]

The lineage of these teachings stems from the sixth lord, great Vajra-dhara, the lineages of the four oral traditions, Jetsun Tilopa, Naropa, Maitripa, Tharlam,[2] Lord Marpa, and Jetsun Milarepa. This lineage was received by Dakpo Dao Shönu, or Gampopa, who was blessed by Milarepa. He attained supreme realization, and by giving these teachings, he sowed the seeds that covered the land of Tibet with realized beings.

Gampopa gave these teachings to the First Karmapa, Lord Dusum Khyenpa, and from him they went to Drogön Repa Chenpo; from him to Loppön Rinpoche Pomdrakpa, and from him to the Second Karmapa, Karma Pakshi. For these teachings, the river of empowerments has not diminished, the banner of maturing and liberating has not fallen down, the current of blessings has not been interrupted, and the plants of enlightenment have not dried up. These teachings have benefited beings impartially; they hold the royal seat of the Kagyu lineage.

In the past, the Buddha empowered the bodhisattva Dao Shönu for the benefit of beings, and he prophesied this bodhisattva's rebirth in Tibet, the Land of Snow. There, Gampopa became the spiritual friend known as Ratna Guru Punya Ratna, or Precious Lama Sönam Rinchen.

He took to heart, with faultless certainty, the instructions coming from glorious Atisha and the great guru Naropa, and he taught them to others. Some of his teachings have been written down here, in a systematic way, by the monk Sherap Shönu.

[2. UNDERSTANDING THE NEED FOR DEVOTION]

The guru, Lord Gampopa, said:[3] In general, in order to practice the dharma, we need devotion, diligence, and wisdom. Devotion is the basis, diligence is the path, and wisdom is the assistant. *The Precious Garland* states:

> *Because of having devotion, one diligently practices*
> *the dharma.*
> *Because of having wisdom, one knows reality.*
> *Wisdom is the foremost of these two,*
> *But devotion is the foundation.*

The *Sutra of the Ten Dharmas* states:

> *Positive qualities do not arise*
> *In people without devotion,*
> *Just like green plants*
> *Do not grow from burned seeds.*

The actual basis is explained in seven points: (1) the causes that give rise to devotion, (2) how to gauge that devotion has arisen, (3) the categories of devotion, (4) the nature of devotion, (5) an analogy for devotion, (6) the activity of devotion, and (7) the way to measure the stability of devotion.

The first point is the four causes that engender devotion.

a. When you read the sutras, devotion arises. It is recommended to initially make an offering and say a prayer, and then read the teachings.

b. Devotion also comes from spending time with friends who have devotion. It resembles the way you get blue color on you when working with blue dye, and red color on you when working with red dye. It is important to have devoted friends.

c. If you rely on a genuine spiritual teacher, that also produces devotion. A real spiritual teacher is someone who knows how to practice without going against any of the teachings. Devotion arises when you associate with someone like that.

d. If you meditate on death and impermanence, you will become devoted to practicing the dharma. You understand that the time of death is uncertain, death comes quickly, change happens rapidly, and there is no time to waste. Devotion arises from being completely certain about this.

The second main point is how to gauge that devotion has arisen. By understanding death and impermanence, you stop taking the world to be real. Through conviction in karmic cause and effect, you are careful regarding positive and negative actions, and diligent in practices of accumulation and purification. Clearly, there is nothing more important to do than practice the dharma, and nothing more important to think about than the teachings of the dharma.

Third, there are three categories of devotion: inspiration, certainty, and aspiration.

Inspiration within devotion comes from seeing true teachers and genuine lamas, and from hearing the teachings. Inspiration also arises from visiting sacred sites that affect you so much that tears fill your eyes and your hair stands on end.

Certainty within devotion arises when you have no doubt about any of the Buddha's teachings, whether detailed or condensed, and so you practice the dharma.

Because of the aspiration within devotion, you long to purify your obscurations quickly to gain the results of your practice. This applies to whatever practice you do, whether it is a little or a lot. You aspire to have the positive qualities and happiness of the higher realms and liberation.

Fourth, the essence of devotion is not mixed with a lack of devotion. It should not be like cold water that is liquid on the surface but frozen underneath, or a container that has flour on top but ashes below. Those with devotion act in wholly positive ways.

The fifth point is an analogy: devotion is like a water-purifying jewel. When this type of jewel is placed in dirty water, the water becomes clear. Similarly, devotion removes defilements so the mind becomes clear.

Sixth, the activity of devotion causes negative deeds to diminish, like the waning moon, and causes positive deeds to increase, like the waxing moon.

Seventh, for the way to measure the stability of devotion, it is said:

> One who does not abandon the genuine dharma
> Due to desire, hatred, fear, or ignorance,
> Is said to have devotion.

As it says, people with devotion do not abandon the dharma due to desire, do not abandon the dharma due to hatred, do not abandon the dharma due to fear, and do not abandon the dharma due to ignorance.

[3. THE MONK WHO QUESTIONED CHENREZIK]

The precious guru said:[4] There was once a novice monk in India who went to the master Dombipa, offered a mandala, and supplicated him. Acharya Dombipa asked him, "What do you want?"

The monk said, "I would like to receive instruction."

The master replied, "You and I do not have a karmic connection. Go to my student Atisha and request instruction from him. There is a karmic link between you two."

So, the novice monk went to Atisha and supplicated him. Atisha said, "What do you want?"

The monk replied, "Acharya Dombipa directed me to you. I am requesting instruction." Then, Atisha taught him a sadhana practice of Chenrezik.

The monk practiced until he achieved signs of accomplishment. He was able to see, touch, and hear Chenrezik, and he could ask him questions about anything. So, Atisha had the monk pose these questions:

1. What is the essence of all dharma practice?
2. What causes obstacles?
3. What should we emphasize in practice?
4. Among all the views, which view is the most important?
5. How many consciousnesses are there?
6. What causes the perfection of the accumulations?

Chenrezik replied:

1. The essence of all dharma practice is bodhichitta.
2. Obstacles are caused by ripening karmic effects. Even the tiniest ordinary action becomes a hindrance when it ripens.
3. The emphasis in practice should be on karmic cause and result.
4. Among all the views, the most important view is the right view.
5. As for the number of consciousnesses, you could say there are six or you could say there are eight. Or, if they are grouped together, you could say there is one. For example, consciousness is like a monkey inside a house with many windows.
6. The accumulations are perfected by the paramita of wisdom.

[4. THE FOUR DHARMAS OF GAMPOPA]

The precious guru said:[5] Whatever good dharma practice you do—whether study, reflection, listening, teaching, keeping the precepts, accumulation, purification, or meditation—should not become just another activity. Instead, dharma practice should be transformative. If you wonder what this means, a scripture says:

> *Attachment, anger, and delusion*
> *And the actions created by them are unvirtuous.*[6]

As well, even virtuous deeds are ordinary actions if they are done to obtain the happiness of gods and humans in this life, or if your intention is degraded or based on the eight worldly concerns.

So that our actions will not be like that, Rinpoche talked about the Four Dharmas: (1) what we call "the dharma" is practiced as the dharma, (2) the dharma becomes the path, (3) the path dispels delusion, and (4) delusion arises as wisdom.

1. In terms of the dharma being practiced as the dharma, there are two approaches: worldly dharma practice and transcendent dharma practice. In worldly dharma practice, you know about death and impermanence, and are certain about the workings of cause and effect. Fearing the suffering of the lower realms, you do all sorts of positive actions to avoid going there in future existences. You practice in order to obtain your own peace and happiness in future lives. For instance, you practice in order to have a good human body or a divine form in the higher

realms, the comforts of a god or a human, or the pleasures of a god. This is called worldly dharma practice.

In the second approach, transcendent dharma practice, you have understood the faults of all of cyclic existence, so you have no attachment whatsoever to the body and the enjoyments of a god or human. Revulsion and sadness arise because you know that samsara is like a pit of fire, a prison, a dungeon, darkness, or a filthy swamp. Being convinced that samsara is an ocean of suffering, you are not attached to any of its joys or qualities, and think, "I want to be quickly liberated from samsara."

While desiring liberation, you also see the shortcomings of the lesser vehicle and the enlightenment of the shravakas. They do all their dharma practice and pass beyond suffering into peace and bliss for themselves alone. Seeing the faults of that approach, you direct your positive accumulation and purification practices toward complete enlightenment. Having the goal of complete enlightenment sums up transcendent dharma practice, the second aspect of dharma being practiced as the dharma.

2. The dharma that becomes the path also has two aspects: the dharma that is the basis of the path, and the dharma that is the actual path. First, in relation to the basis of the path, because of seeing the shortcomings of the lesser vehicle, you do all your practice with the motivation of love, compassion, and bodhichitta. This pertains to whatever you do in terms of accumulation and purification, whether it is a little or a lot. In order to establish all the limitless sentient beings in perfect enlightenment, you think, "I want to attain the three kayas, the five wisdoms, and the omniscience of a buddha." This is dharma as the basis of the path.

In practicing the dharma that is the actual path, you recollect that the relative truth is like an illusion or a dream. You do all your dharma practice, whether it is a little or a lot, with love, compassion, and bodhichitta, and at the same time, you see it as illusory and dreamlike. Since your practice has both skillful means and wisdom, and they are inseparable, your dharma practice is the actual path.

3. The way that the path dispels delusion has two aspects. The first type of delusion is grasping at existence and non-existence, or eternalism and nihilism. This is dispelled by practice in which they are seen as a dream or an illusion. The second delusion is acting for one's welfare

alone and having a Hinayana approach. This is dispelled by meditating on love, compassion, and bodhichitta.

4. Delusion arises as primordial wisdom in two ways, in accordance with the Sutrayana system of the *Prajnaparamita,* and in accordance with the Vajrayana system of the secret mantra. According to the *Prajnaparamita Sutra,* the consciousness that eliminates delusion is part of the relative truth. This makes consciousness itself like an illusion or a dream. The perceiving mind and its perceived objects have never been divided, and their nondual nature is inherently pure. Ultimately, there is no perceiving and nothing to be perceived. When you realize that the grasping and the grasped are completely at peace, beyond any conceptual fabrications, then delusion arises as primordial wisdom.

The way delusion arises as primordial wisdom according to the Vajrayana is like this: all delusion and nondelusion are inseparable from your mind. Not being separate, they are the nature of the mind, the essence of the mind, and the magical display of the mind. In itself, deluded consciousness is nonconceptual clarity. Clarity-emptiness cannot be pinpointed. Clarity-emptiness is uninterrupted. Clarity-emptiness is without a center or boundary. Awareness is baseless and naked.

We need to realize directly and vividly that this is the dharmakaya. The coemergent nature of the mind is the essence of the dharmakaya. The coemergent appearances are the radiance of the dharmakaya. All objects perceived externally as apparent existence, all aspects of samsara and nirvana, are indivisible from the nature of the mind. They are nondual equality and simplicity, which arise as great bliss. To condense this into one point: delusion is unawareness, and once awareness has arisen as wisdom, then delusion arises as wisdom.

[5. THE APPLICATION OF COEMERGENCE]

Lama Rinpoche said:[7] Here are the lama's instructions for applying coemergence in your practice.[8] Coemergence needs to be carried onto the path with two armors: the outer armor of the view and the inner armor of wisdom.

Wearing the outer armor of the view means that you do not commit any negative actions, even to save your life. You constantly act in positive ways.

Wearing the inner armor of wisdom has two aspects: the outer aspect is that you do not reject the sickness in your body, and the inner aspect is that you do not reject the thoughts and emotions in your mind.

In terms of not rejecting the sickness and pain that arise outwardly, there are three approaches: thinking that it could be much worse, getting to the root of it through investigation, and carrying it onto the path.

As for the first way of not rejecting sickness, previously you did not consider your pain to be a small problem, but after you imagine how much worse it could be, you feel better.

The second way gets to the root of the pain by looking for it. To start with, where did it come from? Where does it abide? Where does it go? You find that it does not come from anywhere, it does not abide in any place, and there is no place where it goes. When you see this very clearly, your thoughts subside.

To carry sickness onto the path, see that all good feelings and all bad feelings are inseparable. It is the mind that feels sick, and it is the mind that holds on to the idea of being sick. Seeing this, you think, "I will use this sickness to accomplish something beneficial."

In terms of not rejecting the thoughts and emotions that arise inwardly, you could view your thoughts with gratitude. It would be impossible not to have thoughts. Thoughts, emotions, perceptions, and sensations are quite necessary.[9] Thoughts and emotions are beautiful! It is natural for thoughts to arise. Thoughts are our friends; thoughts are the path; thoughts are fuel for the fire of wisdom.

To start with, do not deliberately focus on thoughts or cultivate them. As your practice progresses, do not let any states of mind linger. Finally, do not hold on to them.

First, in order to not deliberately focus on thoughts or cultivate them, come to the conclusion that whatever occurs in your mind is a thought. View thoughts and emotions as the mind, and view the mind as the unborn dharmakaya. For beginners, it is necessary to use positive thoughts to clear away negative thoughts. However, a meditator is just as constricted by good thoughts as by bad thoughts. It is similar to the sun being just as obscured by white clouds as by black clouds, or a person being just as restricted by gold chains as by iron chains. Here, negative thoughts and emotions are seen to be the mind, and positive thoughts and emotions are seen to be the mind. The mind itself is seen as the unborn dharmakaya. This seeing is called the emptiness of cutting through.

At the intermediate level, the practice is to not abide in mental states. Having cut through all positive thoughts as just described, if your mind becomes fatigued and then becomes peaceful, do not dwell in that peaceful feeling. If an experience of nonthought happens, do not abide in that. If there is a perception of emptiness, do not allow that to remain. Cut through these experiences as mental states. See the mental states as primordial wisdom. See the mind as the unborn dharmakaya.

As for not clinging at the end, having cut through all mental states, do not hold on to the cutting, either. Do not cling to it as the path, do not cling to it as the result, and do not cling to it as the view, meditation, or conduct.

In terms of how various states of mind are mingled with emptiness, there are three analogies: dissolving upon contact, going back, and fire and snakes. First, the analogy for dissolving upon contact is like meeting someone you knew before. As soon as thoughts and emotions arise, you recognize them as the dharmakaya.

The analogy for going back is like meeting someone you had not known before, or like snow falling on a lake. The snow does not dissolve instantly, but it dissolves in a moment. In the same way, you may not immediately recognize the nature of the thoughts, but then understanding dawns because of having previously seen and contemplated this.

The third analogy is fire and snakes. When a fire is small, the wind can extinguish it. But when a fire is big, wind helps the fire to spread. So, when serious accusations are made against you, or you get leprosy, or any terrible situation occurs, and you meditate, you cut through them as mental states. Mental states are decisively seen to be the mind, and the mind is seen and meditated upon as the unborn dharmakaya.

There are four remaining points about applying coemergence in your practice: (1) being able to reconstitute your understanding, (2) being able to transform adverse conditions, (3) being undeluded, and (4) using wisdom to open the door of the dharma.

First, for the ability to reconstitute your understanding, by knowing that one thought or emotion is the dharmakaya, you know that all thoughts and emotions are the dharmakaya. For example, when you drink the water in one area of the ocean, you know the taste of the whole ocean. Similarly, when you see that one straw is hollow inside, then you know that all straws are hollow inside. When you see the way the roots grow on one tsarbu plant, then you understand how the roots grow on all tsarbu plants.

Second, the ability to transform adverse conditions means that by training your mind, all negative conditions become supports for your realization. This is like the wind helping the fire in the previous analogy.

Third, in terms of being undeluded, previously there was delusion because the nature of the thoughts and emotions was not recognized. But when you cut to the root of the various states of mind, you recognize them as the dharmakaya, so there is no cause for delusion.

Fourth, for opening the door through wisdom, the analogy is twirling a spear in the sky. This is the realization that everything is in the state of equality.

[6. THE NATURE OF THE MIND]

The lama Jetsun Rinpoche said:[10] According to the approach of the paramitas, you start by cutting through objects perceived externally. The analogy is a fire made by vigorously rubbing together a horizontal stick and a vertical stick. That fire can burn the whole forest, so that not even ashes remain. Likewise, one can use reasoning, such as "neither one nor many," to investigate phenomena and reach a definite conclusion about them. When one cuts through objects perceived externally, then the mind that perceives them is naturally loosened as well.

In the Mahamudra approach, when one cuts through the perceiving mind, then the perceived objects are naturally loosened. In relation to cutting through the perceiving mind, Rinpoche taught three aspects: the mind's characteristics, essence, and nature.

The mind has two characteristics: it appears as various colorful, outer forms, and it emits various positive and negative mental states. In other words, there is the mind's essence and its two characteristics. These are equivalent to the mind itself and what arises from the mind. In the sky there are various colorful appearances, like thick and thin clouds, which arise from the sky and dissolve back into the sky. In the same way, the radiation of various thoughts and emotions, as well as the appearances of various sense objects—like form, sound, smell, taste, and touch—come from the mind. In this way, appearances are the characteristics of the mind.

What is meant by the "essence of the mind" is your own awareness, that which you think of as "I" or "me." The essence of the mind is clarity-emptiness. It cannot be pinpointed, yet it never ends. Awareness is baseless, fresh, naked, and spontaneous.

What is the essence of the mind like? It is not existent, and yet it is not non-existent. It is neither eternal nor nothing. Free of the two extremes, it is not found in the middle, either. In relation to cutting it, it cannot be cut. In terms of destroying it, it cannot be destroyed. The essence cannot be changed. As for stopping it, it cannot be stopped. At all times, it is free of coming and going.

Since the essence is unbroken throughout the past, present, and future, it cannot be cut. It is uncompounded. It is primordially and spontaneously present, so it cannot be destroyed. It is devoid of form or color. It is not a substance or a thing, which is why it is unstoppable. When you understand what this means, it is called the essence. It is called great bliss. It is called coemergent wisdom. It is called nonduality.

You need to understand that the essence of the mind and its radiance as various thoughts and emotions are not two different things. When you understand that the essence and characteristics of the mind are naturally inseparable, this is called the nature. When you realize what this means, it is the heart essence of all the buddhas of the three times. This nature is present within all beings. A sutra states:

> *The buddha nature pervades all beings.*
> *There is not even one sentient being who is unsuitable.*
> *Generate bodhichitta to the greatest possible extent,*
> *Since all beings have the cause of buddhahood.*[11]

To understand what this means, practice with diligence and devotion, free from distraction. When practicing meditation with characteristics, do not practice formless meditation, and conversely, when doing formless practice, do not have any reference points. It is said that one should tie the elephant of the mind to the pillar of the meditation object with the rope of mindfulness, and then practice with alertness. No matter what type of practice you are doing, try not to get distracted. Whatever the type of practice, apply whichever of the lama's instructions are appropriate at that time. The meditation will never happen if your mind is moving all over, up and down. Understand this to be an obstacle.

[7. THE MEANING OF MAHAMUDRA]

Lama Rinpoche said:[12] For a person to become enlightened in one lifetime, it is important to meditate on Mahamudra. Mahamudra is the nondual wisdom mind of all the buddhas of the three times. If you wonder where to look for it, look at your mind.

Mahamudra is translated as *chagya chenpo* in Tibetan, and it can be understood through the meaning of the Tibetan word. The master Nagarjuna explained the first syllable, *chag*, in this way:[13]

> *Like putting water into water,*
> *Like putting butter into butter,*
> *Chag is one's primordial wisdom*
> *Fully seeing itself.*

The second syllable, *gya* or "seal," has three aspects: the seal of the nature, the seal of experience, and the seal of realization. For the seal of the nature, it is said: "The buddha nature completely pervades all beings."

The seal of the nature refers to the mind's natural state. There are no beings without this nature, even the beings in the lowest hell and the tiniest microbes. The *Hevajra Tantra* states: "Intestinal bacteria, and so on, possess this essential nature."

One might ask, is it sufficient simply to have this nature? No, it is not enough. You also need the experience that comes from meditative wisdom. This is the direct experience of the nature of the mind, the clear light beyond arising and ceasing.

The mind has two characteristics: its radiance as various thoughts and emotions, and its appearance as various colorful, outer objects. These characteristics are not separable from the essence of the mind; they are the magical display of the mind. To condense this into one point: the coemergent mind itself is the dharmakaya, and the coemergent appearances are the radiance of the dharmakaya. All possible appearances of samsara and nirvana, without exception, are completely pure in their essential nature. They are completely accomplished, and free from arising, dwelling, and ceasing. They are beyond any words, thoughts, or concepts. This describes the seal of experience.

Third, for the seal of realization, the reality just described is not produced from causes and conditions. It is not established as a thing or a substance. It is without color or form. It is beyond any kind of assertion or negation, such as being existent or non-existent. It is uncompounded and spontaneously present. To realize this very nature is the seal of realization.

There is nothing superior to this, there is nothing higher, so it is called *chenpo*, which means "great."

In the instructions for realizing chagya chenpo, or Mahamudra, there are four wisdoms that arise in postmeditation.

1. There is greater compassion for sentient beings.
2. There is greater devotion for the lama and the three jewels.
3. One is more careful about karmic cause and effect.
4. All attachment to this life fades away.

[8. SIX POINTS CONCERNING THE CREATION STAGE PRACTICE]

Lama Rinpoche said:[14] In order to bring your practice into experience, keep in mind impermanence and death. Be mindful of karmic cause and effect. Keep in mind the shortcomings of samsara. Remember the shortcomings of the Hinayana, and go beyond that by cultivating love, compassion, and bodhichitta. With that as a basis, the two methods of the creation stage and completion stage practice are the entranceway to the extraordinary great vehicle, the Vajrayana. It is said:

> *For those who are steadfast in the creation stage*
> *And want to undertake the completion stage,*
> *These skillful means, which proceed step-by-step,*
> *Were taught by the perfect buddha.*
> *The meditative equipoise of the two stages*
> *Is the dharma taught by Vajradhara.*

The creation stage practice can be explained in six points: (1) the types, (2) the essence, (3) the definition, (4) the purpose, (5) the measure of stability, and (6) the result.

First, there are three types of creation stage practice: (a) the visualization is created in many steps, according to the particular sadhana, (b) the visualization is created in three steps, or (c) the visualization is created by instantly recollecting the entire form.

Second, the essence of creation stage practice is the transformation of your ordinary thoughts and emotions into the clear appearance of the deity.

Third, there are three parts to the definition of the creation stage: (a) the mind generates the body of the deity, (b) the body and mind clearly appear as the deity, and (c) the deity is known to be a mental imputation.

a. In terms of the mind generating the body of the deity, instead of conceiving of your body as an ordinary, material body of flesh and blood, it clearly appears as the form of the deity.

b. In terms of seeing your body and mind as the deity, you understand that the form of the deity is a display of the mind, like magic or a rainbow.

c. In terms of the deity being an imputation of the mind, the form of the deity is like a magical illusion. You understand that it has no basis. It is merely a name, merely a sign, merely an imputation, merely a designation.

Fourth, as for the purpose of the creation stage practice, it has an overall purpose and specific purposes. The overall purpose is, at best, to attain the realization of nonduality. At a medium or lower level, the overall purpose of the creation stage is to become free of ordinary attachments.

The creation stage practice has twelve special purposes. These are connected with the samayasattva, the jnanasattva, blessings, and empowerment.

First, there are three reasons for generating the samayasattva: (a) your ordinary delusions disappear, (b) you understand that you and your special deity are inseparable, and (c) generating the samayasattva protects your samaya as a vidyadhara.

Second, the jnanasattva fulfills three purposes: (a) you understand that you and your special deity are inseparable, (b) because of recognizing that inseparability, you are blessed by the deity, and (c) it is used to quickly attain the supreme and ordinary siddhis.

Third, blessing the body, speech, and mind fulfills three purposes: (a) blessings transform your ordinary body, speech, and mind into the pure body, speech, and mind of a tathagata; (b) blessings are an excellent protection against harm from human and nonhuman beings; and (c) through blessings, you completely accomplish the kaya of the deity.

Fourth, three purposes are fulfilled by receiving empowerment: (a) it distinguishes the Vajrayana from the Paramitayana, (b) through empowerment, all the emotional obscurations are purified, and (c) through empowerment, you completely accomplish the kaya of the deity.

Fifth, the measure of stability of the creation stage practice has three indications from the practitioner's perspective and three indications from others' perspectives. From your own side: (a) the lowest level of stability is reached when you see yourself as the deity while you are walking, sitting, or sleeping; (b) the medium level is when you see the outer world as a palace, and all sentient beings as yidam deities; and (c) in addition to that, when you see all the deities as a dream, magic, or the moon in water, this is the highest level of stability.

For the measure of stability from the point of view of others: (a) when you are liberated and others see you as the deity, this is the highest level of stability, (b) the medium level is when you appear as the deity all the time, and (c) the lowest level is when the hungry ghosts see you as the deity.

The sixth point about the creation stage practice is the result, which has two aspects, temporary and ultimate. The ultimate result is the arising of the two form kayas. The temporary result has three levels: (a) at best, in this very life, you see the truth, (b) at the medium level, in your next life you become a chakravartin king, and (c) at the lowest level, you obtain a good rebirth as a human or a god.

This concludes the teaching of six points on the creation stage practice.

[9. STABILIZING RECOGNITION OF THE NATURE OF THE MIND]

> *Take advantage of this human boat;*
> *Free yourself from sorrow's mighty stream!*
> *This vessel will be later hard to find.*
> *The time that you have now, you fool, is not for sleep!*[15]

At this time we have attained the precious human body. We have entered the door of the precious teachings. We have heard the precious dharma. We have met the precious, genuine teacher. This is the time to practice the instructions, which takes diligence. It is said: "After stabilizing the root, which is devotion, you should stabilize bodhichitta."

First, for the general path to arise in your being, it is very important to stabilize devotion as the foundation. Then, to firmly maintain bodhichitta, you need to recognize the nature of your mind, because this is the heart essence of the entire dharma.

In terms of understanding this, outwardly there are perceived objects, and inwardly there is the perceiving mind. The internal mind arises as the mind and mental objects. These are said to be the mind's essence and characteristics. "Outer objects" refer to everything outside the mind, including one's own body.

To begin with, the nature of the mind needs to be recognized. In the middle, it needs to become familiar. At the end, there needs to be oneness.

To explain these, first, recognition has three aspects. (1) The essence of the mind is recognized, directly and experientially, as coemergent wisdom; it is clarity-emptiness, which cannot be pinpointed. (2) There is recognition that the radiation of various thoughts and emotions is inseparable from the essence. (3) Then, there is knowing that the various colorful, outer objects are inseparable from the mind. All three of these factors are inseparable.

At the intermediate stage, there is familiarity. This happens by practicing properly and diligently in a solitary place or a charnel ground. Familiarity arises in three stages: (1) meditation and postmeditation are different, (2) meditation and postmeditation are comparable, and (3) meditation and postmeditation are inseparable.

1. Meditation and postmeditation are different when the recognition of the nature is there during meditation, and it is not there outside of meditation. At this stage, the inner thoughts and emotions do not harm you, yet you cannot eliminate them. Therefore, stay in solitude and continuously pray to your lama. Along with having unfailing devotion, it is very important to rest the mind one-pointedly in evenness.

2. Meditation and postmeditation are comparable when the nature is present while meditating, and after meditating, it is unharmed by the four daily activities of sitting, standing, moving, and lying down. You

become decisive that all the radiant thoughts and emotions are inseparable from the nature of the mind. However, sometimes you perceive
outer colorful appearances as illusory and empty, and at other times
you perceive them as real and definite things. At this stage, some meditators get a strong urge and think, "It would be better for me to travel
than to stay here." However, it is very important to remain alone in a
solitary place.

3. In the final stage, meditation and postmeditation are inseparable.
Coemergent appearances are the radiance of the dharmakaya. The coemergent nature of the mind is the dharmakaya. Outer objects and all
phenomena of samsara and nirvana are realized as the great bliss of
nonconceptual equality. There is no difference between meditating and
not meditating. No matter which of the four daily activities you engage
in, you never waver from resting in evenness. All the time, your practice
is like the continuous flow of a river. There is no need to be mindful and
concentrate, or to think and investigate. The nature is simply there all
the time. At this point, it makes no difference whether you travel or remain in one place. Since practice is what meditators do, it is more appropriate to stay than to go. It is said that in general, there are two types
of meditators—one type wears out their shoes, and the other type wears
out their seats. Among these two, the one who stays put is more joyful.

For example, Lama Milarepa stayed in the mountains for forty-two
years. He lived until the age of eighty-four, going from mountain to
mountain. He simply transferred his meditation place from one mountain to another. Our precious teacher Gampopa once asked Milarepa,
"Lama, why do you stay in the mountains all the time?" Milarepa replied,
"For me, there is no difference between staying in solitude and staying in
a marketplace. However, at this time, in this body, I have taken all beings
into my heart, and I am trying to liberate them from samsara. Living in
town is not the real way of a meditator."

Our precious teacher Gampopa acted in the very same way. We need
to practice and train as he did. Let us all be very clear about this.

[10. THE QUALITIES OF A GENUINE TEACHER]

Lama Rinpoche said:[16] After people have begun to experience the general path, if they want to enter the uncommon path of the Vajrayana, it

is very important to attend a genuine Mahayana teacher. A genuine teacher has the following characteristics: (1) a lineage that is connected to the lineage, (2) a lineage that is connected to living words, (3) words that are connected to an authentic transmission, and (4) an authentic transmission that is connected to blessings.

1. A lineage that is connected to the lineage means that the lineage of realized beings has remained unbroken since the time of the perfect Buddha. It must not be a lineage of beings who have transgressed samaya or violated the precepts.

2. A lineage that is connected to living words means that the oral lineage is transmitted from mouth to mouth, from ear to ear, and from mind to mind. It should not be a lineage of black ink on paper, or moldy old books.

3. A lineage that is connected to an authentic transmission means that the lamas have definitely realized the meaning of the teachings and mastered them.

4. An authentic transmission connected to blessings means that since the lineage is unbroken, it contains the blessings that generate virtue in the minds of others.

For these reasons, seek out a lama with these qualities.

In other words, a Mahayana spiritual friend possesses either the eye of dharma or the eye of wisdom. Or the qualified teacher is described in three ways: (1) through great wisdom, the teacher has the ability to lead others on the path, (2) through great compassion, no sentient beings are left behind, and (3) the teacher has not even a hundredth of a hair tip of attachment to the concerns of this life.

Or the lama can be said to have four characteristics: (1) genuine devotion to the three jewels, (2) genuine compassion for sentient beings, (3) genuine realization of the profound meaning, and (4) motivation to teach the dharma with no consideration of personal gain.

We need to attend a lama who has these qualities. A lama who acts like a fox or a monkey is useless as an escort from samsara to nirvana.

[11. HOW TO ACTUALIZE THE VIEW, MEDITATION, ACTION, AND RESULT]

Jetsun Rinpoche said:[17] For a good practitioner who has cut attachment to worldly concerns: (1) the view is connected with realization, (2) the meditation is connected with experience, (3) the action is connected with the time, and (4) the result is connected with benefiting others.

1. The view has two main aspects: the coemergent nature of the mind is the dharmakaya, and the coemergent appearances are the radiance of the dharmakaya. The coemergent nature of the mind, which is the dharmakaya, is present in the mind stream of every sentient being. The coemergent appearances manifest as various thoughts and emotions, and appear as colorful objects. These two aspects—the coemergent appearances that are the radiance of the dharmakaya, and the coemergent mind itself, which is the dharmakaya—are inseparable and completely pure in nature. They are perfect, beyond words or expressions. They are primordially and naturally spontaneous. They are uncompounded—not created by causes or conditions. The basic space of phenomena and primordial wisdom are inseparable. This is the fundamental way of abiding. It is not something that ancient buddhas created, or that clever sentient beings fabricated. This way of being is called the view.

This is something that must be realized. If it is not realized, then it does not help. Lama Rinpoche said: The view that has not been realized is called free of extremes, but this is still a mental construct.

What is to be realized is that the coemergent nature of the mind is the dharmakaya, and the coemergent appearances are the radiance of the dharmakaya. All appearances of samsara and nirvana, without exception, arise as the great bliss of equanimity. This realization is not the wisdom of understanding that comes through study and reflection, but it comes from deep within, through a great deal of meditation. If you have this realization, then the view is connected with realization.

2. In terms of the meditation being connected with experience, what do you experience? You experience realization. Realization is the meaning of experience.

However, there are incidental experiences that are not connected to real meditation. These include coincidences between the inner channels and the wind energy; different appearances seen by the eyes; different sounds heard by the ears; experiences of bliss, clarity, and nonthought while doing shamatha; there being no object to perceive or not experiencing perception; and the feeling of being completely immersed in emptiness, like a completely clear sky. Although these incidental experiences are there for a while, later they are gone. It is taught in the *Lamdre*, or Path with Its Result, that these are circumstantial experiences.

Well then, what experiences are connected with real meditation? These are having a personal experience of the essence, a personal experience of coemergence, a personal experience of the natural state, and a personal experience of Mahamudra. All these refer to knowing the nature of your mind. What is this nature like? The nature of the mind is not something existent, because not even a hundredth of a hair tip can be found. Yet it is not non-existent, because it is experienced and realized. The nature of the mind is clarity-emptiness, which cannot be pinpointed. Clarity-emptiness cannot help but arise and is never interrupted. When this has become apparent, then the meditation is connected with experience. This is also called experience and realization occurring simultaneously.

3. Next, the activity connected with the time has four levels: (a) a beginner acts like a young monarch, (b) a yogic practitioner acts according to the secret Mantrayana, (c) an accomplished master, or siddha, acts according to crazy wisdom, and (d) a wisdom holder acts according to great equanimity.

a. The activity of a young monarch entails observing and not transgressing whatever precepts one has taken, such as the pratimoksha or upasaka vows. One also maintains one's commitment to the bodhisattva training in aspiration and application bodhichitta, and to the samayas of a vidyadhara. The hundred thousand samayas can be condensed into fourteen root downfalls and their branches. One begins by studying and understanding the various vows, and continues to guard them from degenerating. Finally, if a vow is violated, one makes the effort to repair it, purify it, and uphold it.

b. A yogic practitioner of the secret Vajrayana acts according to the path of transformation. This entails practicing in retreat in an isolated place, like a charnel ground. In this kind of practice, the body is transformed into the meditation deity, the speech is transformed into mantra, and the mind is transformed into the true nature. The *Mahamaya Tantra* states:

> *Mantras, forms, and the absolute nature*
> *Are the three yogas.*
> *By means of these three yogas,*
> *One does not become stained by the faults of samsara.*

Transforming one's body into the deity refers to meditating on the stages of generating the illusory body, the form of the deity. Transforming speech into mantra means, at the highest level, to meditate on the wisdom wind of chandali, or Inner Heat. The medium level is to count the ordinary breathing pattern of exhalation, inhalation, and retention. The lowest level is to recite the mantra of the deity. Transforming your mind into the absolute nature means that you engage instantaneously in formless meditation, such as Mahamudra, and practice the various special skillful means of the Vajrayana.

In terms of the secret mantra, what does "secret" mean? It is said that you keep the deity secret, you keep the lama secret, you keep the teachings secret, and you practice by keeping your body, speech, and mind in secrecy.

c. An accomplished master acts in accordance with crazy wisdom. In relation to the yogic activity described above, the siddha's body has been transformed into the deity, the speech has become mantra, and the mind is the true nature. Therefore, it is said that one is able to bring the dead back to life and to make things appear and disappear. These are the activities of a crazy wisdom master.

d. The actions of a wisdom holder reflect the realization of great equality. In all four daily activities, this person acts spontaneously in a state of uninterrupted bliss-emptiness. This is the state of unity of no more learning, beyond meditation and postmeditation. There are no activities to be done or not done. In essence, all action is spontaneous; a wisdom holder has no agenda.

For these four types of people, the higher should not act like the lower, and the lower should not act like the higher. When one's activity is related with one's capacity, then the activity is connected with the time.

4. In terms of the result being connected with benefiting others, for a real yogi, there is no duality of perceiver and perceived. There is no need to be deliberately mindful or think about anything. Without effort, the yogi is naturally immersed in the realization of great equality. At the level of the result, when the nets of the body come apart at death, then the body, speech, and mind become inseparable from the enlightened kaya of great bliss. The result is attained when actualization becomes spontaneous. Then, in terms of how the result is connected with

benefiting others, from the dharmakaya the form kayas naturally and effortlessly arise to act for the welfare of others.

Each of us needs to apply the view and actions described here. Please carefully consider all of this.

[12. THE IMPORTANCE OF RECOGNIZING THE ORDINARY MIND]

Jetsun Rinpoche said:[18] As practitioners, please remind yourselves of death and impermanence. Do not forget karmic cause and result. Recognize the shortcomings of samsara as well as the shortcomings of the Hinayana. Recollect loving-kindness, compassion, and bodhichitta. From now on, if you want to be liberated from samsara, you need to recognize tamel gyi shepa, the ordinary mind, since it is the heart of all the dharma.

What is the ordinary mind? It is your own consciousness, unadulterated by anything, unspoiled by any kind of worldly consciousness. No matter what sort of dullness or thoughts hide it, it remains in its natural state. If you realize it, it is the wisdom of pristine awareness. If you do not recognize it, it is coemergent ignorance. When you realize this, it is called rigpa. It is called the essence. It is called coemergent wisdom. It is called the ordinary mind. It is called the primordial state. It is called free from extremes. It is called luminosity.

If you realize this, you become more qualified than a scholar who knows the five traditional sciences.[19] This is because scholars understand through concepts and words. They may know everything, yet they are stumped on this one point. However, if you understand the ordinary mind, then by knowing one thing, you know everything. Since you have gotten to the real point, your qualities are greater.

It is better to understand tamel gyi shepa, the ordinary mind, than to have shamatha that is so stable that you do not know if it is day or night. That kind of shamatha meditation is common; even the long-life gods, and the prairie dogs, bears, and other animals that sleep in holes have that. The ordinary mind is uncommon; this is why it has greater qualities.

It is better to understand tamel gyi shepa, the ordinary mind, than to receive the four empowerments in sequence, practice generating the deity, and experience the signs of contacting, hearing, and seeing the yidam. Seeing the face of the deity is the pure relative truth, and it is a sign of exhausting one's obscurations. However, knowing the ordinary mind is the ultimate truth, so its qualities are greater.

It is better to understand the ordinary mind than to have the five higher perceptions of the eyes and ears and so on. These higher perceptions come with defilements. Even ghosts and animals can have them. When you understand the ordinary mind, your higher perception is undefiled, so it is more wondrous. A scripture says:[20]

> *Wisdom, wisdom is the great distinction.*[21]
> *One with wisdom understands existence and non-existence.*

It is better to understand the ordinary mind than not to experience perception, or for there to be no perceptible objects, or to have flashes of experience, or to be immersed in emptiness like a completely clear sky. This is because these are generalizations formed through inference. However, the ordinary mind reaches the real point; it is based on direct perception, which makes its qualities greater.

Realizing the ordinary mind is the king of supreme knowing. Since this is not an object of discriminating knowledge, it is said:

> *With great knowledge, in one instant*
> *All phenomena are completely understood,*
> *All phenomena are completely realized.*

This is why it is the king of primordial wisdom. All five types of primordial wisdom are contained in tamel gyi shepa, so it is the wisdom of the basic space of phenomena. Through realizing that the grasper and the grasped are not separate, it is discriminating-awareness wisdom. It is said:

> *In one instant, specifics are discriminated,*
> *In one instant, perfect buddhahood.*
> *In one instant of mind, everything is known.*

There is no need to progress through the five paths, and so on. In one instant, all purposes are accomplished, so it is all-accomplishing wisdom. Since all things in the relative world are realized to be like reflections in a mirror, it is the mirrorlike wisdom. All of samsara and nirvana are equally one's own awareness, so it is the wisdom of equanimity. Therefore, it is said:

> *Buddhahood has no beginning or end.*
> *The primordial buddha has no cause.*
> *The stainless, single eye of wisdom,*
> *The embodiment of wisdom is the Tathagata.*

This is how the ordinary mind is the king of wisdom. The ordinary mind is the king of all qualities. There are no greater higher perceptions than those mentioned above, yet tamel gyi shepa is greater than that. The ordinary mind is the king of all samadhis. Once it is realized, no matter what kinds of samadhi are experienced, they are like outer shells and husks. The ordinary mind is the essence of the entire dharma and the root of all samsara and nirvana, so it all comes down to whether you recognize tamel gyi shepa or not. Therefore, it is very important to recognize the ordinary mind.

[13. THE WAYS IN WHICH A REALIZED YOGI IS FREE]

Jetsun Rinpoche said:[22] For a yogi who realizes Mahamudra: (1) the view is free from two desires, (2) the meditation is free from three stages, (3) the action is free from earlier and later activities, and (4) the result is free from hope and fear.

1. In terms of the view being free from two desires, first, having realized the fundamental way of abiding, we might like others' views to resemble our own, without any disagreement. Second, we might want our practice of the true nature to give rise to one result after another. We need to be free from these two desires.

2. The meditation is free from the three stages. Rather than meditating in some way as the preparation, meditating in some way in the main part, and meditating in some way as the conclusion, at all times one's practice is free from these three stages. It needs to be yogic meditation, like the uninterrupted flow of a river, never moving away from the true nature.

3. The action is free from earlier and later activities. This means being free from thoughts like, "First I will do this, and then I will do that." In brief, one has no agenda. Another way of saying this is that one's actions are free of rejecting and accepting. One is free from wanting to get rid of emotional afflictions and wanting to accomplish wisdom as their antidote. We need to be free of all negating and affirming.

4. The result is freedom from hope and fear. There needs to be freedom from the hope of attaining nirvana and the fear of wandering in samsara. In short, by realizing that samsara and nirvana are inseparable great bliss, there is no wish to rise up to buddhahood and no fear of falling down into samsara.

Please understand that a yogi with realization needs to be like this.

[14. THE IDEAL WAY TO LISTEN TO THE DHARMA]

Jetsun Rinpoche said:[23] In general, listening to the dharma has two aspects: the ideal intention and the ideal application. The ideal intention involves four attitudes. (1) "I wish to listen, not because I want to be famous, but in order to take all beings across the great ocean of samsaric suffering." (2) "I wish to listen, not to obtain honor and gain, but to obtain the wisdom of omniscience." (3) "I wish to listen, not to be victorious in arguments, but to be victorious over the enemy army of my mental afflictions." (4) "I wish to listen, not because I want to expose my teacher's mistakes, but to show respect for my teacher and the teachings."

The ideal application has three parts: the preparation, the main part, and the conclusion. (1) The preparation is motivated by bodhichitta, while knowing that everything is like a dream or an illusion. (2) The main part is to practice all six paramitas while listening to any sort of teaching. (3) The conclusion is to dedicate the positive results of listening toward the perfect enlightenment of all beings.

To practice all these points together, think: "I will establish in enlightenment all the limitless sentient beings, who are like a magical illusion or a dream. For that purpose, I will attain perfect enlightenment. And to accomplish that, I will listen to the precious instructions. I will understand them, I will realize them, and I will practice them." We need to generate this kind of special intention. In general, it is important to have a completely pure intention in listening to the dharma.

[15. PITFALLS IN EXPERIENCE AND
DEVIATIONS FROM THE VIEW]

Jetsun Rinpoche said:[24] Of all the pitfalls, which is the greatest? It is the attachment to worldly things. Unless we turn our mind away from worldly things, there is no way to become a great meditator.

In practicing, there are three pitfalls connected with experience and four deviations from the correct view. Of the three pitfalls connected with experience, the first pitfall is to be concerned about having a comfortable body, a happy mind, and experiences of bliss pervading the body. Through attachment and overt clinging to these things, they become extremely important, and this is the cause for perpetuating the desire realm. If people die in that frame of mind, they deviate by going to the desire realm. After experiencing the bliss and rapture of the desire realm, there is no difficulty in traveling endlessly in the lower realms.

The second pitfall is connected to the experience of clarity that arises in the absence of drowsiness and dullness. By clinging to clarity and giving it the highest importance, one deviates by going to the form realm. After experiencing the bliss and rapture of that realm, there is no difficulty in falling into lower states of existence.

The third pitfall is connected with the experience of being unmoved by the winds of thoughts and emotions. Attachment to that state of mind, and holding it as supreme, is the cause of perpetuating the formless realm. If people die in that frame of mind, they deviate by going to the formless realm. After experiencing the bliss and rapture of that realm, one travels endlessly in the three lower realms.

Even if one does not deviate in these three ways, there are four ways of deviating from emptiness.

1. It is a deviation to treat the ground of being as an object of knowledge. Someone might say, "All phenomena of the grasping mind and the grasped objects are primordially pure and primordially liberated. Right from the beginning, there is enlightenment. Right from the beginning, there is spontaneous presence. Through meditating, things do not get better, and by not meditating, things do not get worse. There is nothing positive or negative. Doing positive deeds does not help; doing negative deeds does not harm. Putting your hand into a black bag and putting your hand into a goat's intestines are equal." Speaking in this way is just

mouthing empty words. This is how one strays from emptiness by turning it into an object of knowledge.

2. One deviates from emptiness by regarding it as an antidote. In general, our study, contemplation, and meditation are geared toward being antidotes to the kleshas. This applies to study and reflection, ranging from the *Karika*, which is the Vinaya text of a novice monk, up to the *Guhyasamaja Tantra*. This also applies to topics of meditation, ranging from death and impermanence up to the unborn nature, and to practices like keeping the precepts, accumulation, and purification.

It is very important to cut the root of the kleshas. If you can cut the kleshas at their base, it is like cutting a tree at its root. If you are unable to do that, then when the five poisons or three poisons arise, you might make assertions, based on analysis, that since their nature is emptiness, they are not truly existent. Although it might seem helpful to meditate on them as unestablished, this would neither lessen nor suppress them, much less cut them at the root. This is the deviation of using emptiness as an antidote to the kleshas.

3. Another deviation is to superimpose emptiness onto phenomena. As an antidote to clinging to things or actions as having substance and characteristics, you might logically analyze them through reasoning such as "neither one nor many," to prove they are empty of existence. Or you might try purifying them with the *shunyata* or *svabhava* mantras. Or you might try to establish them as non-existent by maintaining the nonconceptual supreme knowing of threefold purity. Initially focusing on something as substantial, and later imposing emptiness on top of it to make it non-existent in nature, is the deviation of superimposing emptiness on phenomena.

4. Finally, there is the deviation of regarding emptiness as the path. In general, when the true nature, or Mahamudra, is realized, then all three—the cause, path, and result—are complete in this single nature. The true nature is not produced by the mind; it arises from within. In relation to this, *Chanting the Names of Manjushri* states:

> *Buddhahood has no beginning or end.*
> *The primordial buddha has no cause.*
> *The stainless, single eye of wisdom,*
> *The embodiment of wisdom is the Tathagata.*

Without this understanding, you might think, "By using the meditation on emptiness as the path, I will gain the result—the signs and marks of an omniscient buddha, endowed with three kayas and five wisdoms." This is the deviation of regarding emptiness as the path.

In general, it is very important not to make these mistakes.

[16. ILLUSORY, DREAMLIKE BODHICHITTA]

Jetsun Rinpoche said:[25] In the system of the Mahayana, whatever the level of practice—whether observing the precepts, accumulating and purifying, or giving generously—the things themselves are not of primary importance. The most important factor is one's intention. In any sort of dharma activity, it is very important to start with a pure motivation. To give rise to a special motivation, one generates bodhichitta in an elaborate, medium, or brief way.

The elaborate way of generating bodhichitta is to think: "I must take across the ocean of samsara all the limitless beings, who are like dreams or illusions. I am not going to take them to the shravaka enlightenment or the pratyekabuddha enlightenment of the Hinayana, but I will establish them in unsurpassable enlightenment. Therefore, I myself must attain complete, perfect enlightenment. And to do that, I will perform various types of meditation, practice, and dharma activity."

The medium-length way of generating bodhichitta is to think: "In order to bring to complete enlightenment all sentient beings, who are like illusions or dreams, I will do this and that." The short way of generating bodhichitta is to think: "I will perform this dharma activity to benefit all the illusory, dreamlike beings."

Generally, in relation to whatever accumulations and purifications are done, in the beginning they are motivated by illusory and dreamlike bodhichitta in its expanded, medium, or condensed form. In the main part, the dharma is practiced like an illusion or a dream. At the conclusion, the illusory and dreamlike merit is dedicated for sentient beings. The dedicator (oneself), the object of dedication (sentient beings), and the positive effects of what is dedicated are all illusory and dreamlike, so they are inseparable from one's own mind. All of them are a magical display of the nature of the mind, nondual in essence.

[17. GAMPOPA'S HEART ADVICE TO RETREATANTS]

Jetsun Rinpoche said:[26] All you great practitioners assembled here, if you want to do genuine practice, you must cut the ties to the concerns of this life, to the extent of giving up everything, even your body and life. Reduce your food and clothing to the bare necessities, and then do the practice. In order to truly practice, you need to remain in solitary retreat. The best practitioner goes to the glacier mountains like a lion. The medium practitioner goes to the forest like a tiger. The lesser practitioner goes to the rocky hills like a vulture. Do not skirt the edge of town like a fox ready to sneak into a charnel ground.

Generally, if you are too attached to food and clothes, you cannot stay in the mountains. It is important to be able to wear only one cotton cloth. Rely on just a small amount of food. No matter what purpose you wish to accomplish, whether it is great or small, when life goes well, that is okay, and when things go badly, that is okay. No matter what happens, this is the way to think.

In general, if you are going to practice the dharma, do not expect much from other people. Do not be hard to please or easily annoyed. It is better not to count the number of kind deeds you have done for others. I have not kept track of the kindness I have shown to people, although I do think I have been a great help to all of you.

Generally, whether the students' behavior discredits the teacher, or the teacher's behavior discredits the students, it is all the same. I do not want to disgrace you. The best result would be for all my students to reach supreme enlightenment in this life. Next best would be for my students to become enlightened in the bardo, and at the least, they would be enlightened in a future life.

I ask of you: please do not beat up on yourselves. If you show real kindness to yourself, then things will certainly turn out as I wish.

In general, when you practice the dharma, do not be someone who just talks about practicing, or who practices only a little on the side. Do not look for easy dharma practices, or practice only once a year. Even if you are known to others as a practitioner, and you think of yourself as a practitioner, there is the danger that you could die as an ordinary person. It is very important to meditate on the stages of the path of the three types of individuals, on death and impermanence, and on karmic cause and result. These meditations become the whip of diligence.

Generally, the way it works for those who have entered the dharma is that the best practitioners die smiling, full of joy and deep confidence. They are going from happiness to happiness. At death, medium-level practitioners are free of dread. Lower-level practitioners are free of regrets, without thinking, "I did this and I did that with my body, speech, and mind."

Great meditators stay in solitary retreat because they have given up all their activities, they have given up all their distractions, and they want to do spiritual practice one-pointedly in seclusion. If you are involved in distracting activities, then it seems appropriate to stay in town and live in society. However, if you do go into retreat, do not create more distractions than in the city. Be diligent about your spiritual practice. Because dharma practice is a great, inexhaustible treasure, it is like a wish-fulfilling jewel. Since it is the accumulation of all your lifetimes, it is very important.

Once dharma practice is begun, it needs to be perfected through familiarization. The view needs to be applied in meditation. This will assure the welfare of others. Without doing it this way, acting for others' benefit can harm oneself and make it difficult to be of any help. Therefore, the preliminary step is to accomplish your own purpose. After that, you can nurture students. In order to accomplish your own purpose, it is very important to remain in solitude.

In terms of being able to live in retreat, the Kadampas teach five points:

1. Have conduct that is free of hypocrisy.
2. Ensure that the antidotes hold up under various circumstances.
3. Gain mastery of the instructions.
4. Invigorate yourself through devotion.
5. Have the strength to overcome small problems.

Similarly, our own enlightened teacher, Lord Gampopa, said there are four points involved with staying in retreat:

1. Have confidence in the instructions.
2. Have confidence in your own ability.
3. Have confidence in your experience.
4. Have confidence in the view.

To act according to these points, regard your teacher as a buddha. Supplicate the lama continuously and spend a long time in your teacher's presence. It is not right to snatch the teachings and then take off, like a chicken snatching a bite. On the other hand, do not get too familiar with the teacher. Do not get jaded with the instructions, and do not let your devotion get stale. These points are very important.

We need to think this way: "I have obtained a precious human body, entered the gateway of the precious teachings, received the precious dharma, met with a precious, genuine teacher, and been given precious instructions. I now have the freedom to practice. All these auspicious conditions have come together, so I must meditate." If you meditate at a time like this, it is impossible for the meditative state not to occur. If it does not occur, it is because you are not meditating.

In order to please the teacher, the best type of service is to do the practice. The medium level is to give service through body and speech. The lowest service is to give material things. If the dharma is practiced genuinely, it will fulfill all aims—both your own and others. You will be happy in this life and in all your future lives. Other people will appreciate you. However, if you do not practice like this, then you will suffer. People will scorn you and put you down. It will result in your going to the lower realms.

To practice the dharma in a heartfelt way, generate the power of devotion, respect, joyful effort, and the antidotes. Do not disgrace your lama and your dharma brothers and sisters. Do not be a cause for others to commit negative actions. At the very least, I ask each of you to refrain from a negative lifestyle.

[18. TEN WAYS IN WHICH STUDENTS ATTEND THEIR LAMA]

In accordance with the Kadampa tradition, Jetsun Rinpoche taught ten ways in which students should attend their lama.[27]

1. Attend the spiritual master with devotion, without becoming tired and bored. In doing this, you should follow the example of the mahasiddhas.

2. Attend the teacher by offering material wealth without stinginess. This is similar to what is said in the scripture, the *Fifty Lamas:* "Give even the things which are not given, like your child, your wife, and your own life."

3. Have a flawless and noble intention when attending the teacher. The flaw would be the motivation of a shravaka or pratyekabuddha or

any lesser motivation. Instead, the motivation should be completely pure and noble.

4. Have undeluded wisdom when attending the spiritual friend. This means you should not be confused about the lama's instructions, including the logic involved.

5. Attend the teacher by having respect and not being arrogant. This means seeing the lama as a doctor, yourself as a patient, and the dharma as medicine. Honor your lama just as patients honor their doctor.

6. Attend the teacher with unhesitating service. This means trusting, without a doubt, in whatever the lama says.[28]

7. Attend the master truthfully, without deceit. Give up lies and deception and have heartfelt respect.

8. Attend the teacher by being flexible, rather than rigid and proud. Rather than being hard-edged, or conceited about your background, you need to be humble and peaceful. For example, if you were writing and the vajra master were to ask you to cut off the bottom of the letter *P*, then you would just do it. You need to do whatever the lama says.

9. Attend the spiritual friend with patience and without anger. This means you need to be like Lama Naropa undergoing his twelve trials.

10. Attend the teacher as an extraordinary form of the deity. At all times, see the lama as a buddha rather than as an ordinary person.

In order to attend a lama, it is important to have these qualities. It is inappropriate to simply do whatever you like.

These were some teachings of the precious Lord Gampopa, which were put in writing by the monk Sherap Shönu. May this be virtuous!

Notes

PREFACE BY RINGU TULKU

1. This text is in the *dvags po'i bka' 'bum* (*The Collected Works of Gampopa*), vol. *kha*, 1a–33b.
2. For an overview of the teachings and history of the Dakpo Kagyu lineage, particularly the way it branched out from Gampopa's students to form the four main schools and eight subschools, please see the *Ri-me Philosophy of Jamgön Kongtrul the Great* by Ringu Tulku (Boston: Shambhala, 2006).

CHAPTER 1. THE LINEAGE OF THESE TEACHINGS

1. "Tharlam" is another name for the Indian mahasiddha Kukuripa. Marpa referred to Kukuripa as "the teacher who showed me the path of liberation," *tharpe lamtön* in Tibetan, which can be condensed to *tharlam*. Kukuripa is also known by the Sanskrit name "Jnanagarbha," or "Yeshe Nyingpo" in Tibetan. *The Blue Annals*, written by Gö Lotsawa Shönu Pal in 1476, mentions that Marpa studied the *Guhyasamaja Tantra* with Tharlam in the city of Tulakshetra in western India.
2. There is now a full-length biography of Gampopa in English called *The Life of Gampopa*, by Jampa Mackenzie Stewart (Ithaca, N.Y.: Snow Lion, 1995). There is also a medium-length biography included in the *Jewel Ornament of Liberation*, trans.

Khenpo Konchog Gyaltsen Rinpoche (Ithaca, N.Y.: Snow Lion, 1998). There are also many short biographies of Gampopa on the Internet.

3. *The Life of Milarepa,* trans. Lobsang P. Lhalungpa (Boston: Shambhala, 1985), and the *Hundred Thousand Songs of Milarepa,* trans. Garma C. C. Chang (New York: Harper & Row, 1970).

CHAPTER 2. UNDERSTANDING THE NEED FOR DEVOTION

1. *Dad pa* is the Wylie transliteration of *depa.*

CHAPTER 3. THE MONK WHO QUESTIONED CHENREZIK

1. A mahasiddha is a highly accomplished practitioner.

CHAPTER 4. THE FOUR DHARMAS OF GAMPOPA

1. These are the first two lines of a verse from Nagarjuna's *Jewel Garland:* "Attachment, anger, and delusion / And the actions created by them are unvirtuous. / From nonvirtue comes suffering / And likewise all the evil states. // Non-attachment, non-anger, and nondelusion / And the actions created by them are virtuous. / From virtue comes the happy states / And happiness in all rebirths." This is Erik Schmidt's translation in the *Light of Wisdom,* vol. 1 (Boston: Shambhala, 1995).

2. The six realms of existence are the god realm, the jealous god realm, the human realm, the animal realm, the hungry ghost realm, and the hell realm.

3. This is Sarah Harding's translation, found in *The Treasury of Knowledge: Book Eight, Part Four: Esoteric Instructions,* by Jamgön Kongtrul (Ithaca, N.Y.: Snow Lion, 2007).

CHAPTER 5. THE APPLICATION OF COEMERGENCE

1. The reference to the lama may mean that Gampopa is passing on the instructions that he received from his own teacher.

2. The tsarbu (tshar bu) plant has not been identified in Western nomenclature.

CHAPTER 6. THE NATURE OF THE MIND

1. This quotation is from the *Chandrapradipa Sutra.*

CHAPTER 7. THE MEANING OF MAHAMUDRA

1. This quotation is mysterious since Nagarjuna lived in India in the early part of the first millennium and probably did not use the word *chag* (*phyag*), the first syllable of *chagya chenpo* (*phyag rgya chen po*), the Tibetan translation of the Sanskrit word *Mahamudra*. The Tibetan term *chagya* is two words put together: *chag* usually means "hand," and *gya* has many meanings, but here it would mean "seal" or "symbol." In contrast, the Sanskrit term *mudra* is only one word. *Mudra* is not a word commonly found in Sanskrit; it is a Vajrayana Buddhist term that means "gesture" or "hand signal." The Tibetan word *chenpo* directly correlates with the Sanskrit word *maha*, meaning "great" or "large." *Mahamudra* and *chagya chenpo* are usually translated as the "great seal" or "great symbol."

CHAPTER 9. STABILIZING RECOGNITION OF THE NATURE OF THE MIND

1. This is a quotation from Shantideva's the *Way of the Bodhisattva*, chapter 7, verse 14. The translation is by the Padmakara Translation Group (Boston: Shambhala, 1997).

CHAPTER 12. THE IMPORTANCE OF RECOGNIZING THE ORDINARY MIND

1. This quotation and all subsequent quotations in the root text in this chapter are from the tantra *Chanting the Names of Manjushri*.
2. The five higher perceptions are the divine eye, the divine ear, the knowledge of others' minds, the recollection of past lives, and being able to perform miraculous activities.

CHAPTER 15. PITFALLS IN EXPERIENCE AND DEVIATIONS FROM THE VIEW

1. The *Jataka Tales* are stories of the adventures of the Buddha in his previous existences.
2. The five poisons refer to attachment, aversion, ignorance, pride, and jealousy. The three poisons are attachment, aversion, and ignorance.

3. These mantras state the ultimate purity and emptiness of oneself and all phenomena.

CHAPTER 17. GAMPOPA'S HEART ADVICE TO RETREATANTS

1. This is a reference to worldly dharma practitioners, shravakas, and bodhisattvas.

CHAPTER 18. TEN WAYS IN WHICH STUDENTS ATTEND THEIR LAMA

1. The example in the Tibetan text is "to cut off the bottom of the letter *NA*." This is comparable to cutting off the bottom of the English letter *P*, which would make the letter unrecognizable.

APPENDIX: *GAMPOPA'S GREAT TEACHINGS TO THE ASSEMBLY*

1. This section of the text correlates with the commentary in chapter 1, "The Lineage of These Teachings."
2. See chap. 1, n. 1.
3. This section of the text correlates with the commentary in chapter 2, "Understanding the Need for Devotion."
4. This section of the text correlates with the commentary in chapter 3, "The Monk Who Questioned Chenrezik."
5. This section of the text correlates with the commentary in chapter 4, "The Four Dharmas of Gampopa."
6. See chap. 4, n. 1.
7. This section of the text correlates with the commentary in chapter 5, "The Application of Coemergence."
8. See chap. 5, n. 1.
9. The Tibetan word *namtok* (rnam rtog), which is commonly translated as "thoughts," refers to whatever arises in the mind, which includes thoughts, emotions, perceptions, and sensations. In this sentence, all the meanings for the translation of *namtok* are stated.
10. This section of the text correlates with the commentary in chapter 6, "The Nature of the Mind."
11. See chap. 6, n. 1.
12. This section of the text correlates with the commentary in chapter 7, "The Meaning of Mahamudra."
13. See chap. 7, note 1.

14. This section of the text correlates with the commentary in chapter 8, "Six Points Concerning the Creation Stage Practice."

15. This section of the text correlates with the commentary in chapter 9, "Stabilizing Recognition of the Nature of the Mind."

16. This section of the text correlates with the commentary in chapter 10, "The Qualities of a Genuine Teacher."

17. This section of the text correlates with the commentary in chapter 11, "How to Actualize the View, Meditation, Action, and Result."

18. This section of the text correlates with the commentary in chapter 12, "The Importance of Recognizing the Ordinary Mind."

19. The five traditional sciences are grammar, logic, artistry, healing, and spirituality.

20. See chap. 12, n. 1.

21. All available Tibetan versions of *Chanting the Names of Manjushri* that we checked have a different word in this line than Gampopa's text. In the other versions, line 57 (or chapter 6, line 16) says: *ye shes ye shes 'byung gnas che* (Wisdom, wisdom is the great source). Gampopa's text says: *ye shes ye shes khyad par che* (Wisdom, wisdom is the great distinction). We have translated this line according to Gampopa's text.

22. This section of the text correlates with the commentary in chapter 13, "The Ways in Which a Realized Yogi Is Free."

23. This section of the text correlates with the commentary in chapter 14, "The Ideal Way to Listen to the Dharma."

24. This section of the text correlates with the commentary in chapter 15, "Pitfalls in Experience and Deviations from the View."

25. This section of the text correlates with the commentary in chapter 16, "Illusory, Dreamlike Bodhichitta."

26. This section of the text correlates with the commentary in chapter 17, "Gampopa's Heart Advice to Retreatants."

27. This section of the text correlates with the commentary in chapter 18, "Ten Ways in Which Students Attend Their Lama."

28. See chap. 18, n. 1.

Printed in the United States
by Baker & Taylor Publisher Services